FREE-WILL
and
DETERMINISM

by

Allan M. Munn
B.SC., M.SC., PH.D., F.R.S.A.

*Professor of Physics at
Carleton University, Ottawa*

UNIVERSITY OF TORONTO PRESS

1960

© A. M. Munn, 1960
Toronto: University of Toronto Press
London: MacGibbon & Kee
Printed in Great Britain by
Billing & Sons Ltd.
Guildford & London

Contents

Introduction

A DOG, who, left to himself, might lie contentedly all day long in the shade of a tree, whines miserably if tied to the same tree for five minutes. Tom Sawyer's pals were willing to give up their most cherished possessions for a turn at white-washing his fence, but 'by jingo, they would wail like fettered injuns' if told they must do the same at home. The union steward, who, on holiday, will go tramping across country from dawn to dusk and then spend the evening in the pub, would call a strike if half that amount of energy were required at 'work'. All are protesting the same thing: compulsion, restriction of their freedom to choose what it is they want to do. As Mark Twain philosophized about what Tom could have learned from the white-washing episode: 'If he had been a great and wise philosopher like the writer of this book, he would now have comprehended that work consists of whatever a body is obliged to do and that play consists of whatever a body is not obliged to do. And this would help him to understand why constructing artificial flowers or performing on a treadmill is work, while rolling ten pins or climbing Mont Blanc is only amusement.'

Now while it takes a great and wise philosopher to express it so cleverly, or a great and wise psychiatrist to make full use of it therapeutically, we are all aware of this distinction between play and work and, at least occasionally, use it. If we are a good dog trainer we don't try to teach Imp to fetch the evening newspaper by dragging her on the leash to the letterbox, forcing her jaws open, and, pushing the paper in and forcibly keeping the jaws shut, drag her home again. Instead, chasing a dog biscuit as a game, becomes chasing a stick with the biscuit for reward as a game, and, with a few more steps, this evolves painlessly into the dog's automatically fetching our evening paper with no more reward than an approving pat on the head. When little Rory cannot be deceived into making games out of the drinking of his milk or the running of errands, at least we try to induce in him the feeling that he is choosing to do them for his own future good; that is, that doing them will help him to enjoy his play more at some later time. We must notice that two somewhat sinister elements have put in their appearance: In both the case of the dog and the child, the overt compulsion has been changed into the covert persuasion, and we see that Rory's 'choice' is largely an illusion.

If this is true for Rory mayn't it be true in general? When we as grown-ups 'freely' choose to tell the truth, to rob a bank, to trade our aged last year's model car in on one with the 'forward look of motion', or even to sacrifice our life, if necessary, in converting the hostile Auca Indians of the Ecuadorian jungle to the one true religion, are we really free? It is certainly we who carry out the action and it is certainly we who made the choice to act. The question is: could we have chosen differently? In a number of instances we certainly have no real alternative to the actual choice-act. There may be such overwhelming surrounding physical compulsion that only one possibility exists:—The bound, hooded prisoner with the trap-door under his feet and the noose around his neck cannot choose not to be hanged. The bankrupt nation cannot choose to maintain a modern air force. A Rolls-Royce cannot choose to give birth to Baby Austins. But there are other cases when the immediate spatio-temporal surroundings are not so totally restrictive and some freedom of choice-act seems to exist: I see a wallet dropped on the street. Will I wait till the owner turns the corner, and then pick it up and put it in my own pocket, or will I return it to him? Will the U.S.S.R. try to overtake and exceed the U.S.A. in all fields, or try to get far ahead in certain critical areas only? At the 'Giant Rally for the Defence of the Republic' if I 'find myself getting into the spirit of things' will I 'show enough strength of will' to maintain my independent judgement, or will I go along with the mob shouting: 'Death to all traitors to the Republic'. 'Death to de Gaulle'.

The important question is: In these latter cases is this sense of alternative choice-actions real or illusion? If a supreme intelligence were to know the entire past history of the world would he be able to predict without error that: The wallet will not be stolen. The U.S.S.R. will attempt to exceed in all areas. I will be logically analysing, rather than participating in, the mob's actions? No one doubts that it is sometimes possible to so circumscribe a person's immediate surroundings that his freedom of action is effectively totally destroyed, but there is a considerable range of opinion as to the effect of the past. At the one extreme the strict determinist would not only state that the child's conditioning determines (subject to environmental conditions) the adult's behaviour, but that the non-theft of the wallet today was already implicit in the state of the universe at the time of the fertilization of the egg that developed into the child. That—

> ' . . . *the first Morning of Creation wrote*
> *What the last Dawn of Reckoning shall read*'

The other extreme: that at each instant the Universe is, in effect, created anew, with its future bearing no relation with the past, is so contradicted by the evident orderliness of things that no one can seriously believe in it. However, a number of people believe, and in practice all of us act, as if at each instant a number of different possibilities exist; that, where man and his decision-making is concerned, the particular path followed is dependent upon these decisions, and that an intelligence no matter how supreme could not predict precisely what decision would be made at each instant.

All of us are concerned with this question but it is of particular importance for: the theologian, in his eternal dilemma between a belief in God's omniscience, and his belief, seemingly equally essential to religion, that man has a free choice between sinning or doing good; the judge and the lawmaker, in deciding when a party can rightfully be considered responsible for a certain action; the sociologist, in deciding whether the purpose of prison is: to remove an undesirable element from society, to punish for bad past behaviour, to deter from future bad behaviour, to serve as an example for others . . . ; and, in its most general and simplest aspect, it is the problem of the philosopher: is the world determined or not?

We have begun with the title 'Free-Will and Determinism' but already a number of other related words have put in their appearance, and we can add many others: 'responsibility', 'sin', 'punishment', 'compulsion', 'choice', 'decision', 'guilt', 'liberty', 'predestination', 'fatalism', 'grace', 'causality', 'free will'. Many of these words can be arranged in pairs possessing some sort of logical exclusion: for example, 'compulsion' denying 'liberty', predestination' making 'sin' meaningless, 'determinism' prohibiting 'free will'. This opposition may be real or illusion, but it has long concerned thinking man, and is as much in question today as in Athens 2,500 years ago.

Now as these words are used in common language their meaning is vague and arbitrary. There is little disagreement as to the connotation of 'table', 'red', or 'mankind', but prior to any discussion of a statement like 'the world is determined therefore man does not have free will' there must be understanding and agreement on the meanings of the words used. This is not at all easy to do. So much so that some authors have suggested that the controversial words are essentially meaningless, and should be eliminated from respectable discourse. In particular, they would reject the expression 'free will', and, though perhaps not so readily, 'determinism', 'causality', 'predestination'. This won't do. The baby mustn't be thrown out with the dirty bath water. The words are in use in the language, will continue in use, and man is going to continue puzzling over whether he is a sort of automaton following a predetermined path through life, or whether his path is uniquely his own, in at least the sense that an external observer, no matter how omniscient, cannot make a detailed prediction of it in advance.

If this is going to be a continuing problem we must try to answer it. We cannot expect that our final result will represent absolute truth, or that it will hold for all time. The best that we can do is to build up a world picture compatible with what has been best established in our present-day knowledge. For this, in addition to the virtually countless works dealing with this subject in philosophical literature, we have available the results of the sciences, particularly physics. In this latter, although we are limited to dealing with only the very simplest of problems, we have the enormous advantage that its theoretical formulation, based solidly upon mathematics and logic as it is, permits definitions to be most operationally and transparently clear. For this reason a part of our time will be devoted to an analysis of the structure of Physics. We will find that 'determinism' can be defined inside physics in a way in keeping with its common-sense significance. When we move on through biology to mankind, we will be able to discuss in terms of the world picture we have developed whether man can be said to 'possess free will' or not.

★   ★   ★

The author has tried to steer a middle course between an extreme of rigour that would make the larger part of the book unintelligible except to the specialist, and the other equally undesirable extreme of attempting to so popularize a very serious subject that the book loses any claim to serious study. No apology is really needed for avoiding the first of these extremes, since the belief that one is thereby coming closer to the truth is largely delusion, and the resulting proliferation of details frequently obscures the main lines of the argument. At the other end of the spectrum, many popular books so simplify their subjects, and treat them indirectly by analogy rather than coming to grips with the real difficulties, that they leave the readers with an entirely incorrect picture of what is the actual state of affairs.

In this book, where, as happens from time to time in the development of the argument, it has been impossible to avoid somewhat more difficult mathematical details, these sections have been thrown into a different type, and non-mathematically inclined readers can jump directly to the conclusions, without, in the process, feeling that in any way they are losing the thread of the argument. This book should be intelligible to anyone without specialized training, provided only that he is willing to spend a little more time on the occasional more difficult sections.

To help the reader a number of devices have been employed. Among these are: Each chapter contains a summary of what has been established up to that point in the book and what will be done in that chapter. Since a major part of the argument of the book depends upon Physics, enough physical theory, both classical and modern, has been included to make the discussion intelligible to anyone whose physics is rusty or non-existent. Wherever mathematics is used, it is paralleled with a complete verbal description of what is going on. Wherever possible, illustrations either verbal or figurative have been used to make the abstract argument more concrete and hence more easily understood.

Readers interested in pursuing the subject further should refer to the bibliography listed at the end of the book.

Acknowledgments

THE author is indebted to Carleton University which generously provided him with the opportunity to carry out the studies leading to the preparation of this book, to the Canada Council and the Humanities Research Council for financial support, to many of his fellows who helped him by discussing different parts of the subject, and particularly to Joan S. Munn for her unstinting help in criticizing, editing, and typing. It is a practical impossibility to list all the authors in the bibliography whose works have been consulted during the study. Let this constitute due recognition for their ideas which have been freely used.

FREE-WILL AND DETERMINISM

CHAPTER I

The Child's and the Savage's Evolving Concept of Causality

SUMMARY: In this first chapter we begin our study of determinism by examining some of the aspects of causality as the term is used in our ordinary everyday language. Our approach will be to see how the child, maturing in our civilization, evolves through a spectrum of causal usage which reproduces to some extent the way in which our modern common-sense causality has developed from the causality of more primitive peoples. We will make a classification of cause into four types: 'partial cause', 'total cause' (including preponderating cause), 'original cause', and 'final cause'. Recognizing the practical impossibility of ever completely specifying the total cause of an event, 'total cause' will be replaced by the equivalent concept of 'determinism', in which attention is shifted from the causes of an event to the event itself.

★   ★   ★

'Why' and 'because' are two of the commonest words in the vocabulary of the child and his parents as they try to satisfy his constantly expanding curiosity and to discipline his behaviour. As the child matures, these words are used less and less, but the need 'to know the reason why' vanishes only with death. In time, the average person has been satisfied with more or less pat explanations for everyday events, but the extraordinary always excites his interest to a degree out of proportion to its purely logical importance in his life. Reasons must be found for everything. They may be good or bad, but we must find them before we can be happy to return to our ordinary humdrum (humdrum, when the reasons have all been found) existence. The answers to questions can take on a remarkable variety of forms:

Why did you hit him?   — Because he hit me first.
                        — Because he was going to hit me.
                        — Because I can't control myself.
                        — Because he wasn't careful and he got in the way.
                        — etc.

17

Why aren't you mowing the lawn?	— Because I wasn't told to do it.
	— Because I was told to do it.
	— Because the lawnmower is broken.
	— Because there is no lawn.
	— etc.
Why did John get hurt?	— Because he was driving too fast.
	— Because the car ahead stopped too quickly.
	— Because he is accident prone.
	— Because he wanted a rest.
	— Because he owned a car.
	— Because the road was icy.
	— Because it rained last night.
	— Because there is a low pressure area moving east.
	— etc.
Why does the bicycle move?	— Because the wheels roll.
	— Because the boy pedals it.
	— Because it is made so it will move.
	— Because the boy wants to get home.
	— etc.

A number of the general verbal aspects of 'because-ality' are already apparent from these examples. First, a large part of our time is spent in searching for the 'causes' of events. Second, there is never a single 'cause'. In the case of the bicycle, although it is constructed mechanically in such a way that it can move, the brakes are off so that the wheels can roll, and the boy is present; if the boy wants to stay where he is and not go home, the bicycle will not move. If all four conditions are satisfied, but the road is so soft that the bicycle sinks in the mud, to its axles, the bicycle will not move. And so on. The third characteristic is that there is a considerable difference in form inside any set of answers. The 'cause' may be in the future, the near present, or the past. It may be a physical 'cause', a logical 'cause', or a volitional 'cause'. Fourth, in the backwards direction there is a succession of 'becauses' of 'becauses'. This search backwards along the chain of causality may be cut off abruptly, as by the judge in Butler's *Erewhon*:

'It is all very well to say that you came of unhealthy parents, and had a severe accident in your childhood which permanently undermined your constitution. . . . I am not here to enter upon the curious metaphysical speculations as to the origin of this or that—questions to which there would be no end were their introduction once tolerated, and which would result in throwing the only guilt on the tissues of the primordial cells or on the elementary gases. There is no question of how you came to be wicked but only this—namely, are you wicked or not?' (The crime was tuberculosis.)

but the purely formal nature of any such interruption is evident, as presumably Butler intended it to be. Particularly when dealing with juveniles, the modern court receives both medical and psychological advice and pays as much attention to the origins and motives of an act as to the act itself.

⋆ ⋆ ⋆

As our examples have indicated, 'because-ality' is very much a living concept, and in fact an essential part of our language and thought. In later chapters we will be carrying out a more intensive study of causality as it enters scientific discourse, and as it applies to the problem of freedom in human behaviour. In this chapter we will restrict ourselves to examining its common-sense usage and meaning in present-day adult society. Rather than tackle this latter directly, two somewhat indirect approaches turn out to be fruitful. The first is to study 'cause' as it exists and evolves in children maturing in our society. The second is to examine how primitive peoples go about describing and explaining events occurring about them in the world, and compare this with our own world picture. Both of these subjects are obviously large enough to warrant several large volumes devoted to them alone, but even the cursory study we are limited to here is of value. Let us begin with the child.

Under the twin influences of enlarging experience and social pressure the child develops from his initial unreasoning, totally egocentric state into a more or less standardized (civilized) adult. The why—the cause—of things is of continuing and vital concern to him. Ideally the investigator would like to get directly into the child's mind to learn how he reasons but this is impossible. We have of course the vague and distorted memories adults have of their childhood attitudes, but little trust can be placed in these except as guides in investigation. Hypnotism of the adult has been tried in an attempt to return him mentally to earlier periods of his life, but many reasons, including the customary desire of the hypnotized to please the hypnotist, have combined to make it impossible to obtain consistent, reliable results. The only remaining ways are observation of the child's behaviour, and direct questioning of him as to his beliefs. Many pitfalls are evidently present. The results are affected by the researcher's personal bias, the sort of questions he asks, and the child's capacity for putting into words his feelings about the 'whys'. As he ages his verbal capacity grows, but although he can then attempt more complicated explanations, at the same time he is becoming increasingly straight-jacketed by the necessity to fit his ideas into civilized language.

*   *   *

Among the sources of information on childhood behaviour and attitudes, Piaget is the most valuable for our purposes. He has carried out extensive questioning of children aged from three to fifteen years on their understanding of the world. He is well aware of the difficulties involved in obtaining a true picture of their beliefs. To obtain some appreciation of his approach, here are some of his introductory remarks to *The Child's Conception of Causality.*

'We may thus state the first rule of our method. When a particular group of explanations by children is to be investigated, the questions we shall ask them will be determined in matter and in form by the spontaneous questions actually asked by children of the same age or younger. The influence of the question set must be discounted, that is to say one must abstract from the child's answer the fact that it is an answer. . . . Next, the answers obtained must be stripped of all logical character, and care taken not to introduce an artificial coherence where coherence is of an organic rather than a logical character. Finally, an attempt must be made to strip the answers of their verbal element. . . . When the child is questioned he translates his thoughts into words but these words are necessarily inadequate. . . . Briefly the principle for interpretation . . . is to regard these answers as symptoms rather than as realities.'

Considering the enormous difficulty of the subject, it would be most surprising if Piaget had succeeded in meeting all the requirements he himself sets forth. In particular, he speaks of 'steering a middle course' between 'verifying preassumed hypotheses' and the opposite extreme of 'blind questioning unguided by any pattern'. Now it seems to us that Piaget has strayed rather far from the 'middle' towards the 'verifying of certain preassumed hypotheses'. This is not necessarily bad. The much talked about inductive process, by which a general law is induced from a set of particular observations, does not really exist as a procedure which can be logically specified in the same manner as can the converse procedure of deduction. In actuality there is a logical break between the consideration of the phenomena and the theoretician's proposal of a general hypothesis. The adequacy of this latter can only be tested a posteriori by checking its deductions against experience. It is essential, as Karl Popper points out, that these hypotheses be of such a nature that the subsequent testing could conceivably require their rejection. (An example of an hypothesis that could never be refuted is: 'A blinkim is a cause of all evil', along with the specification that blinkims can never be seen, touched, smelled, . . . etc. No experimental test could ever disprove this theory. Equally of course the theory is valueless. An example of an acceptable hypothesis would be: 'Germs are the cause of all disease', along with specifications as to how both germs and diseases are to be observed.) There are many criteria that must be applied in examining the adequacy of a certain theory and the experimental evidence advanced in support of it, and we will be discussing these at greater length in later chapters. For the moment let us admit that, as a general programme, Piaget's method, which is that of developing certain hypotheses and then finding evidence to substantiate or disprove these hypotheses, while dangerous, is not necessarily improper.

However there are two specific criticisms that must be considered. First, Piaget's habit in the early years of research, of putting aside children whose answers for one reason or another were not interesting to him. (There is no suggestion implicit here that he put aside those whose answers were in contradiction to his theories.) This is a very serious objection and one that Piaget has since accepted. Consideration of it has resulted in considerable modification in his experimental technique which is reflected in his later work. However, while this invalidates statements that might be made as to the conceptual level reached by the bulk of children at any certain age, it does not affect too much the description of the way in which the concept of 'cause' develops in children. Next, there is the question as to what relation the child's verbal presentation of his sense of causality bears to his 'actual' conceptual level. Specifically, since the more 'advanced' concepts of 'cause' require a more developed verbalization ability, it might be the case that while he describes a primitive causality he actually uses a much more sophisticated one that he is unable to state. Now researches carried out by Piaget's group on the child's concept of number, where it is easier to compare his verbal comprehension with his operational comprehension, seem to show that the above is not the situation. If anything, verbalization precedes utilization, rather than the reverse.

In any event, although Piaget might carry out his research differently, and his results might differ in detail, it seems that he would probably come to very much the same conclusions now as then. There is no need for any thorough critique of Piaget; the general picture of the child's development of his sense of cause seems to be clear enough, and it is all we need to know for this book. In the next few pages we will present in a highly condensed form Piaget's results and conclusions, including sample questions and answers.

*   *   *

Piaget identifies some seventeen senses of causality among children. Any one child does not progress in a regular way through numbers one to seventeen, but rather hops back and forth, moving only on the average from earlier to later stages. Similarly, different children at the same age do not hold equivalent views. The seventeen are now listed following Piaget's order which is, on the average, chronological.

1. *Psychological.* As he grows the child separates a 'myself' from the rest of the world. However he does not divide this external world into living and non-living parts. No objects are considered to be entirely inert. They all possess life in some form and are interested in the child's affairs. Since now for the first time he finds himself in conflict with other humans, he is particularly conscious of approval, disapproval and guilt.

'Where do dreams come from?'	'At night from God. God sends them.'
'How?'	'He makes the night come and he whispers in our ears.'
(We asked him to tell us one dream. He had dreamed of robbers.)	
'Why did God send you this dream?'	'To pay me out because I wasn't good.'
'What had you done to have such a dream?'	'I'd been naughty. I'd made mother cry.'

2. *Finalism.* In keeping with his allocation of life to all things the causes of physical events can be in the future (as in human 'purpose')

as well as in the past. Thus the child often sees an inversion of what we would think to be the usual order of cause and effect.

'Why do the clouds move along?'   'Because it will soon be dark.'
'Why does the water in the Arve   'Because it must go and flow into
   go along?'   the Rhone.'
'Why?'   'So that the Rhone can flow into
                                    the lake.'

3. *Phenomenistic.* Things which regularly occur together are regarded as causally connected. Thinking this way the child dreams up reasons which are often most weird, since literally anything may produce anything.

'What holds the moon up?'   'Because it's yellow.'
'What makes the steam engine go?' 'It goes with the fire.   The fire
                                    makes the wheels go by heating.'
'Show me.'   (He draws an engine quite empty
                                    in which the fire can be seen to be
                                    advancing toward the wheels with-
                                    out any intermediary.)

4. *Participation.* Phenomenistic explanations are strengthened by requiring a resemblance between things before they can be causally connected. If they have something in common then they are able to act upon one another even at a distance.

'Why is it dark there?'   'Because it is light there.' (Shows
                                    the other side of the object.)
'Where does the darkness come   'From the shadow.'
   from?'
'And the shadow?'   'From there.' (He points to the
                                    dark end of the room.)

5. *Magical.* Appropriate manipulation of things, words, gestures or even thoughts can influence the behaviour of other objects even at a distance. The connecting link between the two may be verbal or perceptual, or it may be a purely psychological one developed through some chance juxtaposition in the past.

'What makes the clouds move?'

'When we move along they move along too.'

'Can you make them move?'

'Everybody can when they walk.'

'And at night when everybody is asleep do they move?'

'Yes.'

'But you tell me they move when somebody walks.'

'They always move. The cats when they walk and then the dogs, they make the clouds move along.'

6. *Moral.* Nature, which is alive, is under a moral obligation to man and must behave, if treated correctly, in a way to satisfy his needs. There is an atmosphere here of moral *necessity*.

'How does the sun stay up there?'

'Because it wants to give us light.'

'Will this little boat lie on the water or go to the bottom?'

'It will lie on the water because they always must lie on the water.'

7. *Artificialist.* The child, impressed by what he sees people can do, decides that human beings have a hand in other things he doesn't understand. Events or objects are conceived to be the results of human or superhuman creativity.

'How did the wind begin?'

'Don't know.'

'How do you think it did?'

'It's made by blowing.'

'Where does the blowing come from?'

'From God.'

'How does God make it come?'

'With his mouth.'

(Spontaneously on seeing clouds move.)

'It's the mechanic who makes them go.'

8. *Animistic.* The child projects his own life into external objects, and assumes they move, act and think as he does. They act upon one another for human-like motives.

'Why does it (a book we have allowed to drop) not stay in the air?'

'Because it lets itself go.'

'Why does the sun not fall?'

'Because it doesn't want to come down.'

'Why do balloons go up?'

'Because they want to fly away.'

9. *Dynamic.* Things do not necessarily possess life, but they still contain internal forces capable of supporting or moving them.

'Why doesn't the moon fall?'	'The wind pushes it into the air.'
'And the big boats, why do they stay on the water?'	'It's because you make them go with a motor. If the motor stops, the boats go to the bottom.'
'But in port?'	'It's because they're tied up.'

10. *Reaction of the Surrounding Medium.* Here, for the first time, we have the need for continuity and contact. The clouds are regarded as setting themselves in motion, and once started, this motion is self perpetuating.

'Why does the water in the Arve move along?'	'Because there are boats going by.'
'But if there are no boats does it move along?'	'Yes.'
'Why?'	'Because there are big fish which swim.'

11. *Mechanical.* Objects act upon one another by physical contact. There is a direct physical chain of causation extending from the cause to the result.

'How does a bicycle move?'	'You pedal and it makes a wheel go around. There's a chain and it makes the back wheel go round.'

12. *Generation.* The child finally decides that neither he nor other people make all objects, but he may still think of them as born out of each other.

'Where does the wind come from?'	'From the sky.'
'How is it made?'	'From the clouds.'
'What do they do?'	'They open out then they all get together then afterwards they let the air come out.'

13. *Substantial Identification.* The notion of birth is replaced by one of physical reorganization.

> 'The sun and the moon are the same thing, when the sun sets it makes the moon which shinês during the night.'

14. *Condensation and Rarefaction.* Qualitative differences between objects are explained quantitatively.

'What is the sun made of?' — 'There are lots of little clouds.'
'What are clouds made of?' — 'They are all squeezed together.'

15. *Atomistic Composition.* An object is made up of smaller units joined together.

'How do the stones begin?' — 'You put cement, then after you stick them together, and then you hit them with a hammer and that makes them stick.'

'Where do stones come from?' — 'Because the seeds were put in the ground.'

'What sort of seeds?' — 'Seeds of stone.'

16. *Spatial.* Explanations of an abstract geometrical nature are attempted.

'Why is the shadow of this portfolio on this side?' — 'Because the clouds (he believes light comes from the clouds) do not see on this side.'

17. *Logical Deduction.* The reasons are of a highly intellectual nature. In the example given here, the principle of sufficient reason is used.

(Water is poured into a U tube.) 'Why does the water go like this?' — 'If you put a little more in one side it will also come up on the other, because it will go as far as halfway, one part to the left, one part to the right.'

This particular division of causality into different types is, of course, Piaget's, and despite his best attempts at objectivity it is bound to contain a large amount of personal bias. In addition, the questioning was carried out exclusively in French and German, so that questions and responses were limited to ideas expressible in these languages. The differences among some of the latter types seem very small (particularly 10 and 11, and 14 and 15), and taking into account the fact that any one answer usually could be put into any of several different causal categories, it is apparent that a quite different division is possible. A more accurate representation of the answers could be made by setting up a sort of causal spectrum (in analogy with the colour spectrum for light), with Piaget's seventeen different causal types located at various points along this spectrum, the earlier types being at the left, and the later, more mature causal types, at the right. Any specific answer would then cover a certain band of this spectrum, and any instantaneous state of a child's concept of causality would spread over some considerable region. As the child ages this region would move from left to right.

The seventeen senses of causality enumerated by Piaget reflect the child's changing concept of reality as the range of his experiences increases, and as his capacity for analysis and understanding grows. Initially he makes no separation of these experiences into those internal to him, and those coming from an external world, into objects situated in our 'common sense' space and time. The moon is as close to the baby as the rattle above his crib, and the refusal to give him either is met by equal protest. As far as he is concerned the universe has only one function: it is an extension of him and its purpose is the satisfying of his needs. He is not only the centre of the universe—he is the universe itself. This idyllic state is progressively destroyed; he separates off an internal part, over which he has a maximum of immediate control, from an external, the external being composed now of objects which are alive (like himself) and interested in him, but not directly devoted to satisfying his needs. If they are not under his control then he assumes they are under the control of other humans. Later still, he breaks the external world up into some parts which are alive, and more or less like him, and the remainder, which have motion only insofar as they are under the control of some living being.

The responses to Piaget's questions concerning the apparent motion of the moon are most revealing. Presumably we have all had the experience of watching the moon 'move' along in the sky with us when we move, and 'stop' when we stop. The child takes this at its immediate perceptual face value: the moon actually does follow him when he moves. The initial explanation may be that the moon must move in such a manner because the child needs the light (moral). Later, it is thought to move because it is curious about what he is doing (animistic). Development continues, until he finally recognizes that the moon's apparent motion is a trick of perspective. Now characteristically the young child doesn't ask himself whether it moves with respect to other people. When forced to answer this question, he may simply say that the moon follows everybody and doesn't see any reason why it can't. Later he recognizes the logical and geometrical contradictions involved in a situation in which the moon simultaneously follows two people moving in opposite directions, and ultimately the child gives, or at least accepts, the 'correct' answer.

Let us look at some of the typical answers received. Piaget divides them into three stages as the child shows increasing awareness of the relativistic nature of the phenomenon:

State 1. The child believes that the sun and the moon actually are able to follow several different people simultaneously.

'What does the sun do when you go out for a walk?' 'It moves.'
'How?' 'It goes with me.'
'Why?' 'To make it light so you can see clearly.'

'When I go for a walk where does the sun go?' 'It goes with you.'
'If you were to go that way and I this way, what would the sun do?' 'The sun would go with you . . .
'Why?' . . . with me.'

Stage 2. They follow us but without moving themselves.

'What does the sun do when you are out for a walk?' 'It follows us.'
'Then it moves?' 'No, you'd think it did.'
'Then what does it follow?' 'It follows us but it stays in the same place.'
'How does it do that?' 'It stays in the same place (but sends out) its rays.'

Stage 3. The illusion is understood.

'When you are out walking in the evening does the moon move?'	'It's far away and you'd say it was moving but it's not really.'
'Does it follow us?'	'No. I used to believe it followed us and that it ran after us.'

This illustrates the child's shift in attitude from 'subjectivity' to 'objectivity', 'reciprocity', and 'relativity'. By 'objectivity' it is meant that the child is building up a world which, in addition to himself, is composed of other objects and people. In 'reciprocity', he is taking account of perspective. He figures that if he can have an experience of a certain type in a certain place, then another person, similarly located, will have a similar experience. Other people too must have feelings, perceptions, and values like his own. With 'relativity', the child eliminates the absolute nature of substance and quality. The properties of bodies become more and more dependent upon their relation to one another and relative to us.

* * *

A growth in universality and a decrease in contingency is occurring in the child's developing interpretation of the world. In the earlier years the only sense of necessity is a moral necessity for the external world to obey the child, and later, man in general as master and creator. In consequence, laws are arbitrary because of the capriciousness of human will. It is interesting, however, that the child has a reason for everything, although reasons that are contradictory—'the boat will float because it is heavy (i.e. strong); the cork will float because it is light'—can be held simultaneously. Later the contradictions are resolved, as the laws become more general, and change from being 'anthropocentric' and 'moral' to 'physical'. 'Necessity' changes from 'moral' to 'logical necessity', i.e. deducible from 'self-evident' general principles. 'Chance' is now admissible as a valid 'explanation' for some events, and 'caprice' is diminished as an explanation (except where man or gods are concerned), although it never totally vanishes.

Social life is essential to the development of the mature concept of 'reality' in the child. With it, he changes from believing only in his own personal world view, to according significance to all points of view, and finally to considering 'reality' to be that world picture which simultaneously satisfies everyone's point of view. Neither a purely empirical nor a purely a priori philosophy is adequate to explain the changing nature of the child's 'reality'. The child brings to experience (the empirical part) a developing mind capable of certain types of thought (the a priori part), and the two react upon one another under the guiding influence of the surrounding society until the standardized mature adult emerges.

⋆   ⋆   ⋆

All seventeen different usages of the causal concept survive into adulthood, but a number of them are rejected at least theoretically. These include 'phenomenistic', 'participation', 'magic', 'animistic', 'dynamic', and 'generation'. The remainder, with modification, continue in use. 'Finalism' and 'artificialism' appear principally in theology; 'motivational' in psychology; 'reaction of the surrounding medium', 'mechanical', 'spatial', and 'logical', in science. The remarkable success of science in finding 'becauses' for the wide range of phenomena investigated during the last three centuries has emphasized causality in the sense of its scientific usage to the exclusion of the others. This has led to some confusion in investigating primitive societies, where their sense of causality has remained largely in the earlier forms. This is why Kelsen, for example, has denied the existence of any understanding of cause among certain primitive peoples. He states that: 'Personalistic and causal thinking exclude one another. Primitive man traces events which he wishes to understand not to elements of the same kind but to elements of a different kind, not to an object but a subject, not to a thing but to a person.' We reject such a point of view. If a people search for causes, no matter how contingent and personalized they may be, they have a belief in causality.

Particular attention has been paid to the magical and animistic aspects of primitive thought. Now, although the young child in our civilization also uses these in his explanation, there is a considerable quantitative difference between his usage and that of primitive people. Having minds as busily at work as ours, primitive men elaborated these types of causal explanation into structures large and complex enough to provide material for many anthropological Ph.D.'s. However, even the most primitive human must make some use of mechanical causation or he couldn't survive. If the problem is one of shaping a flint to make a hunting arrowhead, our savage craftsman may make certain ritual appeals to the god of stone, but he will most certainly not leave the rough stone for a god to shape. In fact the successful arrow maker has, of necessity, developed quite a sophisticated technique of pressing two stones together at the right angle, and just hard enough, to flake off chips and form a cutting edge; not an easy task as is clearly evident to a modern technician attempting to reproduce the results. The stone age workman certainly has all the notions of necessity, spatial contact, and temporal precedence belonging to a modern mechanical causality.

On the other hand if it is a question of ensuring sufficient rain at one time and adequate sun at another to grow his crops, little of 'advanced' causal thinking will be evident, as any connection between his actions and the course of events is not as apparent as in the case of chipping flint tools. Since good crops are a vital necessity to him, he will make use of what is available. He may pray to God, or threaten him. He may sacrifice a black bull to entice rain or a red one for the sun; or offer up his own son on the altar. Many people have advanced little beyond that stage today. When a volcano erupts, a hurricane threatens, or a war seems imminent, masses of people spend the larger part of their time in 'holy' places, carrying out, what frequently turn out to be, equally futile rituals.

If animistic explanation makes little sense, in terms of demonstrable success, when viewed objectively, it still is sensible in terms of much of the evidence available. The phenomena of life and death, of dreams, of possession by evil spirits, of sickness and madness, of seeing, of consciousness, and of multiple personality, are conducive to the belief that man is composite: a body that is inhabited, and a soul that inhabits. It is a very simple step to extend this notion to animals, and then to inanimate nature. Difficulties only arise when we attempt to elaborate animism into a consistent logical philosophical scheme, and to derive any predicative and testable results.

Every successful people then make use in varying degrees of all parts of the entire causal spectrum. The difference between less advanced peoples and our western civilization of today, is where the emphasis is placed along the spectrum from animistic to mechanistic—the more 'advanced' the group, the farther along in the spectrum the emphasis. An interesting analogy might be drawn between the way the contemporary child's concept of 'causality' develops, as he matures, through stages reproducing the way in which 'causality' appears to have evolved in progressively more advanced human societies into our modern 'civilized' concept, and the way the human foetus in the earlier stages of gestation reproduces the biological evolutionary history of the human animal in his assumed development from a primordial unicell through a succession of intermediate stages to the final human form. The difficulty in developing this analogy lies in deciding upon the particular criteria which must be used in locating societies along the 'primitive' to 'advanced' scale. If one locates them according to technical achievement it is not too surprising that the more 'advanced' would use a more scientific sense of causation. Again, if we located them according to their development of a sense of number or language, the reason for the parallelism would be plain. If we use some more general criterion, such as level of social organization, and if the correspondence survived, then some quite interesting conclusions might be drawn. We will not attempt any inference here.

The overt animism of the primitives contrasts with the covert and mostly verbal formulae of the moderns. Thus the Celts attacked the threatening flood with drawn swords and menacing spears to fight the water god who was apparently turning against them despite their previous peaceful overtures. The Masai threw spears and shot arrows at the moon attempting to devour the sun at the time of an eclipse. West Coast Indians of North America sacrificed slaves to Alaskan glaciers which were invading their fishing streams. Aboriginal Australians do not appear to recognize man's role and the act of intercourse as the cause of pregnancy, but there is still a cause cited:— the bull roarer (a thinly disguised male sex symbol). Today we still speak of 'spirits' of alcohol. A ship is a she, must be named, and properly launched, or she will resent her occupants. We say 'I can't imagine what possessed him', and the law may call in an 'alienist' to decide upon the fitness of an individual to stand trial. However some overt animisms also survive. Even today, in remote country districts of Europe, a peasant when injured by something will attempt a cure, not by attending to the wound, but by treating the offending object. In the most civilized communities there are innumerable superstitions of animistic origin: not walking under ladders, knocking on wood, crossing one's fingers, cherishing good luck symbols of horse shoes, rabbits' feet, four leaf clovers, St. Christopher medals, seven years' bad luck for breaking a mirror, tossing salt over the appropriate shoulder if accidentally spilled, etc.

* * *

Much of the credit for the development of our modern sense of causality must be given to progress in religion. When the world is viewed as peopled by a multitude of gods, with all their individual desires and fears, they will presumably be in conflict one with the other. Though a particular cause for a certain event may be discovered—such and such a stone had a desire to break off from the remainder of the rock and move into the valley—it is usually in retrospect. If this event did not occur it was perhaps forestalled by the god of the teepee being happy with his people and asserting his will against the rock god. With the dehumanization of the inanimate world some advance in universality became possible, but as long as there was more than one god, a conflict between various ones was possible and even common, and no completely consistent pattern of events was believed discoverable. An ancient Greek, therefore, could not truly expect to find the reason for a particular event. Venus, for example, might wish to promote a love affair between two mortals, but it would only come about if Zeus did not interfere. An enormous step forward is made with the belief in a single god. A unique god, never in potential conflict with another, and being truly omnipotent, is assumed sufficiently free of pettiness that an observation of the process of events in the world about us will reveal the pattern of his consistent will. In the case of the Christian culture the differentiation between man and animals is made sharply in terms of possession of a soul in one case and no soul in the other. (These differences are not so evident to, nor in fact even sought for by, the majority of other peoples.) By reducing the part of nature possessing wilfulness, the limiting of souls to man has led to the search for universality of cause, and, with the addition of certain other elements, has eventually led to the relatively recent concept of an entirely universal mechanistic causality.

* * *

Since our contemporary sense of cause has developed out of the earlier anthropomorphic ones, it has dragged along with it notions, which, though a propos in their earlier settings, are meaningless when addended to mechanistic causality. One of these is the notion of some necessary connection between cause and effect. This is understandable in an animistic causality where the cause of some event (such as the floating of a boat) is viewed as a living agent actively bringing about the effect (the god of the stream physically and consciously supporting the boat). However an analysis of phenomena, viewed without any assumed intervention of conscious agents, reveals no such necessary connection. For Hume, the only necessity was a psychological one in the observer, who,

B

having observed a succession of phenomenal conjoints in the past, has got into the habit of expecting the one after observing the other. The same kind of perceptual experience exists in the invariable sequence night-day-night-day . . . , as in striking a match, and observing the flame that follows. In the latter case we say that striking the match causes the flame, but we would never identify the cause of day as being the night. Necessity does not belong in the phenomena but in our interpretation of it.

★   ★   ★

Undoubtably we have not nearly exhausted all the aspects of causality, but we have looked at enough to permit a reduction of our contemporary usage into four kinds of 'cause'. To make this clear, let us return to John's automobile accident mentioned at the beginning of the chapter. The immediate physical event may be: While coming to a stop at a traffic light, John Topely's car is rammed from the rear by another. The resultant abrupt change in momentum snaps his head backward and gives him a sore neck. If we examine the accident a little more closely we find: John, travelling along Olds Avenue in his brand new green 300 SL at a speed considerably in excess of the speed limit, upon seeing the traffic light begin to go through its colour change green to red, slams on the brakes. He takes pride in the quick response of the newly redesigned superior braking system designed by Mercedes Benz and the feeling of driver-with-car identification described in the sports car magazines. Unfortunately a similar identification is not possessed by the ensemble George Hampton—Buick following him rather too closely, and the Buick tries to violate a long-standing logical principle by occupying the same space as the Mercedes at the same time. The net result is that the rear of the Mercedes is thoroughly demolished, the Buick's grill and bumper badly bent, and John Topely gets a very sore neck.

Now this latter would not have happened if: (1) John had not bought the Mercedes. (2) George Hampton's assistant hadn't got a rise permitting him to buy a Pontiac, thus requiring George to sell his year old Chevrolet (which would have stopped in 25% shorter distance) and buy a Buick. (3) If the brakes on the 300 SL hadn't been adjusted with such loving care by the German mechanic specially brought over by The Speed Merchants Garage to service their sports cars. (4) If the engineers at General Motors had been permitted by the salesmen in the advertising department to put as much attention into the designing of superior brakes as in increasing the horsepower of their engines. (5) If John had been less obsessed with a feeling of his own omnipotence and been paying attention to the car behind him. (6) If the traffic light relay had closed two seconds later, which it would have if there had been a little more rust present, which there would have been if the weather were damper, which it would have been if so many trees hadn't been cut down by farmers which . . . (7) If a snow storm hadn't occurred the night before and the road not been somewhat slippery.

For this particular accident, then, if any one of this list had been as stated above the accident would not have occurred. This is our first sense of causation: *partial cause*—as an example, one (partial) cause was the slowness of the reflexes of the driver of the black car. Tracing back from the event to the causes, we recognize that each of the partial causes was a necessary condition for the particular event. Next, for the accident to happen we must have slowness of reflexes of the one driver, plus non-attentiveness of the other, plus slipperiness of the road, plus all the rest. We call the sum of all the partial causes the *total cause* of an event, and we will identify it as the necessary and sufficient condition for that particular event. Now let us take one of these partial causes—example, the slipperiness of the road—and search back along its history. If it hadn't snowed the road wouldn't have been slippery. If the sanding truck had come by on time the road wouldn't have been slippery. The truck would have been in good order and able to keep up to schedule if the mechanic had got to his job on time. The mechanic wouldn't have been late for work if . . . etc. Now such a list may extend backwards in time indefinitely or we may decide it potentially comes to an end at a certain point. In this case it may be that the mechanic wakes up at the usual hour, deliberates between getting up or going back to sleep and, if we are believers in 'free will', 'freely' decides to sleep rather than go to work. This decision can be called an *originating* cause for the event. Our fourth aspect of cause is *final cause*. Our black car driver is speeding along this slippery road faster than is safe in order to get to his appointment. The appointment can be called a *final cause* of the event. One more sense of cause remains. The accident would not have occurred—if the road had not been there, if automobiles had not been invented, if gravity did not exist to keep the car on the road, if the planet earth did not exist. . . . However, all these factors are so constant over space and time that in practice one does not bother mentioning them in describing the causes of this particular accident. The set of causes that must be specifically mentioned in giving the why for a certain event can be called the *preponderating cause*. It constitutes a subset of the set of causes constituting the total cause.

* * *

Let us summarize. The 'cause' can be:
  (1) partial cause (necessary but not sufficient);
  (2) total cause (necessary and sufficient), including preponderating cause;
  (3) originating cause (the causal reverse trail stops at a certain point);
  (4) final cause (teleological—one of the causes is an event in the future).

In physical science we are concerned principally with the first and second, 'total cause' being of central theoretical importance. However, as we have seen in our examples, the search for the 'total cause' of any event generally takes in such a large territory, both spatially and temporally, that rarely can all the 'partial causes' be enumerated. Thus, science may use the concept of 'total cause' without actually ever being able to specify all the individual 'causes' making it up. It seems preferable then to introduce the word 'determined'. Rather than saying ΣC_i (the sum of all the individual partial causes, C_i) is the 'total cause' of an event E, we say that E is determined—meaning by this that we believe there is a set of earlier events determining that E and no other must occur even though we are not able in practice to specify the entire set. This will become clearer in later chapters when we will concentrate our attention upon particular problems. After this, when we speak of 'cause' we will be referring to (one of the) 'partial causes' of a certain event.

'Originating cause' plays no role in science although it is an important concept elsewhere, as, for example, in moral philosophy or legal theory. When we use 'cause' in this way we mean that there exists a causal sequence of events—A,B, ... C,D—and that there is no causal precursor to A. 'A' would then be the 'originating cause' of D. Since B invariably succeeds A, B itself is determined and cannot be an 'originating cause' of D (even though B is a (partial) cause). In our discussion of the automobile collision the decision of the snowplough mechanic to sleep, rather than work, is an example of such a cause, provided we assume he might have 'freely' chosen to do one or the other, and there is nothing in his previous history to determine that he do the one he did. (A full-fledged discussion of 'free', used in the sense above, is postponed to Chapter 8, by which time we will have at our disposal much more information and analysis.)

'Final cause' is a concept of considerable theoretical importance in fields ranging from Biology, through Psychology, to Theology (it is also known under the equivalent names of equifinality, teleology, etc.) which are specifically concerned with the behaviour of living organisms. It has to do with that particular kind of behaviour in which an entity's attention seems to be directed towards a certain end-goal, and the entity's actions are adjusted towards achieving that end. The means used depend upon the general situation, and can take on a multitude of different forms. Thus, in the sequence A,B,C, . . . D, it is the D that is important and could be called the 'final cause'. In other cases the sequence could be $A,B_1,C_1, . . . D$ or $A,B_2,C_2, . . . D$, etc. The D is fixed, but the sequence leading up to it is variable. (An example of this would be an animal seeking food.) This used to be considered to be a characteristic peculiar to living beings and to be inexplicable in physical terms. However, although this end-directed behaviour is not so evident in the phenomena of non-living entities, it does exist, and the development during the last several decades of automated devices has produced many instances of it. These devices frequently make use of a feed-back technique in which the separation between the instantaneous state of the device and the desired end-state is measured, an appropriate correction is made, and the process is repeated until the goal is achieved. One well-known example of this is the 'homing' rocket. Its 'brain' continually corrects the rocket's path for changes in the internal functioning of the rocket, changes in the state of the surrounding atmosphere, and evasive action of the enemy, to 'home-in' on the target. Among other examples are Ashby's 'Homeostat' and Grey Walter's 'Tortoise'. This latter wanders about 'exploring' the environment until it becomes 'hungry' (its battery runs down), it looks around for and heads for 'food' (a battery charger), groping around obstacles in its path in 'a most life-like manner'. Thus, we see there is nothing peculiarly mysterious about 'final cause'. In a penetrating theoretical study Braithwaite shows it to be a special kind of the more ordinary, temporally prior cause, as our examples above have illustrated.

If we return to the surviving senses of cause accepted in our civilization, we see that the common-sense man takes up a position somewhere between the extremes of total mechanistic determinism and indeterminism. With animism eliminated, he assumes that inanimate nature is physically determined, but, where life and particularly man is concerned, a non-reducible indetermined element enters the picture. He recognizes the effect of past events in developing the character of an individual, but believes that, except in special cases where the effect of past environment has been too harsh, the exercise of sufficient 'will power' will permit him to do what he (as originating cause) wills, within the limits, of course, of immediate compulsion. Man believes that he can not only do what he wills but can will what he will.

CHAPTER II

Percept and Concept.
The Structure of a World Picture

SUMMARY: We have seen in the first chapter that 'cause' is a most important concept in man's everyday language and that it is used with a wide variety of different meanings. As long as these different senses of the word are not contradictory this does not bother us in most of our ordinary affairs, where in fact some ambiguity enhances the aesthetics if not the clarity of discourse. However, in a philosophical study greater precision is necessary. We have made a first step by establishing a classification of cause according to: 'partial', 'total', 'originating', and 'final'. We introduced the scientific term 'determinism' as equivalent to 'total cause', and dropped 'finalism' as being simply a special type of 'prior cause'. In the sequel, then, we will be working only with 'partial cause', 'determinism', and 'originating cause'. There is little disagreement about the existence of partial causes of events. The real question revolves about whether events in the world are determined or not. Much more work needs to be done before we will be ready to talk about this.

Now whatever else 'cause' and 'determinism' may be they are words, and to understand them we must understand the function of words and language; how words combine with one another to make meaningful statements, and how these statements correspond to events in the world around us. It is beyond the scope of this book to carry out a thoroughgoing analysis of this. In particular, we will make no attempt to study the details of language or mathematical grammar. However there are three things we must do. In order they are: First, by recreating the method by which our concept of reality is built up, to examine the nature of our present-day common-sense—scientific—philosophical world picture; second, to study the construction and operation of symbolic systems in general (of which language is one example); third, to understand the functional relation between the two—our experiences of the world and our symbolic representation of it.

* * *

Like the doubting Descartes with his 'Cognito ergo sum' ('I think therefore I am') the reflective man begins with a fundamental certainty: the existence for him of a continuing flux of his own thoughts. A verbal description of the nature of this basic experience is very difficult since words only appear at a much later stage when this 'raw stuff of the imagination' has been shaped, disciplined, and forced into the restrictive mould of language. Though the child for the first few months of his life operates close to this basic level, the adult can only be fleetingly aware of it at such times as, for example, the first moments of consciousness after an operation or a severe shock. It is a continuum of sounds, colours, smells, tastes and tactile sensations not yet organized into our common sense reality and conceptualized as: 'This pine tree', 'The sun', 'Morgan's bark', 'Rory's crying', . . . etc. 'My desk' does not exist as such yet. There is only a certain colour complex of yellows, greens, and dark browns in visual space, certain sensations of hardness and pressure in tactile space, and possibly some smells, tastes, and sound sensations in their various sense spaces. (To be quite correct we would have to recognize that these sense spaces have not even been disentangled from one another at this early stage of pure perception.) Introspective examination shows that this, our basic experience, is continuous, both throughout our sense space, and in time. In fact, the very notion of gaps, voids in which there is simply nothing, is both incomprehensible and indescribable in our language. It is continuous and gapless but not uniform. In the middle of the large patch of yellow in visual space is a patch of green. Two long thin patches of brown are adjacent to the yellow, with a large patch of red in between. On the other side of the yellow is a large patch of blue. Beyond the blue is . . . The same holds true for the other sense spaces but description of them is even more difficult. Although some of these perceptual differentiations hold a relatively constant relationship with respect to one another, in general they change as time progresses. A convenient label for this raw experience (before the mind begins its organizing action upon it) is: 'The changing differentiated continuum of immediately apprehended experience'. The significance of the various words in this label should be quite clear by now.

The existence of this 'changing differentiated continuum' is not here considered to be an assumption open to discussion, but a fact. With a few exceptions (such as the rejection by some mystics of the differentiations as being illusion—Maya) the certainty of its existence is fundamental to all world pictures. Nothing else is equally certain. Thus even Descartes' 'Cognito' is open to doubt since it goes one step further:

namely, the assertion of an 'I' that experiences, rather than simply the immediately existing experiences themselves. This 'I' is a postulate, and may be valid or not, but it is not part of our basic certainty.

Individual differentiations in the perceptual continuum will be called *percepts* (as examples: a patch of yellow, b flat played at a certain instant by the cello, a rotten egg smell, the mouth-pursing taste of raw lemon, the softness of a kitten's fur). However, as adults, it is only rarely that we can be directly aware of percepts in themselves. As we have observed the process going on in the child, the mind is constantly working on the raw material, organizing this basic experience into a world picture comprehensible to itself. In the first step of this process, observing that certain complexes of percepts seem to persist and move as more or less invariable units against the continuum background, the mind makes the simplification of considering that these grouped percepts are just various aspects of the same *thing*, and we have the simplest class of *concepts*: desks, doors, trees, pussycats, . . . After a few years of this sort of conceptualization, it is difficult to remember or even recognize the considerable amount of theorizing that has gone into the formation of these elementary concepts which form the basis of our symbolic world picture. However they are concepts, and they represent a first stage of abstraction away from basic experience. This introduces for the first time a possibility of error not existing in the pure percepts themselves. This is part of the reasons for the attempt in science to reduce the final check on theories to the simplest types of concepts, such as juxtapositions of pointers with marks on scales or, even more simply, counting procedures. (However this simplification in testing usually results in a compensatory elaboration in the theoretical part of the symbolic structure—witness physics.)

* * *

Now we have been presenting percepts and concepts as if they were as distinguishable as black from white, and this is not really the case. In fact, all intermediate shades of grey exist. A convenient representation of percepts and concepts would be as a spectrum ranging from pure percepts at one end, totally devoid of cognitive action, to pure concepts at the other, containing no sensory component whatsoever. In actuality, of course, we are never dealing with the pure extremes but rather some intermediate hybrid.

* * *

We make a rough but necessary division of percepts and the concepts formed from them into two general classes. The first is called sensory, and the second, introspective. To differentiate qualitatively between the two in words is very difficult. We could say that the sensory class is composed of those that persist regularly in time and can be organized into a consistent conceptual scheme, while the introspective consists of those that do not satisfy these above requirements; while these latter may form meaningful patterns for a time, they soon change in unpredictable ways. It is apparent that any such verbal division is far from sharp, and this is reflected in the fact that there frequently is disagreement among different people as to where certain percepts belong. Regularity, organizability, persistence, it is not at all easy to make a distinction in words between sensory and introspective, while in fact everyone understands what we mean by the distinction: assuming our conceptual scheme includes an 'I' separated from the rest of the universe but receiving information from it through a set of sensory receptors, we can say quite simply that the sensory group consists of those percepts resulting directly from stimulation of our 'sense organs' by processes in the 'external world', while the introspective are of 'internal' manufacture.

In science we restrict our attention as much as possible to the sensory group of percepts. There are two reasons for this. The first is that in science we are concerned with 'objective reality', with what can be observed by everyone, and this would obviously limit us to 'public' percepts. The second reason, however, is the eminently practical one that up to now relatively little success has been attained in organizing the introspective percepts into a conceptual scheme that works except occasionally and imperfectly. Thus, among the countless attempts by amateurs and professionals alike at basing predictions on dream analysis, it takes a Joseph analysing a Pharaoh's dream to produce a verifiable result comparable with those attainable by a modern scientist in his field; and the Josephs have been rare. Workers in the field of introspective percepts and concepts are the first to admit the very elementary state of their knowledge.

★   ★   ★

Patches of colour, sensations of hardness, heaviness, loudness, bitterness, are percepts, whereas 'I', the 'sun', a 'tree', the 'diatonic scale' are experience plus a considerable amount of mental operation—concepts. The naïve realist's belief that, for example, there exists an external object corresponding to the concept 'desk' possessing in fact all the properties of colour, shape, susceptibility to termites and fire, ability to stand up under heavy loads . . . that we associate with it inside our symbolic system, certainly works. This holds true for the larger part of our common-sense everyday reality, otherwise neither this reality concept nor man would have survived to the present day. The development of this common-sense scheme into physical science proved to be equally satisfactory, and it was not until the twentieth century, when the instrumental extension of our senses brought us into a new range of experience—the very small, the very large, the very fast (the very slow may be yet to come)—that serious difficulties arise.

As an example of this, consider the question: 'Is an electron a particle or a wave?' This query is an entirely legitimate one at the common-sense level and also for classical physics, where 'x' can be one or the other, but not neither nor both. However no one answer could be found. There are three possibilities: (1) there is no electron; (2) physics is 'wrong'; or (3) the question assumes a conceptual scheme not corresponding to reality at this level. If we take the first answer, we have left unexplained a large set of physical experiences—cloud chamber tracks, clicks in geiger counters, and, as part of the large organized scheme of microscopic theory, atomic and hydrogen bomb explosions. If we accept the second, the 'wrongness' of physics, then we would be rejecting a theory which has been one of the most successful universal theories of all time, and we have nothing to substitute in its place. The third possibility, that the question is illegitimate, is the one we must accept. This question will be taken up and discussed in detail in succeeding chapters.

*   *   *

In case all this argument about the distinction between percepts and concepts may seem to be purely academic and without any practical importance, as it must to the average common-sense man and his philosophical counterpart—the 'naïve' realist, let us look at some of the evidence justifying such an analysis. Ideally, we need an enormously precocious child who, in the first moments of life, would be able to tell us his sensations and describe the mental operations leading to concept formation. This, of course, is not a possibility. We do have available the work of such artists as the 'impressionists', who describe their work as being close to what we experience in immediate sensation. There is no doubt, however, that a considerable amount of sophisticated interpretation goes into their work, and it cannot be taken as a really close approximation to the 'differentiated continuum of immediately apprehended experience'. Fortunately some very useful although controversial experimental evidence exists in the studies carried out upon people who, congenitally blind, gain their eyesight, following eye operations, at an age when, in contrast to the infant, they are perfectly able to speak and describe their visual sensations as they construct, laboriously and painfully, a visual world. Now, the results are not clear-cut, nor can they be taken as equivalent to what goes on in the developing baby, as the recently blind do have already available to them a concept world formed from the sense material of the other senses, and during the period of blindness they may have irrevocably lost some visual ability, but still it represents probably the best evidential picture we can get of what goes on.

The recently blind have little difficulty in learning to recognize and correctly name patches of colour; however, weeks of practice are required before they can learn to perform quickly the act, so simple for the normal adult, of distinguishing a triangle from a square. They report that the first stage in their learning to do this comes when they can start to identify and count corners. If they close their eyes and use their hands to feel the geometrical figures, they can recognize them without difficulty. Experiments on animals kept in totally dark enclosures from birth and then exposed to controlled visual experimental situations lead to conclusions paralleling the above. This groping and piecemeal identification is to be compared with our normal 'instantaneous' identification or, in fact, that which the previously blind themselves are able to execute after some months of practice. As a common example of this for the 'seeing' we are all familiar with the sort of trick pictures in which we are asked to pick out certain objects hidden in a maze of others. Once we discover them there is no difficulty in hanging on to them or in finding them later with much less difficulty.

Now let us consider some instances of the converse situation, namely, that in which an object which is not there at all is conceptualized out of an incomplete set of percepts. We consider studies reported by Hebb. When one occipital pole of the brain has been destroyed, the patient becomes blind in one half of his visual field. However, if a simple symmetrical object, such as a billiard ball, is suspended at midway the patient nevertheless says that he sees all of it. That he actually does not, but in fact is completing a conceptualization, is shown by presenting him with only half a ball so located that the missing half is on the blind side. The patient still 'sees' it all. More familiar instances are those in which people's 'overwrought' imagination see dangerous figures where none are present.

Another even more startling example of the amount of mental construction involved in our apparently direct perception of the world appears in the results of investigations carried out in distorting rooms. These are so constructed, following the laws of perspective, that when empty they look normal to the 'naïve' observer. However, in actuality, the one corner is much farther away than the other. If now a subject unknown to the observer walks about in the room he appears to shrink and grow in a most mysterious manner as he walks from one corner to the other. The observer maintains the belief that the room is an ordinary one, with the far wall perpendicular to his line of sight, and can only explain the perceived change in subject size by a growing and shrinking. However the really extraordinary phenomena appears when a subject is used with whom the observer is 'emotionally' involved. The previous situation is reversed, the subject looks 'normal', his change in size is interpreted correctly as a change in distance from the observer, and the room is seen as distorted.

As a final example there is the very simple experiment in which children are asked to estimate the size of a plain white disc by matching it visually against standard discs. It is found that if the disc has acquired some significance to the children, by, for example, being previously used as a candy token, it is estimated as being larger (as much as 14%) than if it is neutral.

There are many more examples. The reader who is still unconvinced is advised to spend some time with the extensive literature on the subject of Perception (particularly the work of the Gestaltists).

* * *

So far we have used the word 'reality' several times. Before we go any further we had better come to an understanding as to what we mean when we use this word. There appears to be at least four different ways in which 'reality' can be defined:

(i) As we have already noted, for the naïve realist the ordinary everyday world of doors and dishes, water waves and billiard balls, as described in our language, is what 'really is', and is 'reality'. There are three serious objections to our adopting this as our definition. First, as we have mentioned above, this conceptual scheme doesn't work for the new range of perceptual experience we are encountering in the twentieth century. Second, as a general objection, there is no way that this 'really is' can possibly be verified operationally, since this would require some independent method of obtaining information about the 'really is'. Third, different peoples disagree with one another in their description of this 'reality'.

If we make a division of our universe of discourse into four parts (*a*) concepts organized into a world picture, (*b*) percepts that we are taking account of, are 'attending' to, (*c*) the totality of our raw percepts, and, (*d*) for a fourth element, the commonly made assumption of a 'source' of these experiences, we find that there are three more sophisticated possible definitions:

(ii) 'Reality' is the 'source of experiences'.
(iii) 'Reality' is the differentiated continuum of perceptual experiences.
(iv) 'Reality' is the particular conceptualization scheme that we are using at any one moment.

Any one of these is potentially acceptable but it is necessary for us to make a choice. If we mean by 'reality' this 'source' of experience, we are talking about something that in itself is unknowable and undescribable, and is much more of an assumption than experience, percept, or even concept. If we mean by 'reality' the raw experience itself, then it is most certainly what 'really is', and in this sense is an absolute which may be amplified but is otherwise unchangeable. The disadvantages are that this end of the percept-concept spectrum is by definition undescribable, and worse, it is far from the way in which the common-sense man would answer the question: 'What is reality?' He would promptly talk about chairs and tables and not about patches of colour. This objection is satisfied if we take for our meaning of 'reality' the symbolic world picture. The disadvantage of this definition is that 'reality' is then not something permanent for all time, but instead somewhat arbitrary, varies from person to person, and changes as the conceptual picture changes. These objections are outweighed by the fact that it is entirely describable, operationally applicable, and is very close, in verbalization at least, to the common-sense meaning. This is the definition we will use. In using this we are not denying in any way the 'existence' of a 'source' of experience.

'Reality' then is our conceptualized representation of experience as organized into a systematic picture. It is not actually what 'really is', but something we have created rather than discovered. For any one person it is built up partly consciously and partly unconsciously as the result of the interaction between the maturing child's modes of thought and his continuing experience; and it is shaped and disciplined by his social environment. By defining 'reality' in this way we are not denying the realness of experience. It is the final truth against which our conceptual structures and predictions are checked, and the resulting verification or refutation serves as a criterion for preferring one system to another. The better one is the one in better agreement with experience.

★ ★ ★

The first stage in the construction of a world picture is the conceptualization of the percepts into things. The second stage is the representation of these things by names or, more generally, by symbols. The third stage is the organizing of these symbols into a comprehensive system. Now non-human animals too make use of signs and symbols. The dog delimits his territory and advertises his presence by lifting his leg and leaving his smell. By means of an elaborate dance, only recently interpreted by zoologists, the honey bee tells her co-workers the direction and distance of a new find of honey-makings, and the greater the potential of the discovery, the more frenzied her dance. However, man alone has a special ability at inventing symbols and weaving them into patterns. The human child with his babbling is unique among young animals, even among the anthropoid apes closest to mankind. The apes make noises, but principally in response to specific stimuli or to induce particular behaviour in their fellows, while the human baby makes a large variety of sounds apparently for the pure joy of making them. As he matures, the sounds are channelled and restricted according to the local social usage, and finally develop into common speech. Our language symbolic system, along with certain social signs, painting, music, and mathematics, which is our most precise form, is largely responsible for the development of our civilization of today, but at the same time this systematization restricts our capacity for thought. The thoughts we can have, the deductions we can make, and the concepts we can form, are limited not only by our mental structure but also by our symbolic apparatus.

· Here's an example. If we use a logic in which there are only two values for statements, 'true' or 'false', it is difficult to consider statements which might be neither 'true' nor 'false', but have some third, fourth or fifth value. Multi-valued logics of this sort would be rejected by the man in the street as just so much nonsense. However, as we have mentioned above, questions which cannot be answered by a simple 'true' or 'false' have appeared in modern physics. The translation of languages furnishes another even simpler example. The change in the relationship between people characterized by shifting in conversation from the 'vous' form to 'tu' (to 'tutoyer' someone) in French, or among the three forms 'tu', 'lei', and 'voi' in Italian, has no significance in English, and is a constant problem for the tourist or the translator of stories and plays.

                              ★   ★   ★

Symbolizing by man, then, has both advantages and disadvantages. That it must be predominantly an advantage is proven by the persistence of our species. We can contrast the ape who will reach for a banana with a stick as long as he can see both banana and stick simultaneously, but rarely otherwise, with the human child who can hold onto the concepts of banana and stick simultaneously by means of the words, and from this symbolic association proceed at any time to the physical. More advanced than either monkey or child is the engineer designing a bridge on a piece of paper.

   A liability in the use of symbols is that the existence of words as sounds or marks representing a certain concept is often extended into some sort of assumed physical existence. Such a confusion has already been seen in the child. In the extreme case, among some peoples their gods or even the people themselves are known only by nicknames. Their real names are closely guarded secrets, for they believe that anyone finding out these names would have absolute power over their owners. As further examples, we find primitive peoples slaughtering black bulls to bring on rain or red bulls to stop the rain, praying to different specific gods (that they themselves have invented as symbols) depending upon the specific trouble they are in or expect to be in, and, in one case, parading about a city and blowing horns in an effort to make the walls fall down. . . . If a dog in a psychological test behaved analogously we would be most startled and probably pronounce him neurotic, particularly in view of the pragmatic fact that such attempts at using symbols directly to control the environment have been unsuccessful in the past, according to any reasonable criterion of reliability.

   As we have seen, man's mind never simply experiences. It immediately acts upon the continuum of experience, fitting it into a conceptual framework. Experience has been reduced to a set of concepts, and each concept is represented by a symbol. This seems to be an unavoidable procedure so far as man is concerned, but in the process much of the immediately apprehended perceptual experience has been lost. As a general rule, from the initial infinitely complex experience only what has significance to us has been retained. This is apparent among animals when we try to interest them in things not related to food, shelter, or sex. It can be done with much effort, but any trainer knows the advantage of having a pocketful of biscuits or a handful of raw liver when teaching his dog some new trick. There are many instances at the human level: the experienced hunter sees the deer and takes a shot at it while the amateur marksman sees only a jumble of brush and trees; the professional football coach appears to see all the movements of the players in both teams, while the afternoon T-viewer is barely able to follow the ball. . . . Only when certain details have significance (sign worthiness) for a person will he invent symbols for them.

★　★　★

In this first part of the chapter we have looked at the process by which our 'changing differentiated continuum of immediately apprehended experience' is reduced to a set of symbols. Our next job is to study how these symbols are combined with one another to form a logical system which can be handled deductively, and manipulated so as to predict the nature of future experience. In later chapters we will study one example of such a system—physics—in some detail, but in this chapter we will examine the general characteristics essential to all symbolic systems. For this we will make use (without following it rigorously) of the scheme developed principally by Charles Morris and Rudolf Carnap. In their method of analysis a symbolic world picture, which they call a *semiotic*, is divided into three parts:

(1) The primitive symbols plus the set of hypotheses, laws, axioms, premises, postulates, or codes (call them what you will) arrived at inductively, intuitively, or revealed mystically. The study of these and their relation to their user is called *Pragmatics*.

(2) The methods of deductive thinking, more or less formalized, which combine elements in (1) above to form particular statements and theorems—*Syntactics*.

(3) The correlation of the theoretical scheme with experience itself. This is the decisive test for the adequacy of the system. If this test is

satisfied, then particulars obtained deductively in the Syntax become predictions for future experience. This division of semiotics in which symbols and experience are correlated is called *Semantics*.

Now although semiotics has been broken up into three divisions, this must be considered merely a device for making analysis easier. The three flow together, and a full understanding of any system requires not only investigations into its pragmatics, syntactics, and semantics separately, but, in addition, a study of how they function jointly. If we examine any actual semiotic we will see that its initial inspiration was some particular set of conceptualized experiences and hence semantic; that an attempted understanding of these events led to hypothesis formulation and syntactical elaboration; that semantic comparison with the facts showed deviations; variations on the orginal hypotheses were tried, and the process repeated, until the entire system proved in some measure satisfactory. This tripart analysis is enormously useful a posteriori for picking a system apart, seeing its flaws and weakness and strengths, and, most importantly, suggesting the place where modification may be made to improve it. Let us look at each of the three.

In *pragmatics*, the words 'arrived at inductively, intuitively, or revealed mystically' are used in order to emphasize the fact that the hypotheses (laws, axioms, premises, codes) are not obtainable logically, and most definitely not deductively. Induction is sometimes defined as a process which is the reverse of deduction, but this does not make clear the radically different nature of the two. Deduction can be formalized, definite rules laid down so that any person starting with the same postulates will arrive at the identical conclusion. This cannot be done in the same unique way for induction. Although Bar-Hillel and Carnap, among others, have been working to develop a formalized 'inductive logic' the probabilistic calculus is required in the 'induction' and we must recognize the existence of a sharp discontinuity between the consideration of the particular events and the formulation of an hypothesis designed to 'explain' them. We can emphasize this by appending the word 'jump' to 'inductive' thus: 'inductive jump'. In addition, it seems established that for any finite set of facts an infinite number of distinct sets of hypotheses could be used to integrate them into a coherent system and the particular set chosen is a matter of personal choice and genius. At the time when Einstein formulated his theory of relativity all the component ideas existed: four dimensional space-time geometry, Fitzgerald-Lorentz contraction, the Michelson-Morley experiment showing the absence of measurable ether velocity, and so on. Many were working on the problem, proposing and testing hypotheses, but it was Einstein's luck or genius that his hypothesis set was the one finally adopted as being the most satisfactory. If a machine were carrying out an induction we could imagine it running through a succession of trial postulational systems until it arrived at the best one, but the process is not really so simple, particularly when we take into account the already mentioned infinity of possible sets. Anyway, no matter how it is done, the problem is to find a set of hypotheses whose logically deduced consequences will fit the set of particular phenomena being explained. When the process is 'intuitive' the only difference is that the search has been carried out largely unconsciously and appears to be instantaneous as far as the 'conscious' is concerned. The mystical can be considered a special case of the intuitive.

In the past, distinctions have been frequently made between axioms and postulates. Axioms were considered to be universal rather than restricted to any particular system, and to be 'self-evident truths', while postulates were concepts assumed as true to form the basis of some special system. Thus, as examples of axioms we have: 'things equal to the same things are equal to each other'; and, 'the whole is the sum of its parts'; while 'through two distinct points only one straight line can be drawn', and, 'any straight line can be extended indefinitely' are postulates. However we can find no justification for drawing distinctions between the two; they are all hypotheses intended to be elaborated logically. Any or all may be changed since we can prove none of them in the sense of any logical or mathematical proof.

In the *syntactic* part of the semiotic, the primitive symbols are combined with one another according to specified rules of formation so as to derive new entities. The manipulation is entirely symbolic, and a 'true' theorem or sentence is simply one formed correctly according to the rules of the system. We are all familiar, or were, with the rules of English grammar and those of traditional logic, among others: *identity*, A is A; *contradiction*, A cannot be both B and not B; and *excluded middle*, A is either B or not B. But a syntax does not have to follow these. It may follow any set it pleases as long as certain criteria of independency and consistency are satisfied.

In *semantics* a correlation is made between the entities present in the syntax and our experiences. Memory is essential, and our most important tool is the pointing finger. It should be quite apparent from our consideration of the percept-concept spectrum that it is not necessary that all the concepts be directly correlated with experience. In fact, it is probably impossible to form a semiotic that doesn't contain some such non-correlatable elements. Thus in English and traditional logic, relational elements like 'and', 'or', 'is', 'implies' have no immediate perceptual significance in themselves, but only as part of the entire statement which contains them. Another example is universals. At least one group of semanticists recognizing this characteristic of universals has refused to admit them into their language. They emphasize that while Smith, Jones, and Doe exist, 'man' does not. Even more, Smith of 1957 is not the Smith of 1958, nor is the science of 1957 the science of 1958. They push this consideration back into the syntax, and insist that words of this type be qualified if sentences using them are to be legitimate. Thus the sentence 'science states that . . . ' is considered by them to be 'untrue', that is, not a proper sentence syntactically. Whereas 'Science (California, 1953, . . .) states that . . . ' may be true or false but at least it is correctly constructed. Questions of this kind are rather technical, and far beyond the scope of this book. We will content ourselves with only two remarks. (1) An attempt at greater precision of this sort leads quickly to an impracticably cumbersome syntax. (2) Our discussion of the formation of concepts from percepts has demonstrated the amount of abstraction involved in the formation of even the simplest concepts. There seems to be no particularly good reason to be intimidated by the additional amount required for universals and any other non-directly correlatable concepts from the pure concept end of the percept-concept spectrum. There is no logical objection to the introduction into a semiotic of any element that will help in the succinct testable description of experience.

To some extent the correlation between symbols and experience is arbitrary, although in forming a useful semiotic many restrictions are necessary. Since the symbols are united together in the syntax, the perceptual experiences must follow an analogous pattern. As a simple example of this: once 'Smith' is correlated with a particular subset of experiences, we cannot correlate 'Jones' with the same or, on fact, most intersecting subsets. Next, with 'Smith' and 'Foot' correlated, no independent correlation exists for the symbol 'Smith's Foot'. The instance here is trivial and the problem becomes more acute as the system becomes more complicated. Thus, in physics, we find that once length, time, and force have been individually semantically correlated with certain percepts, mass cannot be arbitrarily correlated, and, if we look back into our syntax, we find this is because mass is a defined function of the other three.

⋆   ⋆   ⋆

Certain restrictions are imposed upon the semiotic. Some of these are:

(1) The syntax must rigorously follow some system of logic, with precisely defined rules of analytic definition and logical inference.

(2) The hypotheses are considered to be exactly that—hypotheses. They are accepted as a satisfactory basis for the entire conceptual scheme only as long as they work; that is, as long as their predictions for future experience are verified.

(3) The better system of hypotheses among several is the one which in practice is able to make more detailed and successful predictions, and permit its user to have a greater degree of control over the environment.

(4) The semiotic must be comprehensive, in that it organizes a wide range of experience into a relatively small and actually usable symbolic system.

(5) The semiotic must be universally confirmable. Any intellectually and technically equipped individual must be able to use the system, make predictions, and verify them.

(6) No independent subset of the concepts exists which is completely lacking in semantic correlation with experience.

In practice, such rules are only an ideal to be aimed at. It would be unreasonable to believe that any actual working scheme has been put into such a tidy state that it conforms perfectly to all possible demands, but it still represents a goal towards which we work. Nor is it likely that anyone would seriously set forward a scheme of thought violating all of these principles. In fact, it would be impossible to do so, since the very formulation of a system necessitates some sort of syntactical framework, some set of hypotheses, and some pragmatic justification for continuing to use the system.

⋆   ⋆   ⋆

A common query about any statement or theory is: 'Is it true?' There would appear to be four principal kinds of *truth*:

(i) The first of these is *logical truth* inside the structure of the system. Here a given statement is true or false depending upon whether or not it is constructed according to the syntactic rules of a system, or, another way of saying the same thing, is obtained by following the accepted rules of inference from the fundamental postulates. Consider:

'That man's husband is hungry.'

This statement is syntactically 'true' in English in that it follows accepted rules of grammatical construction. Or:

'The exterior angle of a triangle is equal to the sum of
the interior and opposite angles.

This is a logically 'true' deduction from the postulates of Euclidean geometry.

(ii) The second truth is *semantic truth*. Using the above examples, we make a correlation between the syntactical logical system and the assumed external real world. We would reject the first statement as 'untrue' in that 'husband' is not a possible attribute of man because of the way the two are semantically associated with objects in the world. As for the exterior angle of the triangle, the truth can only be checked by an actual measurement, and this can never constitute more than a partial verification.

(iii) *Pragmatic truth* is the third. A set of hypotheses is pragmatically true for an individual or a group of individuals when its use as the basis of a syntactical-logical deductive scheme leads to particular statements, which, when semantically correlated, are demonstrably true. Or, to put it more simply, when the system is successful, according to its users' definition of success.

It can be asked: Does not semantic verification of a set of hypotheses show them to be absolutely true? That this is not so can be shown by an example set in the form of a classical syllogism. We begin with a postulate and a definition:

'All stones are nourishing.'
'Bread is stone.'

Combining these two we make the deduction:

'Therefore bread is nourishing.'

The deduction follows accepted principles of logical inference and the conclusion is certainly semantically true. Nevertheless the premises are false inside our usual language system. Thus we have a situation where a logically deduced conclusion which is true does not in the slightest furnish proof of the truth of the original premises.

(iv) The fourth truth we have already encountered—that of the existence of experiences. There is no need here to elaborate on this further.

* * *

In our definition of 'pragmatic truth' above, we used the words 'hypotheses true for an individual'. These words imply the non-existence of any absolute standard of 'truth'. This we believe to be the case. Thus, opposing and contradictory systems can all be 'pragmatically true' if they are accepted and put to use by different individuals. The standards of acceptibility vary widely according to the values and orientation of different people. Thus the scientist has an entirely different point of view from a theologian, and this can be the source of much conflict unless they can both accept the relativity (which we saw to be an increasingly important characteristic of the maturing child's conceptualization technique) of 'pragmatic truth'. The modern scientist insists on the observability of his fundamental entities and chooses between rival equally semantically true systems using Occam's razor—that system is best which is simplest in structure and in application. Here, the all-important word is 'simplest', and the decision as to what is the simplest is very much a matter of individual choice. The theologian has different but equally valid criteria.

Let us take as an example the Ptolemaic Theory of the universe as opposed to the Copernican-Keplerian. If the mathematics in use at that time had been adequate, the Ptolemaic Theory of planetary motion, as a set of cycles and epicycles with the earth at the centre of the universe, could have been correlated with Tycho Brahe's observations. The Keplerian system became accepted as true by the mathematicians of the time, because calculations using it were enormously simpler. To the theologian the mathematical simplicity of the Copernican-Keplerian theory was more than counter-balanced for him by the conceptual simplicity of a theory in which God created the universe for mankind, and necessarily then must have put man's earth at the centre, with the other bodies revolving about in Platonic perfect circles. However this was not all there was to the Copernican-Keplerian Theory. It was developed by Newton into an all-encompassing mechanical theory which described the solar system with the same mathematics that were used to calculate the fall of a stone through the air or the motion of the tides on the earth. Eventually this became too much for the opposition, and by 1800 no one, theologian, philosopher, or scientist, held onto the anthropocentric universe. (It was not until 1822 that the Roman Catholic Church finally and formally accepted the Copernican Theory.)

*   *   *

Let us summarize what we have established up to now:

(1) Common-sense 'reality', the world of you and me and objects moving about in space-time, is neither given empirically (i.e. a part of our initial perceptual experience) nor is it an inevitable consequence of man's mental make-up. It is a conceptual structure evolved partly consciously and partly unconsciously, in a give and take exchange between man and experience. The fact of man's persistence as a species is evidence that this reality possesses considerable adequacy in organizing everyday experience, but there is no guarantee that varieties of experience outside this range will be equally well assimilated without making considerable modifications to this common-sense world picture.

(2) Our world picture can be analysed semiotically into three parts—a set of postulates used by man, the *pragmatic*, a method of combining and making particular deductions from the postulates and definitions, the *syntactic*, and a set of well-defined epistemic correlations between elements of the syntax and experience, the *semantic*.

(3) The only absolute truth is the certainty of the existence of experience itself. Other than this there is only truth relative to a system. *Syntactic truth* simply means that a certain combination of primitive elements follows the rules. *Semantic truth* is the agreed or tested correlation of symbols with experience. *Pragmatic truth* means that a semiotic system is an adequate system (according to the user's definition of adequacy) for organizing experience.

*   *   *

Now we must apply some of these results to the concept of causality. In particular, we must locate and define the function of 'cause' inside a semiotic. ('Determinism' we will continue to equate to 'total cause'.)

If we check over the examples given in the first chapter such as:

'The slippery road is a cause of that accident',

we see that 'cause' always appears as a relation connecting something caused with one or more causers. It thus has the same semiotic status as other relational elements of language and logic such as: 'and', 'or', 'is', 'implies', and has no direct perceptual correlation in itself. 'Cause' is thus quite unlike a concept such as 'John Smith' which can be immediately and uniquely identified among our percepts, and is also different from universals like 'evil' which can be identified in extension as: 'John Smith's temper is an evil' (coupled with a pointing finger at an example of it), 'Stealing candy from a baby is an evil', etc. . . . In a statement including cause, the causer has perceptual correlation, the caused has perceptual correlation, and the statement asserts that a certain perceptual relationship holds between the two.

However, the statement is also making assertions about a certain set of other hypothetical physical situations. In the example:

'The slippery road is a cause of that accident'

the direct perceptual relationship being asserted is that a temporal sequence of slippery road and accident is part of our actual experience. The statement, however, is indirectly describing another physical situation, namely, one in which the road is dry, and, all other features of the situation being the same, the accident not occurring. Verification of the correctness of the statement requires, therefore, not only the check that the actual situation is as described, but experiments verifying the prediction as to what happens when the road is dry. This last, of course, is vastly more difficult to establish than the first.

A statement including the relation 'cause' is thus logically equivalent inside a syntax not to a single situation but to a set of perceptual situations. It will be easier to understand this if we use a symbolic shorthand. We will consider all the physically possible joint states of 'causer' and 'caused', identify those which are asserted to be actual or possible, and those rejected as impossible.

Let 'S' stand for slippery road, and 'A' stand for accident. Our initial statement about the accident will be written in the form 2.1. If we check back through our above remarks, we see that 2.1 is equivalent to saying that the three perceptual combinations of 'S' and 'A' given in 2.2 are possible, but that the case 2.3 will not occur. In logical terms we would say that: 'S' is a cause of 'A' asserts that 'S' is a necessary although not sufficient condition for the occurrence of 'A'.

Next, we collect all the partial

' "S" is a cause of "A" ' 2.1

is equivalent to:

'S' and 'A'
'S' and 'no A' } actual or
'no S' and 'A' } possible . . 2.2

'no S' and 'A' } impossible
                 . . . . 2.3

' "ΣC_i" is the cause of "A" ' . . 2.4

is equivalent to:

'ΣC_i' and 'A' $\left.\right\}$ actual or
'no ΣC_i' and 'no A' $\left.\right\}$ possible . 2.5

'ΣC_i' and 'no A' $\left.\right\}$ impossible
'no ΣC_i' and 'A' $\left.\right\}$ 2.6

causes of the accident (in theory they would be infinite in number, but, in practice, we can assume an average state of the universe and only take into account a finite number of preponderating causes) and call them 'ΣC_i'. We can write expression 2.4 where 'ΣC_i' is now the total cause of the accident. Analysis of this shows that 2.4 is equivalent to saying that the two perceptual combinations 2.5 are possible, and those in 2.6 are impossible. In logical terms we would say that 'ΣC_i' is the necessary and sufficient condition for 'A', or, alternatively, say that 'A' is 'determined'.

Thus, although 'cause' is not something that is to be sought for and discovered directly in experience, it is possible, at least in principle, to test the adequacy of a causal theory designed to correctly describe experience. For example, if the theory makes a statement of the type shown in 2.1 (' "S" is *a* cause of "A" ') the observational 'proof' would consist in noting that in at least one instance (1) 'S' and 'A' both occur ('A' after 'S'), (2) 'S' occurs but 'A' does not, (3) neither 'S' nor 'A' occurs; and that in no instance does (4) 'S' not occur and 'A' occur. In the situation purportedly correctly described by 2.4 (' "ΣC_i" is *the* cause of "A" ') confirmation would be obtained if it is observed that in at least one instance (1) 'ΣC_i' occurs and 'A' occurs, (2) 'ΣC_i' does not occur and 'A' does not occur; and that in no instance does (3) 'ΣC_i' occur and 'A' not occur, (4) 'ΣC_i' not occur and 'A' occur. Now, statements like (4), which require that in *no* instance does a certain phenomenon occur, would require an infinity of time for verification and thus the 'final' proof of a causal statement could never be completed. However this is the usual situation with any general hypothesis and does not constitute grounds for rejecting the particular concept of 'cause'. As Karl Popper has pointed out, the really important criterion for the admissibility of an hypothesis is the existence of tests by which it could be refuted. Since one instance contrary to the causal prediction would constitute such a refutation, 'cause' is entirely admissible as part of a semiotic structure.

We will spend no more time here on the question of testing hypotheses. The practical problems are always severe. Later on when we come to consider 'determinism' and 'cause' as they function inside physics we will consider the problem of verification and refutation of hypotheses in more detail.

CHAPTER III

Classical Physics
and its Determinism

SUMMARY: We have studied the way in which man's mind works upon the 'changing differentiated continuum of immediately apprehended experience' in an effort to force it into a pattern that will be meaningful and manipulatable. Individual 'percepts' are mentally combined to form 'concepts', the concepts are represented by symbols, and the symbols are organized into a symbolic world picture. This picture is what we will be referring to when we speak of 'reality'. Since it is dependent upon the nature of our experience, and our method of organizing percepts, it is not fixed for all time. It has changed in the past, and is very much in flux at the present time. The symbolic world picture, called a semiotic, is broken down for analysis into three interlocking parts: the set of assumed postulates which form the basis of the system—the pragmatic part, the logical elaboration of the postulates into individual theorems and statements—the syntax, and the correlation between elements of the syntax and particular perceptual events in experience—the semantic part. Our ordinary language and physics are two examples of such semiotics.

The 'proof' of any world picture can only lie in its continuing successful prediction of perceptual experiences. In each test it is always the entire theory that is subject to verification or refutation. Continued verification leads to our placing increasing reliance upon the theory, refutation (and it is essential that a good test place the theory in jeopardy) requires the modification of at least some part of the theory. However, in general, a predictive failure does not specify the particular part needing modification, only the need for some change.

This analysis is applied to 'causality'. We recognize that 'cause' is a relational type of concept far along towards the pure concept end of the percept-concept spectrum, and without any direct denotatum in experience. In consequence, when looking for 'cause', we must examine the semiotic used to represent experience symbolically, rather than go searching through the experiences themselves. A semiotic may be causal-deterministic or not. It happens, as we have seen, that our common language is causal, but there is no a priori necessity that a successful theory be so.

In this chapter we will turn our attention to that most remarkably successful semiotic: classical physics. Its limited field of application, as compared with language, plus its emphasis upon a mathematical-logical formulation, will permit us to be more rigorous in our study of causality than has been practical in the first two chapters of this book. We will arrive at a much more precise definition of determinism, and in the process decide whether or not classical physics is deterministic.

For the first time we are forced to become somewhat technical. To assist the non-specialist, whose knowledge of physics may have become hazy over the years, we will develop (in a way different from that customary in either popular or specialist books) enough of classical physics to make the succeeding discussion comprehensible to him. A new difficulty is now present which was absent from our previous discussions. The use of mathematics, with its attendant conciseness and logical clarity, is an essential part of physics and is at least partly responsible for its success. Thus a purely verbal exposition of physics is unsatisfactory. This will present real difficulties for the non-mathematically inclined reader, which we will attempt to resolve in two ways. The one will be to employ the most elementary mathematics possible, consistent with some reasonable degree of accuracy and rigour. In most parts of the discussion we will be able to get along with the simplest algebra, and, where calculus and differential equations are required, we will restrict ourselves to ordinary derivatives. For the reader for whom even this is too much we will employ an additional device. Wherever mathematics is being used, the page will be split vertically, the right hand side being devoted to the mathematical analysis, and the left hand side to a simultaneous verbal description of what is going on. Thus though it may be impossible for some readers to verify all the details of the discussion, they should still be able to follow the general line of the argument without particular difficulty.

★   ★   ★

From the earliest days of formalized thinking men were fascinated by numbers, and by the apparently inexorable way axioms led to their consequences in mathematical systems. Mathematical and logical arguments were subject to seemingly undeniable verification or refutation, in contrast to verbal debates, where no decision between opposing conclusions had the same feeling of finality. Contrast Euclid's Theorem, 'The exterior angle of a triangle equals the sum of the interior and opposite angles', with 'Democratic chaos is preferable to organized despotism'. It was inevitable that thinkers would try to extend these mathematical systems of seemingly absolute truth to theories of the world and of the cosmos.

Historical examples of this are known to every school boy: The Pythagorean discovery of the mathematical ratios connecting lengths of plucked strings playing notes in the diatonic musical scale led to a harmonic theory of the astronomical spheres; Plato's notion of perfect geometrical figures was used in the Ptolemaic Theory of the Universe; the five regular solids were used by Kepler in constructing a model of the Solar System . . . and so on. Though some progress was made in isolated instances at elaborating these into world systems, no really significant and verifiable success was achieved in reducing the complexity of a large chunk of our experience to a small set of quantitative mathematical laws until Newton produced his *Principia Mathematica* in 1687.

This, as it developed into Classical Mechanics, was probably the greatest achievement in human thought in the world's history—at least so far as scientific philosophy is concerned. A small set of definitions and laws encompassed a mathematical description of phenomena ranging from the motions of the planets, the stars, and the galaxies, to Brownian Motion, just visible under high-powered microscopes. In a constantly expanding field of application, problem after problem was solved with such uniform success that the other subject divisions of physics took mechanics as their ideal. During the two centuries following Newton's Principia, theoreticians worked to derive mechanical theories of heat, light, sound, and electricity. Though complete success in this was not achieved, enough progress was made to lead to the materialist belief of the nineteenth century that eventually all phenomena (and this was extended by mechanistic philosophers to problems of living beings, including man) would be reducible to physical mechanics. Thus, in our study in this chapter of the place of determinism in Classical Physics we can legitimately confine our attention to Mechanics.

* * *

Although in its basic principles mechanics is very concise, in fact it uses all the laws, postulates and apparatus of mathematics, classical logic, and our everyday language, so that any really exhaustive presentation of it is virtually impossible. We will present only those parts that are of particular importance to our subject. In this we will follow neither a chronological account of how it developed historically, nor will we use the obvious semiotic device of first expounding the pragmatic basis, then the syntactic development, and finally the semantic correspondence rules. It will be simpler for the non-physicist if we take a small easily understood part, and expand from this to the more general laws. ·

In the logical syntax of physical theory we begin with a set of primitive elements. Since they are logically primitive—the building bricks of our physical edifice—there is no way in which they can be defined within the syntax itself. We digress for a moment to talk about 'definition'. In an analytical definition, a complex quantity is defined by breaking it down into the simpler components which make it up. In turn, these latter are defined in terms of more elementary quantities, until we arrive at quantities so fundamentally simple that they have no constituent elements, and analytic definitions of these beome impossible. Thus a cow is defined as a four-legged, one-tailed, one-headed, one-uddered . . . animal. In turn the tail can be defined in terms of vertebrae, skin, etc., and (science aside) these latter elements eventually become fundamentally so simple that they cannot be further defined. 'Hair? Why hair is just hair! Anyone knows what hair is!!' Later on we will consider the process of operational definition by means of which these fundamental entities acquire meaning through rules of semantic correlation with percepts.

In Mechanics the basic, primitive, elements will be represented by the symbols 'm', 's', and 't'. We will adopt a rule of subscripts by which, for example, 's_1' is one particular value of 's', 't_1', one particular value of 't', and (s_1, t_1) constitutes a set, (s_2, t_2) constitute a second set, and so on. In the particularly simple system that will initially be considered here, 'm' will be taken to be a constant quantity, and, consequently, one needing no subscript. Our primitive elements thus consists of 'm', 's', and 't'.

Now at this stage it is as if in the process of setting up some new game of 'superchess' we had carved out the pieces, but as yet

Primitive quantities:

m

s

t

(s_1, t_1)

(s_2, t_2)

Rules of combination:

$$+$$

$$\times$$

$$\div$$

$$\sqrt{}$$

etc.

Analytic definitions:

$$\frac{v_2+v_1}{2} = \frac{s_2-s_1}{t_2-t_1} \quad \ldots\ldots\ldots\ldots 3.1$$

$$a = \frac{v_2-v_1}{t_2-t_1} \quad \ldots\ldots\ldots\ldots\ldots 3.2$$

$$f = ma \ldots\ldots\ldots\ldots\ldots\ldots 3.3$$

Manipulations:

Divide 3.1 by 3.2:

$$\frac{\frac{v_2+v_1}{2}}{a} = \frac{\frac{s_2-s_1}{t_2-t_1}}{\frac{v_2-v_1}{t_2-t_1}}$$

Cross-multiplying:

$$\frac{v_2{}^2-v_1{}^2}{2} = a(s_2-s_1) \quad \ldots\ldots\ldots 3.4$$

Multiply 3.3 by (s_2-s_1):

$$f(s_2-s_1) = ma(s_2-s_1) \ldots\ldots\ldots 3.5$$

Substitute 3.4 in 3.5:

$$f(s_2-s_1) = \tfrac{1}{2}mv_2{}^2 - \tfrac{1}{2}mv_1{}^2 \ldots\ldots 3.6$$

had neither board to play on, nor rules of permission and restriction on the variety of moves open to the pieces. For this we adopt the entire logical body of deductive mathematics with its usual meanings for addition, multiplication, division, etc. Now we can combine our primitive elements to form complex structures, i.e., to 'define' new quantities. In principle any sort of definitions might be used, but the choice is usually made with a specific purpose in mind, in this case its prospective function in Physical Theory. In 3.1, 3.2, and 3.3 we analytically define 'v', 'a', and 'f' in terms of the basic elements 'm', 's', and 't'. The subscript 1 on v, shows that it belongs to the set (s_1, t_1), and v_2 to the set (s_2, t_2). Since 'a' and 'f' are without subscripts, like 'm', in this system, they are unchanging, and belong to no single set.

We have now reached a stage equivalent to that of Euclid when he had completed the formulation of his axioms; or, as in our analogy with a 'superchess', had our board set up with pieces and were now ready to play a game. Just as Euclid proceeded from his axioms to deduce a wealth of theorems, we may combine the expressions shown in 3.1, 3.2, and 3.3, according to the rules of mathematics, to find new results. As for example, we derive here the three

'Theorems', equations 3.4, 3.6 and 3.7. Now it is true that these are already implicit in equations 3.1, 3.2, and 3.3, so in a way we have obtained nothing new, but this is simply a mark of good logic, and is the basis for the feeling of inevitableness we have when we contemplate a mathematical proof.

Multiply 3.3 by (t_2-t_1):

$$f(t_2-t_1) = ma(t_2-t_1)$$

Substitute for $a(t_2-t_1)$ from 3.2:

$$f(t_2-t_1) = mv_2-mv_1 \dots \dots 3.7$$

Note particularly that this is entirely a bit of paper-mental work. As yet there is no reference whatsoever to physical experience. Equations 3.4, 3.6 and 3.7 are 'true' in the sense that they have been rigorously deduced from the set of initial definitions. It will be remembered that this is one of our three kinds of truth—syntactic truth.

* * *

So far, then, this has been entirely an exercise in mathematics and logic. Since however the purpose of any practical system is to make statements about experience, we must now pass on to the semantic part of our total semiotic—the establishing of epistemological correlations between the symbols present in our syntax, 's', 'm', 't', 'v', 'a', and 'f', and particular physical events. Since 'v', 'a', and 'f' are analytically defined inside the syntax in terms of 's', 'm', and 't', once these latter are correlated with experience, we are no longer free to arbitrarily correlate 'v', 'a', and 'f'.

Ideally the primitive elements of the physical semiotic (including, among others, m, s, and t) would be correlated directly to pure percepts so as to reduce the potential for error in this part of the semiotic to zero, but, as must be evident from the discussion of the previous chapter, this is both a practical and theoretical impossibility. However, in physics every effort is made to relate the fundamental quantities to entities and events as simple as possible, to ones close to the pure percept end of the spectrum, and, consequently, containing a minimum of conceptualization. Nevertheless we are correlating the symbols with concepts rather than percepts, and this means that we are necessarily introducing into our physical semiotic the entire conceptual scheme which uses these concepts. This process takes place so naturally and easily that we are hardly aware we are doing it. This was the case in Classical Physics which took over the whole apparatus of language, logical, and mathematical

C

syntax, plus our everyday conceptual scheme of an 'I', other observers, and a universe of solid bodies. This included the assumptions that, at least in principle, an observation can be made of the behaviour of any body without interfering with it, that these external solid bodies possess more or less fixed characteristics, and at each instant are at certain definite locations in space and are moving at certain definite velocities. This was all accepted into the structure of Classical Physics without serious criticism, and it is only in the twentieth century that we have been forced to re-examine these assumptions.

Although Classical Physics was thus closely linked conceptually with our everyday common-sense world picture, it took the enormous step of finding ways to describe objects and phenomena by numbers. Thus instead of saying: 'John is heavy', 'It is hot outside', 'Toronto is far away', 'It is late'; the physicist says: 'John has a mass of 208 pounds', 'the temperature is 108° Fahrenheit in the shade', 'the distance Toronto to Ottawa is 280 miles', 'it is 1.30 a.m.' To describe with precision how it is done would keep us busy for many pages, and it is doubtful that the resultant rigour would justify the time spent. We will content ourself with a much simpler description of how this quantification of experience is carried out.

We will begin with 'S'. In words, 'S' will be called the 'length of a certain object', or, the 'distance from one identified point to another point'. We establish the stretch between two marks on some solid body as a physical example of length, and simultaneously, as our standard of length. For simplicity, we will initially restrict ourselves to bodies fixed in position with respect to the observer, assume the ordinary common-sense semantic meaning for coincidence of two points, and state that a space interval has the same length as our standard if it can be placed in coincidence with it.

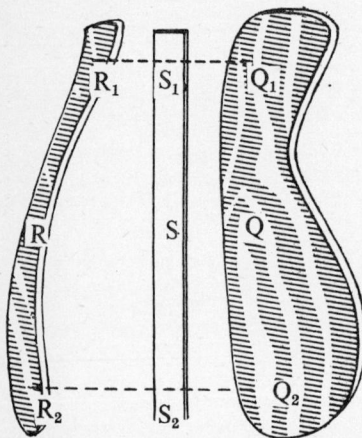

In the illustration shown, if point 'S_1' on our standard coincides with 'Q_1' at the same time as 'S_2' coincides with 'Q_2', we say that the two stretches '$S_1.S_2$' and '$Q_1.Q_2$' have the same length.

We find experimentally that stretches of this kind are symmetric and transitive. That is, if 'Q' has the same length as 'S' then 'S' has the same length as 'Q'; if 'Q' has the same length as 'S', and 'R' has the same length as 'S', then 'Q' has the same length as 'R' (i.e. they can be put into length coincidence with each other). This completes the first step. We now know how to find out if two space intervals have the same length, or are equal in length to our standard.

It is an easy exercise to move on to the second step of giving meaning to the statement that: ' "Q" is longer than "S" ', or, 'shorter than "S" '. The third step is to learn how to measure space stretches, and give their lengths in multiples and fractions of the standard. We first subdivide the standard into a number of equal parts commensurate with the accuracy we desire to reach in our measurement. We begin, by placing our standard so that 'S_1' is at one end of the length being measured, 'Q_1', and mark the point in 'Q' reached by 'S_2'. Next we shift the standard along the curve until 'S_1' is at the point formerly occupied by 'S_2' and mark the new point reached by 'S_2'. This process is repeated until the standard covers the final point on the object being measured. In our illustration, the length

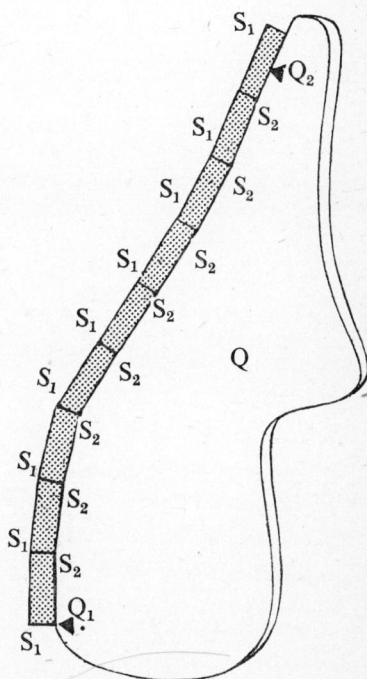

$1 = 8\frac{1}{2}$ standards

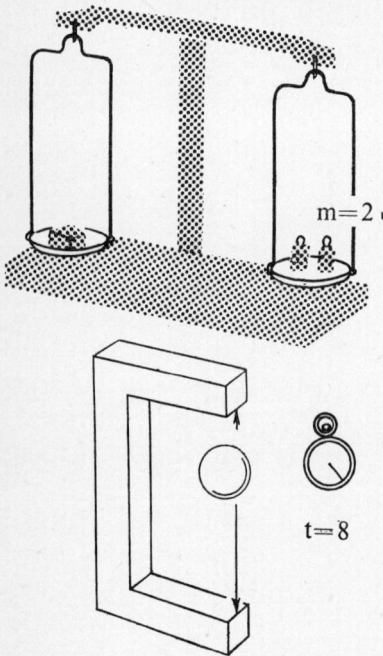

along the curve from 'Q₁' to 'Q₂' is 8½ units.

The same procedure is used in measuring 'm', which will be called the 'mass', or 't', the 'time'. In the first of these, the object whose mass is being measured is put in one pan of an equal arm balance, and standard masses, and fractional standard masses, added to the other pan, until the whole system balances. For measuring time, the process being investigated is compared with the number of ticks of a standard of time—a clock. There are all sorts of practical problems in the actual measurement of 'm', 's', and 't', when we are dealing with more complicated systems, the very small, or the very large, but these will serve to illustrate the process.

This then is the method by which we give operational definitions to the fundamentally primitive quantities of a semiotic. We specify, and here a most important tool is the pointing finger, the sequence of operations required to give a numerical value for the quantity being measured.

* * *

As we have already said, since 'v', 'a', and 'f', which will be called 'velocity', 'acceleration', and 'force' respectively, are defined analytically in terms of 'm', 's', and 't' inside the syntax, we are not free to choose independent operational correlations for them. The most obvious way to determine them is through the definitions, and through our already operationally specified means of measuring 'mass', 'position', and 'time'. Because of the particular ways in which they have been defined this will prove to be not quite so easy as it initially looks, and has been the source of much philosophical dispute. We will outline in some detail how we would go about obtaining a value for 'v'.

Let the physical situation be one in which a body travels from 'S₁' to

'S_2', i.e. a distance 'S_2-S_1', measured with a standard of length, in time 't_2-t_1', measured with a standard of time. Searching through our analytical definitions, we see that we can begin by using 3.1 to obtain the quantity $\frac{v_1+v_2}{2}$ by the purely mathematical operation of dividing the known number 'S_2-S_1' by the known number 't_2-t_1'.

$$\frac{S_2-S_1}{t_2-t_1} = \frac{v_1+v_2}{2} = (\text{ v average})$$

Notice that no standard of velocity has been introduced in this determination. The customary name for this quantity is 'average velocity', and it is what we are speaking of when we say, for example, that, driving the 280 mile distance from Ottawa to Toronto in 4 hours, our (average) velocity was 70 miles per hour. We know, however, that this does not mean that our car speedometer was continuously reading 70. Although much of the time it may have been hovering around 70, it will have fluctuated over a range of values from 0 up to 90 say, and at any particular instant, for example the moment when the car is passing a white birch on the open stretch of highway west of Perth, it will have a certain specific value, say, 85. Such a particular value of 'v' is called the 'velocity at a point' and we must now go on to define it, and show how it is to be computed.

Since it is a very difficult concept, we will begin with a non rigorous, approximate definition, follow this with a description of how it might be measured experimentally, and only then attempt to give a reasonably rigorous definition. First, the approximate one: 'The "velocity at a point" is the average velocity over a small interval of distance surrounding that point, a distance so small that the velocity remains approximately constant during the time taken to travel that distance'. (The obvious objection to this definition is that it is circular—it contains as part of itself the quantity we are trying to define.) Next, the operational description of how it might be measured: We measure out a small distance, ΔS_a, including the point S at which we wish to obtain the velocity, measure the time, Δt_a, required to cover this distance, and calculate the average velocity, v_a,

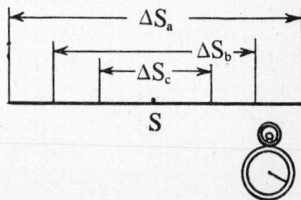

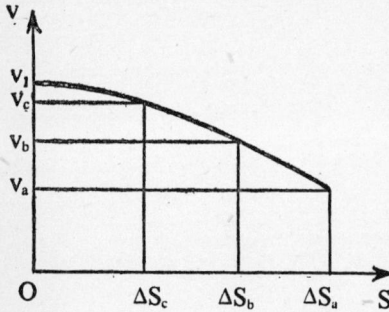

$$v_a = \frac{S_2 - S_1}{t_2 - t_1} = \frac{\Delta S_a}{\Delta t_a}$$

$$v_b = \frac{\Delta S_b}{\Delta t_b}$$

$$v_c = \frac{\Delta S_c}{\Delta t_c}$$

$$v_d = \text{etc.}$$

$$v_1 = \text{limit of } \frac{\Delta S}{\Delta t}$$

as ΔS approaches 0

(This is called by mathematicians the derivative of 'S' by 't'.)

using 3.1. This process is repeated with successively smaller intervals $\Delta S_b, \Delta S_c, \ldots$, and the average velocities $v_b, v_c \ldots$ are calculated and plotted on a graph of v against ΔS as shown. A smooth curve is drawn through these points and extrapolated to $\Delta S = O$. The point where the extrapolated curve intersects the v axis is the 'velocity at the point S_1'. For increasing accuracy we would increase the number of points.

The more rigorous verbal definition evolves naturally from this operational one. 'The "velocity at a point" is the limit approached by the average velocity, computed over a small interval of distance surrounding that point, as the distance interval approaches zero.' Historically, a study of this question of defining 'velocity' led Newton to develop a new branch of mathematics that finally resulted in Calculus.

We must note that there are other more practical methods of determining 'v', remember that v is analytically defined in terms of s, m, and t, and appears at many places inside the syntactical development of the theory. However we will put off for the moment any further discussion of 'velocity at a point'. It will be coming up again in later chapters.

* * *

What have we so far?

(1) A syntax using the rules of ordinary language and mathematics, a set of primitive quantities 'm', 's', and 't', a set of defined quantities 'v', 'a', and 'f', and an extensible set of theorems logically derived from the fundamental definitions.

(2) A set of assumptions including those of mathematics, traditional

logic, and the realist common-sense world picture of external objects possessing relatively fixed properties, and being at each instant at precise measurable positions, and moving with precise measurable velocities.

(3) A set of semantic correlations between the theoretical symbolic structure and certain experienceable events.

★   ★   ★

We have made several steps forward in our development of physics: we have gone through the qualitative stage—deciding upon significant quantities which will be investigated, and the quantitative, the measurement stage—setting up standards of measurements. If our operational descriptions are adequate, anyone can now check the statements that John's mass is 208 pounds, the temperature is 110°, that the distance Ottawa to Toronto is 280 miles, or that it is 1.30 o'clock. This is all very nice, but physics does more than this. We must go on now to look at the procedure by which predictions about the future or retro-predictions about the past are made; e.g. 'John will weigh 260 pounds in two months if he continues to eat like this'. This is the most difficult stage in a mathematical science. It is relatively easy to carry through the first two in a direct straightforward way, and from the earliest period of man's social intercourse some sort of standards of measurement have existed, while, as we have already mentioned, a system capable of making accurate predictions over a wide range of phenomena has only existed since Newton's time.

Let us study what is involved in terms of our sample syntax developed earlier in the chapter. We have described s_1, v_1, and t_1 as constituting a set, and spelt out in words through our semantic correspondence rules that this amounts to stating that some object has a measurable position s_1, and a measurable velocity v_1, at the time t_1. For prediction then, we want to be able to calculate that at some time still in the future, t_2, the object will be at the observable position s_2, and will have the observable velocity v_2.

We can take our defining equation, 3.2, and solve it for v_2. Doing this we see that v_2 is expressed in terms of v_1, a, t_1, and t_2. So if these latter quantities are known, v_2 may be calculated mathematically 'f'—3.8. Now v_1 can be found by a measurement at t_1, and t_2 is the

$$a(t_2-t_1) = (v_2-v_1) \quad \ldots\ldots\ldots 3.2$$

Solving for v_2 we get:

$$v_2 = v_1+a(t_2-t_1) \ldots\ldots\ldots 3.8$$

$$\frac{v_2{}^2 - v_1{}^2}{2a} = s_2 - s_1 \quad \ldots \ldots \ldots \quad 3.4$$

Solving for s_2 we get:

$$s_2 = s_1 + \frac{v_2{}^2 - v_1{}^2}{2a} \quad \ldots \ldots \ldots \quad 3.9$$

known future time at which we want to calculate v_2, so v_1, t_1, t_2 are known quantities. Only 'a' remains unknown. Similarly in equation 3.4 we can solve for s_2, 3.9. Again we see that s_2 is expressed in terms of a measurement at time t_1, of s_1 and v_1, and also is dependent upon 'a'. 3.8 and 3.9 then can both be solved (in that order) for the future position and velocity only if the acceleration 'a' is known. 'a' serves as a parameter connecting the measured values of observables at a present time with predicted values for them in the future. To finish the story, we note that equation 3.3 can be solved for 'a' in terms of 'm' and 'f', 3.10. 'm' is the 'mass of a body', and 'f' the 'force acting upon it'. So the final result of all this is: that equations 3.8, 3.9, and 3.10 can be simultaneously solved for the future position, 's_2', and velocity, 'v_2', of a body at time 't_2', if at the instant 't_1' its position 's_1' and velocity 'v_1' are measured; its mass 'm' is known; and if we know the force 'f' acting upon the body.

$$f = ma \ldots \ldots \ldots \ldots \ldots \ldots 3.3$$

$$\therefore a = \frac{f}{m} \ldots \ldots \ldots \ldots \ldots \ldots 3.10$$

$$v_2 = v_1 + a(t_2 - t_1) \ldots \ldots \ldots \quad 3.8$$

$$s_2 = s_1 + \frac{v_2{}^2 - v_1{}^2}{2a} \quad \ldots \ldots \ldots \quad 3.9$$

* * *

A number of additional (pragmatic) assumptions must be made, and these constitute classical Newtonian physics. A few of these are:

—The mass 'm' of a body is constant with change in location, velocity, or time. (Thus there are no subscripts on m.)

—There exists certain bodies, called 'rigid bodies' (including our standards), whose lengths are constant with change in location, velocity, or time.

—Expressions for the force function 'f' are discoverable, such that when they are substituted into equation 3.10, and the result used in 3.8 and 3.9, these equations give verifiable correct predictions for future values of position and velocity. These 'f's are not invented in some magical way, nor are they obtained as a gift from heaven. They are found by a process of trial and error, the correct 'f's being those that give right answers. Three of these are:

(1) Newton's law of Universal Gravitation: Every body attracts every other body with a force varying with the product of the masses and inversely as the square of the separating distances.

$$f = G\frac{m_a m_b}{(S_a - S_b)^2}$$

(2) Hookes's Law: In an elastic body strain is proportional to stress.

$$f = k_1(S_2 - S_1)$$

(3) The currents remaining constant, the force between parallel current-carrying conductors varies inversely as the first power of the separating distances.

$$f = k_2\frac{I_a I_b}{S_a - S_b}$$

There is no inherent limitation on the form of the force function. It can be, and usually is, dependent upon the positions and velocities of a number of bodies, and it can be both implicitly and explicitly a function of the time. The latter would take care of the eventuality that the laws of the universe are changing with time. The only restriction upon the 'f's is that they are discoverable for all possible phenomena, and that they are few enough in number, that for any particular problem, given a reasonable time, the necessary ones can be discovered.

⋆ ⋆ ⋆

Now back to the set of equations 3.8, 3.9, and 3.10. We examine the physical problem, go through our lists of forces acting, identify those that must be considered, and add them up to obtain the total force 'f'. We insert this into equation 3.10 to find the acceleration 'a', put this 'a' into 3.8 to find 'v_2', and the result into 3.9 to find s_2. We

$$v = \frac{ds}{dt} \quad \dots\dots\dots\dots\dots 3.1^1$$

$$a = \frac{dv}{dt} \quad \dots\dots\dots\dots\dots 3.2^1$$

$$f = ma$$

$$= m\frac{dv}{dt} = m\frac{ds^2}{dt^2} \dots\dots\dots 3.3^1$$

have made our predictions. We wait until the time t_2 and measure s_2 and v_2, and compare the results actually observed with our predictions. For a happy ending, let us suppose that they agree, within reasonable values for the experimental error involved.

We have dealt here with a particularly simple type of problem—one in which the force and hence the acceleration is a constant. Essentially the same procedure is used where 'f' and 'a' vary. The only difference is that equations 3.1, 3.2, and 3.3 are replaced by equivalent ones using Calculus. They become 3.1^1, 3.2^1 and 3.3^1.

★ ★ ★

This process of identifying the forces acting, and solving Newton's Equations to predict the future, was successfully repeated many times, and by 1750 the degree of confirmation of Newtonian Physical theory was so general it was accepted as a true system. This is, of course, true in the sense of being pragmatically true—the system was universal, comprehensive, succinct, and its predictions agreed with experiment.

★ ★ ★

A few lines above we have used the rather sinister words: 'that they agree within reasonable values of the experimental errors'. To understand what this means, we must spend a little time discussing the theory of experimental error in classical physics. Prediction and measurement will usually not agree exactly. Even a repetition of the same experimental measurement on an unchanging object will, in general, produce a different result. In physics one tries to reduce this and the observer's subjective bias to a minimum, by using the simplest possible types of observation—a simple counting, or coincidences of pointers and scales; but even in these cases there will be some spread in the results obtained. As an example, consider the simple operation of measuring the length of an object. In the first instance we will use a simple meter stick. We place the meter stick against the object, read the meter stick at the two ends of the object, and subtract these two values to get the length. The meter stick is taken away and we repeat the measurement trying not to be biased by the result of measurement No. 1. An even better technique would be to have the measurement repeated by a number of different observers, who do not communicate their results to one another until all are completed. We attempt to keep all factors constant that might produce a systematic variation in the result: temperature; pressure; presence of magnets, if either the standard or the object are made of a magnetic material; etc. Despite these precautions a number of different values for the length will be obtained. Call them 1_1, 1_2, 1_3 . . . etc. We count the number of times 1_1 is obtained, N_1, the number of times 1_2, N_2 . . . etc. We plot N against 1 and obtain the bell-shaped curve familiar to statisticians. This curve is called the

$$N \qquad N = N_4 e^{-k(1-1_4)^2}$$

Error Function or Gaussian curve, and is represented mathematically by the expression shown above the diagram.

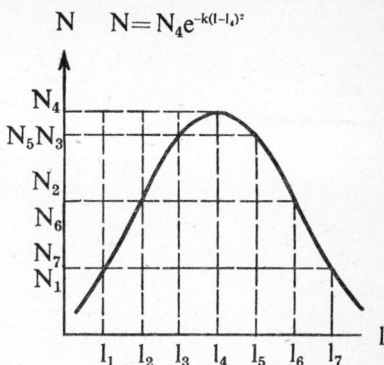

In Classical Physics (where this test is applicable) two assumptions are made: (1) If a Gaussian curve is not obtained, some disturbing factor is present which must be eliminated before we consider that a satisfactory measurement has been made. If the curve is a Gaussian, the best answer for the 'true' length is the peak of the curve. Now, this latter point is not uniquely determined, since for any finite set of points many different curves may be drawn, all with slightly different maxima. However, as the number of measurements increases ($N \to \infty$) the determination of the maximum becomes more precise. (2) The other assumption is: that as instruments of increasing sensitivity are used (in the case of our length measurement we might next use calipers, then a travelling microscope, and finally a Michelson interferometer), the resulting Gaussian curves will fall within one another, and, at least in principle, any degree of accuracy in finding the peak can be attained by simply refining the measurement techniques.

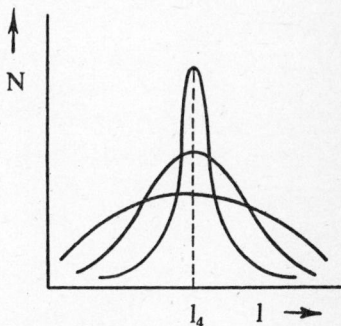

* * *

Since it will come up later, we might as well mention another thing now. It was recognized in Classical Physics that the measurement affected the observed object, but it was assumed that this effect could be either reduced to zero or compensated for. This means that, in principle, any two variables could be simultaneously measured, and their 'true' values obtained, to any degree of accuracy. The pair of particular importance, as we have seen in our example problem of prediction, is the position and velocity of a particle.

★　★　★

Now, up to now we have assumed that prediction and measurement have agreed. Let us shift our historical location to 1850, after Newtonian physics had been operating successfully for 150 years, and suppose some predicted result had not agreed with observation. Would we have rejected Newtonian physics? No, certainly not. We would assume that either a mathematical or observational error had been made, or else that some type of force was acting which we had not taken into account. With every disagreement, we could invent a new kind of force which would restore harmony between theory and observation. It is important to realize that physics is an open theory in this respect. The only restriction on the introduction of new forces is the pragmatic one that if a new force is needed for every new situation the theory is of no real help in problem solving, since we could never know in advance what force would be needed, and predictions would become impossible.

★　★　★

The equations 3.6 and 3.7 that were syntactically derived earlier in the chapter were obtained with a very definite purpose in mind. They lead to the laws of conservation of energy and conservation of momentum respectively. In later chapters we will be making use of these, so we must spend a little time discussing them here. Let us begin with the second of these, 3.7. Interpreted semantically, it tells us that: the product, 'force', times, 'time of action of the force', equals the change in the quantity 'mv' of the body—the final value, 'mv$_2$', minus the initial value, 'mv$_1$'. This quantity 'mv' appears sufficiently often in physics to be

$$f(t_2 - t_1) = mv_2 - mv_1$$
$$\text{i.e.} = \Delta(mv) \ldots\ldots\ldots 3.7$$

(Where $\Delta(\ )$ stands for 'the change in $(\ )$')

given a special name—'momentum'. In the case where no force acts upon a body we see that its momentum remains constant. Now let us go on to the case where there are two bodies exerting forces upon each other. One of the assumptions of Newtonian mechanics is that these forces are equal and opposite. We write equations like 3.7 for each body, add them up and obtain equations 3.11 and 3.12. In words, 3.11 would be interpreted to read: 'When two bodies are acting upon one another, although each of their momenta will change, the total change in momentum is zero'. 3.12 reads: 'The change in momentum of the one body is equal in magnitude but opposite in direction to the change in momentum of the other body'. These results can be generalized,

For two bodies, the force on one is equal to minus the force on the other

$$\therefore f(t_2 - t_1) = \Delta(mv)_A$$
$$-f(t_2 - t_1) = \Delta(mv)_B$$

$$0 = \Delta(mv)^A + \Delta(mv)_B \qquad \ldots\ldots\ldots 3.11$$

or:

$$\Delta(mv)_A = -\Delta(mv)_B \quad \ldots\ldots 3.12$$

For a system of bodies we would generalize 3.11 to read:

$$\Sigma\Delta(mv)_i = 0 \quad \ldots\ldots\ldots\ldots 3.13$$

(where Σ_i stands for 'the sum of')

(3.13), to a system of any number of bodies, and we obtain the law of conservation of momentum: 'In a closed system, no matter what internal changes in momentum may occur, the total momentum remains constant unless some outside force is brought to bear upon that system'.

* * *

We go on to a consideration of equation 3.6. In our everyday world we use the concepts of work and energy in a qualitative way. We associate work rather vaguely with the exerting of force through some distance, and say we have expended a certain amount of energy in performing that work. This, like our other common-sense concepts, is formalized and quantified in physics. The product of force and distance (more correctly, the product of the component of the force in the direction of motion times the distance) is called the work done. In equation 3.6

$$f(s_2 - s_1) = \tfrac{1}{2}mv_2{}^2 - \tfrac{1}{2}mv_1{}^2 \quad \ldots\ldots 3.6$$

derived earlier in this chapter this is the quantity '$f(s_2-s_1)$', and our equation equates this work done to the change in the quantity '$\frac{1}{2}mv^2$'; i.e., the final value, '$\frac{1}{2}mv_2^2$', minus the value at the initial position, '$\frac{1}{2}mv_1^2$'. These last quantities must have the same dimensions as '$f(s_2-s_1)$', namely energy, and since they depend upon velocity, '$\frac{1}{2}mv^2$' is called the kinetic energy of the body. In this case then the work done upon the body equals the change in its kinetic energy.

Now let us examine a case in which we are lifting a body against the force of gravity. The force we have to exert equals the weight of the body ($f = mg$, g is the gravitational constant at the surface of the earth), and, if we lift the body from a height 'h_1' above the earth's surface to a height 'h_2', we do a total amount of work equal to force times distance moved, namely, '$mg\,(h_2-h_1)$', and the body has acquired energy of position. We call it potential energy. If the body is now released it falls towards the earth, losing its potential energy but gaining an equivalent amount of kinetic energy. If its initial velocity at height h_2 is v_2, and its final velocity at h_1 is v_1, the gain in the kinetic energy is $\frac{1}{2}mv_1^2-\frac{1}{2}mv_2^2$. In equation 3.14 we equate the change in the potential energy (equal to the work done in raising it initially) to the change in the kinetic energy. If we transpose two of the quantities in 3.14, we obtain equation 3.15, which states that the initial potential energy plus the initial kinetic energy, i.e. the initial total energy = the final total energy.

Work done = $mg(h_2-h_1)$
= Potential Energy gained

Loss in Potential Energy = gain in Kinetic Energy

$\therefore mg(h_2-h_1) = \frac{1}{2}mv_1^2-\frac{1}{2}mv_2^2$ 3.14

or:

$mgh_2+\frac{1}{2}mv_2^2 = mgh_1+\frac{1}{2}mv_1^2$ 3.15

or:

Initial total energy = final total energy

Thus, in this process of a drop from h_2 to h_1, although height and velocity are both changing, at all times the total energy remains constant. We generalize from this and other examples to the law of conservation of energy which states: 'If no outside force is acting upon a system, its total energy remains constant regardless of whatever internal changes may occur'. This became a universal law of Newtonian physics. Supposing now in one case we find the total mechanical energy not remaining constant, would we reject Newtonian mechanics? Again no. We would search for some other kind of energy.

In practice this was done, and by 1900 in addition to mechanical energy there was heat energy, chemical energy, magnetic energy, electrical energy. How then could Newtonian Mechanics ever be shown wrong? The criterion lies in the notion of pragmatic truth. If the number of different sorts of energies had proliferated to such a point that in practice problems could not be solved, the theory would become pragmatically useless, i.e. pragmatically false.

* * *

It is a fact that at the macroscopic (human-sized) scale of phenomena such an event did not occur. With two hundred years of continuing success, the theory became an ingrained habit of thinking, and Newton's Laws acquired the nature of absolute laws. (This idyllic state was abruptly disrupted at the turn of the twentieth century, but discussion of this will be postponed to the next chapter.) The success of this theory in dealing with the relatively simple problems of mechanics led to an attempted extension of the mechanical mathematical approach to all phenomena. Considerable success was realized in the 'mechanization' of heat, but not elsewhere in physics. However, where success was not immediately attained, the failure was attributed not to any weakness in the theory but to the complexity of the phenomena, particularly for those involving living beings.

Pierre Simon Laplace expressed the prevailing scientific and philosophic feeling of his time in the following words:

'Consider an intelligence which for any given instant would know all the forces animating nature, and the instantaneous positions and momenta of all the objects composing it. If this intelligence were powerful enough to analyse all this data, it would be able to embrace in one formula the movements of all bodies from the largest to the smallest. Nothing would be uncertain for it, and the future, like the past, would be equally present to its eyes. Human knowledge, in the perfection it is able to give to astronomical calculations, offers a feeble illustration of such an intelligence.'

Spelt out more analytically, and with the reference to the supreme intelligence removed, this would become: 'A knowledge of the positions and simultaneous momenta of every body in the universe, plus a complete knowledge of all the laws of the universe, would permit a prediction of the position and momentum of any particular body for all future times and all past times'. This was intended to apply to both inanimate and animate bodies, including man. It was believed that all other physical phenomena—light, heat, sound, electricity, magnetism, and all the more psychical phenomena—would be ultimately reducible to mechanical measurements. With one change—Laplace intended his statement to apply to the 'real world', while we will, following our earlier discussion, consider it applicable only to the conceptual world picture—this can be taken as a fair statement of the classical determinist belief.

A number of apparently valid objections to Laplace's principle have been raised. One example will suffice: 'No actual supreme intelligence exists, and no single man or group of men could gather the enormous mass of simultaneous information needed'. Now this is obviously a practical true limitation to the applicability of Laplace's principle, and to understand why we will reject it we must return to our earlier semiotic study. Just where does determinism fit into a world conceptual picture? The only possible place is among the assumptions. This assumption must be consistent with the other assumptions if a logical development of them all is to be made in the syntax. Thus, if we hold with Laplace, we will be restricted in our search for laws to those of a certain, i.e. determinist, nature. Like all the hypotheses, the determinist one is not to be tested directly, but only as it develops syntactically in combination with the other hypotheses into specific statements about the form our experiences will take. Laplace's Principle, then, is not intended to be a statement about actual experiments, but rather is a statement about the nature of physical theory. It does not mean that in actuality someone is going to measure the positions and conjugate momenta of all the particles of the universe, and then fit them into appropriate equations, solve them, and actually make such a Laplacean prediction. Rather, it is a statement that the pragmatic and syntactic structure of physics is constructed in such a way that the insertion of the m's, s_1's, v_1's at t_1, and the f's into the mathematical equations of the theory uniquely determines the s_2's and v_2's at any t_2.

This can be seen more easily if we solve Newton's equation in its differential form where we take into account the usual case in which the force is not constant. This can be put into an integral form, giving explicitly the position at any time 't', if it is integrated twice. In the first integration we get an expression containing 'v_1', the initial velocity of the particle. The second integration introduces 's_1', the initial position—3.17. Thus, we have the position, 's_2', of the body under investigation as a function of its initial position 's_1', initial velocity v_1, and the double integral of force with respect to time. This last quantity represents the effect of every other body in the universe upon the particular one being studied, and depends for its value upon the relative locations and velocities of all the bodies. Similar

$f = ma$; or, using calculus notation:

$$f = m\frac{dv}{dt} = m\frac{d}{dt}\left(\frac{ds}{dt}\right) \quad \dots\dots 3.3$$

Integrating:

$$\int f dt = m\frac{ds}{dt} - mv_1$$

Integrate again:

$$\int(\int f dt)dt = ms_2 - ms_1 - mv_1 t$$

Or, rewriting:

$$s_2 = s_1 + v_1 t + \frac{1}{m}\int(\int f dt)dt \quad \dots 3.17$$

equations to 3.17 can be set up for every body in the universe. The f's relate the equations one to the other, and in principle they can all be solved simultaneously. Any difficulty in using this equation is the purely practical one of performing such an enormous mathematical operation. This is Laplace's Principle, and it is true, then, that the theoretical structure of physics is of this deterministic nature.

* * *

Now of course there is more to physics than a logical mathematical exercise; it makes verifiable statements about experience. An additional assumption of physics is that the interaction forces between bodies fall off sufficiently rapidly with distance so that the double force integral can be evaluated for any particle in any particular situation by taking into account only a small number of local bodies. As physics developed, it established methods of deciding how much of the external universe must be considered in solving a given problem. This provides us with a semantic test for the applicability of our theory. Pragmatically and syntactically it may satisfy all the rules, but unless it works it is a purely logical exercise. Our question, then, is whether or not classical deterministic physics was semantically verifiable. The answer was 'yes!'

Two hundred years of success gave it considerable pragmatic weight and one example will suffice here—one that Laplace would surely approve of. This was the purely theoretical prediction of both the existence and the location of the planet Neptune. The outermost planet known at that time, Uranus, had a number of irregularities in its orbit which could not be explained by the pull of the planets closer to the Sun. A transuranic planet was postulated. Next, Adams and Leverrier used these irregularities to calculate the orbit of the planet. Upon the receipt of Leverrier's paper, the Berlin Observatory began the hunt. That same evening they observed a 'star' in the correct location, which did not exist on the star maps. By the next evening it had moved against the background of stars and was identified as a planet belonging to the solar system. A certain amount of luck had been involved, because Leverrier's calculations were rather makeshift, but the fact remains that the discovery was made on this basis. It subsequently turned out that Neptune had been noticed and recorded on star maps from time to time during the preceding century without even being identified as a planet.

   In the sense of 'total cause', the motion of Uranus was subject to gravitational forces from the Sun and the inner planets, all the rest of the galaxy and outer galaxies, and, theoretically, even influenced by whether or not I sneeze or hold my nose. In practice, and following our concept of 'preponderating cause', only a very few factors had to be considered.

*   *   *

We have mentioned earlier in this chapter that the remarkable success of Mechanics in reducing an enormous range of phenomena to a very small number of physical laws led to attempts at mechanical interpretations of the other branches of physics. We will consider only what is probably the most successful of these: the Kinetic Theory of Gases. It is a simple and good example of 'mechanization', and at the same time it constitutes an initiation into the new class of physical situations that will be considered in future chapters where our capacity to make deterministic predictions is severely limited.

   The problem is to express the two special variables of Thermodynamic theory, 'pressure' and 'temperature', in mechanical terms. In Kinetic Theory, a gas, which at the macroscopic scale appears to be continuous, is assumed to be made up of a large number of very small particles, called molecules, in violent motion. At normal temperatures and pressures, a single cubic centimetre is assumed to contain some 30 billion billion molecules, moving with velocities of some hundreds of metres per second. The 'pressure' (force per unit area) is interpreted as resulting from the continual bombardment of any surface immersed in the gas by the molecules of the gas, and the 'temperature' (which was introduced into thermodynamics to 'conserve' the law of conservation of energy), as being simply another term for the mechanical kinetic energy possessed by the molecules. Derivation of an expression for the pressure is so simple that it is worth giving here. Initially, for simplicity, we assume that all the molecules are travelling at the same velocity and that the molecules are divided up into three sets, moving in each of the three possible directions shown in the drawing. The equation 3.7, derived earlier in this chapter, equates change in momentum, to the force exerted, multiplied by the time of action of the force. Thus, if we calculate the total momentum change per second experienced by the molecules in bombarding a wall, we will get the force exerted; and, since the area of the wall is taken as 1 square centimeter, this force is numerically equal to the pressure. To get this total momentum change per second, we must multiply the change in momentum per molecule, *by* the number of times it strikes one wall per second, *by* the number of molecules travelling in that direction. If we carry this out we get equation 3.18.

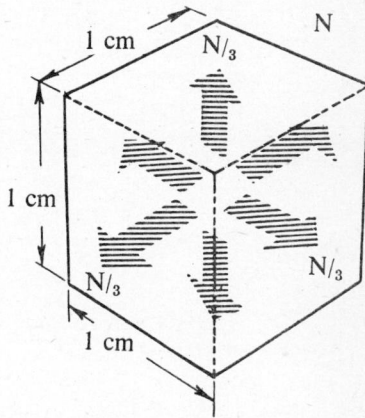

Now because of the collisions between molecules and between molecules and wall, the velocities of the molecules do not remain at the constant value v; nor do we have exactly ⅓ travelling in each of the three principal directions. For large surfaces immersed in the

$$f(t_2-t_1) = mv_2-mv_1 = \Delta(mv)$$
$$\dots\dots\dots\dots\dots 3.7$$

If $t_2-t_1 = 1$ second and the area = 1 sq. cm. then

f = the pressure = $\Delta(mv)$

(*a*) Change in momentum per molecule:

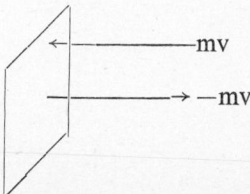

$$\therefore \Delta(mv) = mv-(-mv) = 2mv$$

(*b*) Number of collisions per second = velocity divided by the distance travelled between collisions $= \dfrac{v}{2}$

(*c*) Number of molecules travelling in each direction $= \dfrac{N}{3}$

$\therefore$ Total momentum change per second $= 2mv \times \dfrac{v}{2} \times \dfrac{N}{3}$

$$\therefore P = \tfrac{1}{3}Nmv^2 \dots \dots \dots 3.18$$

Or, more accurately:

$$\overline{P} = \tfrac{1}{3}\overline{N}m\overline{v^2} \dots \dots \dots \dots 3.19$$

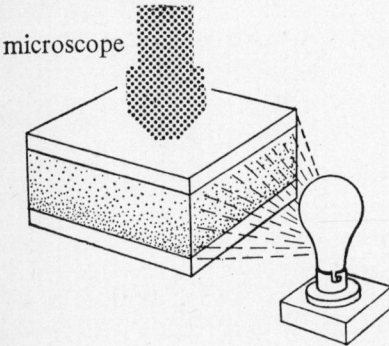

microscope

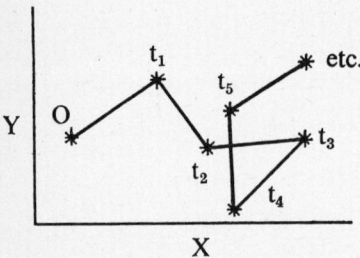

The location of the Brownian Particle at different times: t_1, t_2, t_3, etc.

fluid, however, the number of molecules striking it per second is percentage-wise so regular that to a high order of approximation we change N to $\overline{N}$, the average number of molecules per c.c., and replace v^2 by the average of the squares of the velocities. 3.18 is then rewritten as in 3.19.

Kinetic Theory goes on to develop the Ideal Gas Law, Van der Waal's Law, etc., that were considered as 'primitive' inside thermodynamic theory. It is not necessary to discuss these further here. Instead, we will consider a phenomenon that could not be fitted at all into the framework of Thermodynamics. In Brownian Motion, so named after its discoverer, tiny particles (only barely visible under high-powered microscopes) suspended in a fluid are observed to move about in a jerky unpredictable way, and no thermodynamic explanation in terms of convection currents, heat radiation, etc., could be found. Kinetic theory explains that these apparently random motions are due to the irregular bombardment of the particles by the molecules of the fluid. For small enough bodies the fluctuations of 'N/3' and 'v^2' around the average values, which could be ignored at the macroscopic level, are now proportionately large enough to produce observable effects. At the quantitative level it is a practical impossibility to trace out the paths of all the individual molecules, and Kinetic Theory contents itself with a statistical theory which predicts the motion of an average Brownian particle. More specifically, the theory as used by Rayleigh and Einstein gave the average square distance a particle would travel in any given time. This theory has been well confirmed experimentally. Of course, it is statistical, and makes no prediction as to the precise distance travelled by any one molecule in a given time.

* * *

We are thus confronted in thermodynamics with a situation quite different from those considered earlier in this chapter. In those, any uncertainty as to the exact value of some future observable is due to a lack of sufficiently precise information about the present state of the system, or the laws governing its motion, and, at least in principle, this uncertainty can be reduced to any desired value. This is impossible for Brownian motion, where a complete knowledge of the macroscopic state of the gas: its pressure, temperature, volume, plus a knowledge of all the pertinent laws, will not yield any prediction for the location and velocity of the Brownian object at any future time. We have here, then, an indeterministic theory as far as the variables of thermodynamics are concerned. However, if one switches one's attention from the variables of thermodynamics to the variables of kinetic theory, at least in principle the complicated motions of individual molecules could be traced out, and then a summing up of their individual momentum exchanges would permit precise predictions to be made for the motion of the Brownian particle. Such a theory is called a hidden variable theory. The uncertainty, the indeterminism, at one theoretical level is assumed to be due to a fluctuation of a set of unmeasured variables. If, however, one is able to take into account the hidden variables, determinism would be restored.

This is only one example of an indeterministic theory in physics. It was assumed in classical physics that all such theories were of the above hidden variable type, where it was simply a question of discovering an improved technique, or carrying out a more detailed analysis, to restore determinism and precise prediction. It came to be felt that determinism was an essential part of any scientific theory, and that any indeterminism in a theory was a mark only of our temporary ignorance. In the next several chapters we will study a number of phenomena in which this assumption seems unjustified.

CHAPTER IV

The New Phenomena resulting from the Instrumental Extension of Man's Unaided Senses

SUMMARY: In the first three chapters we have been studying the concept of reality (i.e. the set of concepts symbolically represented and organized into a semiotic world picture) as it existed in western thinking at the turn of the century. Agreeing that causality-determinism is part of the postulational structure of a semiotic rather than something to be looked for directly in experience, we examined language and classical physics and decided that causality-determinism is explicit in the first of these and implicitly part of the general semiotic structure incorporating classical physics, in the second. While our language-common-sense conceptual scheme permits some violations in the 'inexorable chain of cause and effect', particularly where man is concerned, we found that classical physics is rigidly deterministic in principle, if not everywhere in practice. In Mechanics, which was considered to be the most advanced division of Classical Physics, as well as its most ideal form, determinism was defined as meaning:

(1) That the mathematical-syntactical structure of the theory is such that the insertion into it of a set of numerical values for the observables 'm', and 's_1' and 'v_1' at some 't_1', and an analytical expression for 'f', leads to a determination of unique values for 's_2' and 'v_2' at any other 't_2'.

(2) That semantically the 's's', 'm's', and 'v's' are suitable observable quantities to describe experience, and can be simultaneously measured to any desired degree of accuracy.

(3) That in practice suitable expressions for 'f' can be discovered such that, when combined with an actual measurement of 's_1' and 'v_1' at 't_1', correct predictions for future positions and velocities can be made for all bodies in every possible kind of physical situation.

By 1890 classical physics had attained success unprecedented in the world's history in organizing a wide range of phenomena into a concise, unified, and quantitative conceptual structure. This range at that moment contained only the inanimate, and in fact only the simpler parts of that, but there was every reason to believe that extension to the more complex inanimate and the animate was only a matter of time and perseverance. A distinguished scientist expressed the feeling of the time, at an important international scientific conference, when he stated that the broad theoretical developments of Physics had been completed, and that the future scientists' job was only the 'fleshing in of the skeleton,' and the adding of further significant figures after the decimal point. There were several outstanding problems, particularly that of a theory covering black body radiation and an explanation for the Michelson-Morley experiment, but it was felt that in time they would be integrated into the existing structure.

It was not to be so. As with the proverbial fish out of water, the instrumental extension of man's senses was bringing him into new realms of experience for which nothing in his several hundred millennia of past environmental development had prepared him. Modern time distortion and microscopic motion picture photography have made vividly evident how different the world would be if our senses were of different magnitude. In time lapse photography we see a world of plants growing, lashing about, and fighting each other for their existence. At the other extreme we see the complicated high-speed motions which permit a humming bird to hover, or the cat to shift his maximum of moment of inertia from front to back and front again while he executes the 'impossible' manoeuvre of turning about during a fall to land on his feet. In the microscopic world we see the confusion of Brownian Motion, bacterial division and redivision, and the living-non-living viruses, all behaving in ways never encountered at our macroscopic common-sense level of phenomena. Now, these phenomena, though too fast or too slow, too small or too large, to be directly apprehended by our senses, affect us indirectly but surely at the macroscopic level, and consequently cannot be ignored in any world picture purporting to be universal.

In this chapter we will direct our attention specifically to the conceptual difficulties that began to turn up in physics from 1890 on. The previously successful picture of bodies of fixed mass moving about in an absolute space, and an independent absolute time, at each instant occupying a specific measurable position and travelling with a specific simultaneously measurable velocity, no longer seemed applicable. The concepts of body and wave, mass and energy, space and time which were distinct in Classical Physics, now seemed to blur into one another. It is neither practical nor necessary to give a complete historical discussion of all of these phenomena, but some at least must be presented in sufficient detail to appreciate the very real inter-phenomena occurring. We will find the same 'thing' at some times acting like the small rigid body of classical mechanics and at other times like a wave. The law of conservation of energy, and the separate law of conservation of mass, must be changed into a fused law: the law of conservation of mass-energy, since occasionally mass vanishes to be replaced by an equivalent amount of energy, and, conversely, at times raw energy materializes into mass. The space and the independent time of Classical Mechanics have to be replaced by a four dimensional space-time continuum, where space intervals and time intervals transform smoothly into each other. It is true, of course, that most of these phenomena occur in regions outside of that directly apprehended by our senses, and this means that the interweaving of theory and experiment, necessary in order to arrive at a satisfactory conceptual scheme, is more apparent here than at the macroscopic level. Thus, for example, the conceptualization chain extending from a string of water droplets in a cloud chamber, or from a click in a Geiger counter, to the concept 'electron' is considerably longer than that leading from certain direct visual and tactile percepts of shape and colour to the concept 'table'. But still, 'table' is no more an immediate percept than 'electron'. The practical difference is that with familiarity we have forgotten our conceptualization for 'table', while necessarily we remain very much aware of it when we are trying to understand 'electron'.

We will begin our account of these critical inter-phenomena with a description of some of the experiments and theory which seemingly imply a corpuscular nature to waves. Since historically Planck's Theory of Black Body Radiation was the first of the strange new physics, and since it is fundamental to the others that will subsequently be discussed, we begin with it. It is unfortunate that it also happens to be mathematically more complicated than the remainder that will be discussed in this chapter.

*   *   *

CORPUSCULAR NATURE OF WAVES

BLACK BODY RADIATION

One of the outstanding theoretical problems during the latter half of the nineteenth century was that of deriving from basic physical theory a satisfactory formula describing the characteristic emission spectrum of a 'black' body. We will give the two inadequate formulae which were obtained classically, and then outline the method by which Planck was able to derive a successful formula by abandoning some of the classical concepts.

Every body, except at a temperature of absolute zero, is in continuing thermal interaction with its environment. It emits a characteristic radiation 'E', which is a function of the nature of the body and its temperature, absorbs a certain fraction 'A' of the radiation coming to it from the environment, and reflects the rest. A 'black body' is defined as one for which $A = 1$ (and, in consequence, none of the incident radiation is reflected). Its emission spectrum is found to be particularly simple, in contrast to coloured bodies or gases with their complex line and band spectra.

Black bodies radiate energy continuously over the electromagnetic spectrum in a way that depends only upon the temperature. By using a spectroscope we are able to measure the energy given off at each frequency, and if we plot a curve of energy versus wave length we obtain a shape like that shown in the diagram. If we now heat the body to a higher temperature, and then once more plot the energy —wave length curve, we obtain a shape generally resembling the first, but with its maximum shifted along towards shorter wave lengths. (Incidentally, this explains why heating a body causes it first to become red hot (wave length = 7×10^{-5} centimetres), then orange, yellow, blue (4×10^{-5} centimetres), until it finally becomes white hot (all the colour present)).

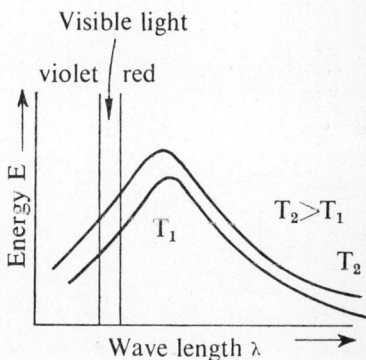

Now that the physicist has the experimental facts on hand the theoretician takes over. His task is to derive from basic physical principles a mathematical expression relating energy and wave length which agrees with the curve obtained experimentally. Once this is done the physicist can feel that the phenomenon has been 'understood' and fitted into the semiotic of physics. In the case of black body radiation, two quite separate approaches using the semiotic of classical physics were used.

We will not go into detail in our discussion of these since neither was completely successful.

In Wien's theory the black body was modelled as a 'gas' capable of absorbing and emitting radiation. He assumed that each molecule sends out radiation whose wave length and intensity depends only upon the velocity of the molecule. It then follows that the amount of energy existing at a certain wave length would be proportional to the number of molecules travelling at the corresponding velocity. He then used the kinetic theory of gases to calculate the proportional numbers of molecules at different velocities as a function of temperature, and finally derived equation 4.1 for the energy distribution.

$$E_{Wien} = \frac{C_1}{\lambda^5} e^{-C_2/\lambda T} \dots\dots\dots 4.1$$

$$\left. \begin{array}{l} C_1 \\ C_2 \end{array} \right\} \text{Constants}$$

T = Temperature

$e \approx 2.72$

λ(lambda) = wave length

This equation agrees with the experimentally obtained radiation curve for a region extending from the short wave length end of the spectrum up towards the visible blue, but fails progressively more and more as it approaches the longer wave lengths of the red and infra-red.

In the second approach using Classical Physics, Rayleigh assumed for the mechanisms of radiation a set of standing waves in the body. (A standing wave occurs when a travelling wave is so enclosed inside a reflecting boundary that the regions of maximum and minimum oscillation come to be fixed in location.) For a given wave length, the energy present would be proportional to the number of standing waves of that wave length which could be set up in the body. He finally obtained equation 4.2. This expression agrees with the actual spectrum in

$$E_{Rayleigh} = \frac{C_3 T}{\lambda^4} \dots\dots\dots 4.2$$

C_3 = Constant

the far infra-red (long wave lengths), but is completely wrong in the near infra-red and the visible.

Looking at this situation in retrospect, it is interesting that a 'wave' theory satisfied the experimental facts in one part of the spectrum, and a 'corpuscular' theory in the other. This suggested that some 'truth' lay in each theory, and some combination was necessary.

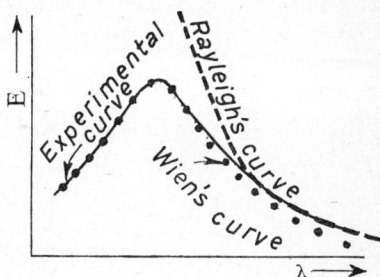

* * *

Planck set about making the minimal number of mathematical modifications of classical theory that would result in a successful theoretical expression. For the moment he put aside any attempt to make conceptual 'sense' out of what he was doing.

For his first step, he treated the radiation inside the solid in the same way as Rayleigh, as a set of standing waves. This is the same sort of calculation as is made in figuring out the frequencies that will be produced by an organ pipe. When such a pipe is in the resonant condition, a standing wave is set up with a point of zero oscillation (a node) at the closed end, and a region of maximum oscillation (an antinode) at the open end. An infinite set of standing waves will satisfy these conditions. The fundamental is shown in the first figure, and we see that the length (l) of the organ pipe is $\frac{1}{4}$ of a wave

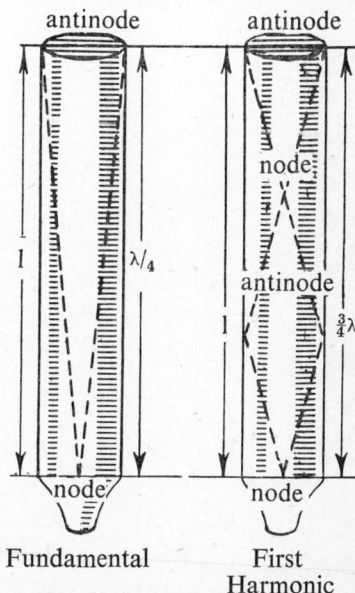

Fundamental

First Harmonic

$$\nu_1 = \frac{c}{\lambda_1} = \frac{c}{4l} \quad \nu_2 = \frac{c}{\lambda_2} = \frac{3c}{4l}$$

(c = wave velocity

ν = frequency

λ = wave length)

$$\nu \text{ (nu, frequency)} = \frac{c \text{ (the velocity)}}{\lambda \text{ (wavelength)}} = \frac{c}{4\lambda}, \frac{3c}{4\lambda}, \frac{5c}{4\lambda}, \ldots \text{ etc.}$$

length. In the next possibility the length of the pipe is $\frac{3}{4}$ of a wave length, then '$1\frac{1}{4}\lambda$', '$1\frac{3}{4}\lambda$' and so on. Each of these corresponds to a different frequency which can be calculated from the basic formula: In the case of a three dimensional system as for the solid black body the calculation is more complicated, but the same principles are used. Using some mathematical ingenuity, which we won't distract the reader by presenting here, it is possible to work out the number of different ways, 'N', in which waves of a certain frequency, 'ν', and velocity, 'c', can be fitted into a body of unit volume (equation 4.3). Then, the energy contained in the body in radiation at this frequency is obtained by multiplying this number, N, of standing waves by the average energy, $\bar{E}_\nu$, of each.

$$N = \frac{8\pi\nu^2}{c^3} \quad \ldots\ldots\ldots\ldots\ldots 4.3$$

$$E = \bar{E}_\nu.N$$

$$= \bar{E}_\nu.\frac{8\pi\nu^2}{c^3} \quad \ldots\ldots\ldots\ldots 4.4$$

$\bar{E}_\nu$ = average energy in each standing wave

$$= \frac{h\nu}{e^{h\nu/kT}-1} \quad \ldots\ldots\ldots\ldots 4.5$$

(h = Planck's Constant

k = The Boltzmann Constant)

$$E_\nu = \frac{8\pi h\nu^3}{c^3}.\frac{1}{e^{h\nu/kT}-1} \quad \ldots\ldots 4.6$$

But $\lambda = \frac{c}{\nu}$

$$\therefore E_\lambda = \frac{8\pi hc}{\lambda^5}.\frac{1}{e^{\lambda kT/hc}-1} \quad \ldots 4.7$$

The second step requires an evaluation of $\bar{E}_\nu$. Planck assumed that the radiation was being produced by mechanical oscillators whose energies could not take on a continuous range of values as in classical physics, but were 'quantized' to the particular values o, hν, 2hν, etc. The average energy comes out as shown in equation 4.5. If this $\bar{E}_\nu$ is substituted into equation 4.4. we obtain Planck's equation 4.6 which gives the distribution in energy in black body radiation as a function of frequency, and finally equation 4.7 which gives it as the required function of wave length. We now proceed to compare this with Wien's and Rayleigh's expressions and with the experimental curve.

For *small* values of λ the exponential term in the denominator $(e^{-hc/\lambda kT})$ is much larger than 1, so, if we ignore 1 in comparison with it, we can simplify the equation to the approximate expression shown in 4.8. If we then take the exponential up into the numerator we come out with equation 4.9, identical to Wien's equation, which as we have noted above agrees with experimental results for short wave lengths.

For *large* values of λ the exponential term can be written approximately as shown in 4.10. Substituting this approximation, Planck's equation may be written in the simplified form 4.11, which now agrees with the Rayleigh-Jeans expression, already found to be correct for large wave lengths.

$$E_{\lambda small} \approx \frac{8\pi hc}{\lambda^5} \cdot \frac{1}{e^{-hc/\lambda kT}} \quad \cdots \cdots 4.8$$

$$\approx \frac{8\pi hc}{\lambda^5} e^{-hc/\lambda kT} \quad \cdots \cdots 4.9$$

$e^{hc/\lambda kT}$ for large values of λ

$$\approx 1 + \frac{hc}{\lambda kT} \quad \cdots \cdots \cdots 4.10$$

$$\therefore E_{\lambda large} \approx \frac{8\pi hc}{\lambda^5} \cdot \frac{1}{\dfrac{hc}{\lambda kT}}$$

$$\approx \frac{8\pi kT}{\lambda^4} \quad \cdots \cdots \cdots 4.11$$

Thus Plank's equation agrees with the experimentally obtained curves for black body radiation throughout the whole range of the spectrum. Though the mathematically 'correct' expression has been obtained, the problem of understanding what this quantization of energy meant still remained. If the energy of each oscillator is restricted to this set of discrete values 0, hν, 2hν, ... then in passing from one level to another it can only emit or absorb energy in multiples of hν. Since this energy is emitted as electromagnetic radiation, such an abrupt change in oscillator energy implies that an equal bundle of electromagnetic energy has been produced. Now, classically such a 'bundle' makes no sense for wave phenomena where the energy transformations are always continuous, however, abrupt discontinuous changes of energy do take place in, for example, collisions between particles.

While in itself this does not necessitate assuming there is a corpuscular nature to waves, Planck's Theory of Black Body Radiation was followed almost immediately by Einstein's Theory of the Photo-electric Effect, where the corpuscular aspect of radiation was more specifically needed to understand certain characteristics of the phenomena.

THE PHOTOELECTRIC EFFECT

In the classical theory, light was described by four independent characteristics—frequency (ν), wave length (λ), velocity (c), (related through the equation $\nu = \dfrac{c}{\lambda}$), intensity, and state of polarization. For all classical phenomena, changes in frequency have a qualitative, all or none, effect, while the quantitative effects are produced by changes in intensity. Thus the eye looking at a source of light responds or not according to the frequencies (colours) present, but once it does respond the magnitude of the response is a function of the intensity. Again, photographic paper (ideally) does not respond to yellow light but is very sensitive to blue, while the density of the latent image produced is proportional to the intensity of the light.

With the discovery of photoelectricity the situation was entirely reversed. In this effect, light falling upon certain surfaces causes them to give off electrons. The energy of each electron is dependent only upon the frequency of the light and is entirely independent of the light intensity. The only effect produced by changing the light intensity is to change the number of electrons emitted—doubling the intensity doubles the number of electrons emitted—but each one has the same energy as before. If this same held true for water waves, doubling the amplitude of the waves would result in twice as many ships bobbing up and down, but each would bob up and down through the same distance as before. While the photoelectric phenomena seems strange using a wave theory of light, it is easily understood according to a corpuscular theory. Light then would consist of a shower of corpuscles, the energy of each corpuscle would depend upon the frequency, and the intensity of the light would be proportional to the number of corpuscles present. One corpuscle of light would be swallowed up by one electron, which would then go off with an equivalent amount of energy. Doubling the intensity would double the number of corpuscles and hence double the number of emitted electrons. For the magnitude of this light corpuscle energy (henceforth called a 'photon'), Einstein used the energy differences (hν) of the oscillators in the Planck Black Body Radiation Theory. Applying the law of conservation of energy, Einstein wrote that the kinetic energy of the electron equals the energy of the photon minus a certain quantity of energy characteristic of the material (φ), which represents the energy required for

Kinetic Energy = corpuscle energy minus surface escape energy 4.12

i.e. $\frac{1}{2}mv^2 = h\nu - \varphi$ 4.13

the electron to escape through the surface. This very simple equation is in excellent agreement with the experimental results.

THE COMPTON EFFECT

Following the discovery of X-rays in 1895, much work was done to establish whether they were wave-like or corpuscular. The evidence then available pointed towards waves. X-rays were unaffected by electric or magnetic fields; they were reflected and refracted by crystals; polarization effects occurred. Later on with more refined instrumentation it became possible to measure the wave length of the longer X-rays by the same sort of grating spectrometer as was used for light waves. For the shorter X-rays, crystals, with their regular alignments of ions, functioned as satisfactory gratings, and in a few years about as much was known about the X-ray spectra of elements as their visible spectra. It seemed clear enough that X-rays were waves.

However, there was one problem that eluded solution: that of deriving a satisfactory theory of X-ray scattering. This is basically the same phenomenon that makes visible the passage of a beam of light through a cloud, smoke fumes, or air filled with dust particles. The individual particles suspended in the air intercept a portion of the light and reflect it in all directions, and it is this that one sees. Now X-rays, like all other radiation in the electromagnetic spectrum, are scattered in passing through substances. However, a new effect appears that is not present in the scattering for the visible region of the spectrum. The scattered radiation contains, in addition to the wave length originally present in the incident beam, an additional X-ray component of longer wave length. The wave length of this modified radiation is dependent upon the angle of scattering, but is completely independent of the nature of the scattering substance.

The job of the theoretician was to derive a mathematical expression giving the intensity and wave length of this secondary radiation as a function of angle. Since it was independent of the kind of substance used as a scatterer, the anomalous scattering had to be produced by something which was a common constituent of all matter. This limited the possibilities to the only two subatomic fundamental particles known at that time: electrons or protons. Since, as we will see later in the discussion of the Bohr Atomic theory, the protons are in general only to be found in the nucleus, where they act jointly with all the nuclear particles and would thus produce a scattering dependent upon the substance, we are left with electrons as the only remaining possibility for the scattering particles. All attempts to obtain a correct formula, using the same methods as were successful in considering the ordinary scattering of light particles, failed.

As we shall now show, A. H. Compton was able to obtain a theoretical expression, agreeing with the experimentally observed values of angle and frequency, by treating X-rays in the same way as Einstein did visible light in the photo-electric effect, i.e. as small corpuscles moving with the speed of light, each possessing a specific amount of momentum and energy. Thus, in Compton's interpretation, an X-ray photon strikes an electron, the photon bounces off in some new direction making an angle θ_x with the old, and the electron goes off at some angle θ_e. The whole process is analogous to a collision between two billiard balls. Assuming that the collision is totally elastic, the laws of conservation of energy and momentum can be used in obtaining the solution. Using the first, we equate the initial energy, '$h\nu$', of the incident X-ray to the sum of the energies of the reflected X-ray, '$h\nu^1$' and the struck electron, '$\frac{1}{2}mv^2$', equation 4.15. When we apply the law of conservation of momentum, we actually have two equations, since this is a two

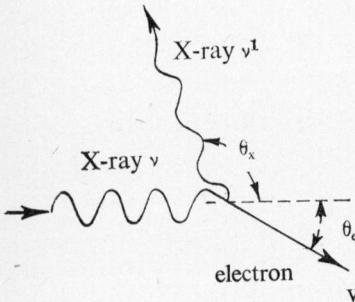

$$h\nu = h\nu^1 + \tfrac{1}{2}mv^2 \ \ldots\ldots\ldots 4.15$$

dimensional problem and momentum in both directions must be conserved. For the momentum of the X-ray we use the standard expression from classical electromagnetic theory, the energy divided by velocity, $\frac{\text{`h}\nu\text{'}}{c}$, and for the electron, the expression obtained in Chapter 3, mass times velocity, 'mv'. We write the two momentum equations, 4.16 and 4.17. (To be more correct, we would have to use the relativistic equations for the energy and momentum of the electron, but as it happens the final result is unchanged.) These three equations can now be solved to obtain the energy of the electron, the frequency or wavelength of the scattered X-ray, and the direction of motion of the electron, as functions of initial X-ray frequency and angle of scattering of the X-ray. The results are given in equations 4.18 and 4.19. These equations are in excellent agreement with the experimental results.

$$\frac{h\nu}{c} = \frac{h\nu^1}{c}\,\text{Cos}\,\theta_x + mv\,\text{Cos}\,\theta_e\,.\,4.16$$

$$0 = \frac{h\nu^1}{c}\,\text{Sin}\,\theta_x - mv\,\text{Sin}\,\theta_e\ \,..\,4.17$$

Solving equations 4.15, 4.16, 4.17 simultaneously we get:

$$\nu - \nu^1 = \Delta\nu = \frac{2h\nu^2}{mc^2}\,\text{Sin}\frac{^2\theta_x}{2}$$
$$\dotfill 4.18$$

Or, written in terms of wave length:

$$\lambda^1 - \lambda = \Delta\lambda = \frac{2h}{mc}\,\text{Sin}\frac{^2\theta_x}{2}\ \dots 4.19$$

⋆ ⋆ ⋆

In the actual experimental measurement, short wave-length X or γ (γ = gamma) rays of a definite known wave length are incident upon some solid body such as graphite, the scattered radiation is observed, and the scattered wave lengths determined spectrally. The effect, however, can be more vividly demonstrated if extremely low intensity X-rays are allowed to pass through a cloud chamber. (Let's take time out to describe the cloud chamber. In this device, the sudden expansion of a volume containing water and alcohol at 100% humidity results in

D

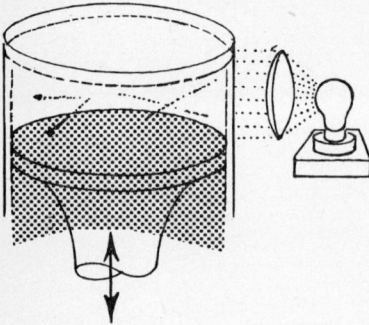

an abrupt drop in temperature and the consequent condensation of water droplets on any ionized molecules present. The passage of certain high energy particles—alpha rays, protons, electrons, etc.—produces a trail of ionized molecules, and, if the chamber is illuminated, this track becomes visible as a white line, thin or dense depending upon the kind and energy of the particle.) In the case of the X-rays, the ray itself produces no visible track, but its passage is marked by a set of short electron recoil tracks produced by Compton collisions between individual X-ray photons and electrons present in the chamber.

THE WAVE NATURE OF WAVES

Now although in these three examples—black body radiation, photo-electric effect, and Compton effect—satisfactory theoretical expressions have been obtained only by considering electromagnetic waves as corpuscles, they are peculiar 'particles' in that they always travel at the same velocity, regardless of the magnitudes of their energy and momentum, and these latter quantities depend upon a *frequency*. In addition, while taking account of these corpuscular aspects of waves, we must not

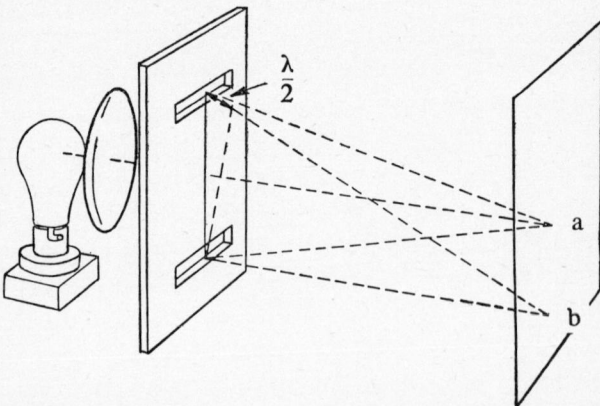

forget the countless experiments only satisfactorily explainable by the wave theory. The two most important of these are interference phenomena and reflection-refraction.

As an example of interference, consider the grating spectroscope. In this, an incident beam is split up into a number of individual rays, and these combine (as shown in the drawing) to produce a bright or a dark region according to whether the various waves arrive in phase so that they reinforce another (position a), or out of phase, cancelling one another (position b).

When radiation is incident upon a surface, the initial ray is broken up into two parts. The one is a reflected ray bouncing off the surface at an angle equal to the incident one, and the other is a refracted ray which penetrates into the material at some different angle.

No satisfactory corpuscular theory of these typically wave phenomena has ever been developed. A corpuscular explanation of interference would require the rather odd result that *one* corpuscle *plus one* corpuscle *equals no* corpuscle at some places and *four* corpuscles at others. In the second situation, an incident corpuscle must split up into two parts, the one being reflected and the other part refracted. While this would not in itself seem too unusual, further experiment shows that in the reflected and refracted beams only whole corpuscles are present.

To sum up: In general, the macroscopic behaviour of electromagnetic radiation is describable by a purely wave theory, but when sensitive measurements are made at the microscopic level, new phenomena appear which are only explainable by introducing a corpuscular theory. The opposite situation holds for material particles, and this will now be discussed.

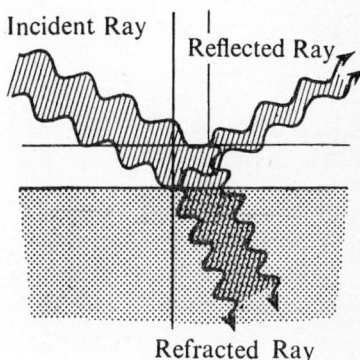

WAVE CHARACTERISTICS OF CORPUSCLES

DE BROGLIE WAVES

In Classical Physics, two equations in widely different parts of the theory resemble each other strongly: the Principle of Least Action in Mechanics, and Fermat's Least Time Principle in the Theory of Light. Each of these equations is fundamental in its respective field and has been amply verified.

Fermat's principle states: 'A light ray in going from one point to another will follow that path which makes the time of travel a minimum.' It is not at all difficult to develop its mathematical form. We begin with the simplest case of a single medium where the ray velocity is constant. The time taken will be obtained by dividing the path length, 'S', by the velocity, 'u', 4.21. It is obvious that in this instance the least time will be with the shortest path, and this will be the straight line drawn from P_1 to P_2. The next case will be that of a succession of different media in each of which the ray will travel at a different constant velocity. Following our first result, the path in each medium will be a straight line, and the entire path will then be a succession of these straight lines. The total time for any path would be calculated by writing a term like 4.21 for each medium and then adding them all up. . . . 4.22. Fermat's Principle requires that the actual path followed by the ray will be that one for which the sum, 4.22, is a minimum. There are sophisticated mathematical techniques for finding the minimal time path, but, in principle, it could be found on a trial and error basis by drawing a large number of such trial paths and choosing that one making the

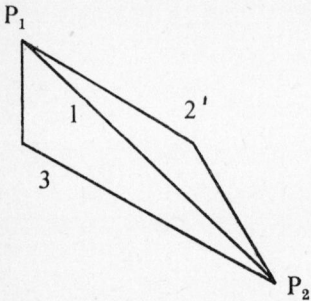

$$t = \frac{s}{u}, \text{ a minimum} \quad \ldots \ldots \ldots 4.21$$

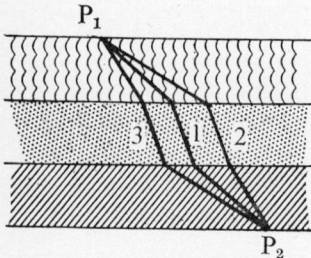

$$t = \Sigma \frac{S_i}{u_i} \ldots \ldots \ldots \ldots \ldots 4.22$$

to be a minimum

(Σ = 'Sum of'

S_i = Path length in medium i

u_i = Velocity in medium i)

time a minimum. When we consider the most general case of a medium of continuously varying index of refraction, we must replace the sum in 4.22 by an integral . . . 4.23. Again, the actual path could be found graphically by an extension of the method used in 4.22, or the minimum integral could be found analytically by using the Calculus of Variations. Finally, when the index of refraction (defined as the ratio of the velocity of light in a vacuum, to the velocity in the particular medium being considered, $\mu = c/u$) is introduced, we obtain the usual mathematical expression of Fermat's Principle . . . 4.25.

In problems concerning the motion of a particle, rather than solving Newton's Equation, it is sometimes more convenient to use the mathematically equivalent Least Action Principle. In words, this reads: 'A particle in going from one point to another, moves along such a path that the average value of its momentum over the entire path is a minimum.' Jumping immediately to the general case, we write equation 4.26 for the mathematical expression of this principle. Now this momentum is a function of the particle's location in the field of force. From the Conservation of Energy principle we obtain 4.27, giving the momentum as a func-

$$t = \int_{P_1}^{P_2} \frac{dS}{u} \quad \dots \dots \dots \dots \dots 4.23$$

to be a minimum

(ds = an infinitesimal bit of path length
u = the instantaneous velocity at a point)

Since the velocity in a medium equals the velocity in a vacuum divided by the index of refraction (usually represented by the Greek letter 'μ' (mu)):

$$u = \frac{c}{\mu} \quad \dots \dots \dots \dots \dots \dots 4.24$$

we can write 4.23 as:

$$t = \int_{P_1}^{P_2} \frac{\mu}{c} dS \quad \dots \dots \dots \dots \dots 4.25$$

to be a minimum

$$\star \quad \star \quad \star$$

The Least Action Principle is:

$$\int_{P_1}^{P_2} (mv) dS \quad \dots \dots \dots \dots \dots 4.26$$

to be a minimum

Total Energy = Kinetic Energy plus Potential

$$\therefore E = \tfrac{1}{2}mv^2 + V$$
$$\therefore \tfrac{1}{2}mv^2 = E - V$$
$$mv = \sqrt{2m(E-V)} \quad \dots \dots 4.27$$

Put this in 4.26 and we get:

$$\int_{P_1}^{P_2} \sqrt{2m(E-V)} \, dS \quad \ldots \ldots \ldots 4.28$$

(to be a minimum)

★ ★ ★

$$\frac{h\nu}{c} = mv \ldots \ldots \ldots \ldots \ldots 4.29$$

but $\lambda = \dfrac{c}{\nu}$ 4.30

$$\therefore \frac{h}{\lambda} = mv$$

or $\lambda = \dfrac{h}{mv}$ 4.31

★ ★ ★

$$\int_{P_1}^{P_2} \frac{\mu}{c} \, dS \quad \ldots \ldots \ldots \ldots \ldots 4.25$$

(to be a minimum)

tion of the potential field 'V'. Substituting 4.27 into 4.26, we get equation 4.28. Equations 4.28 and 4.25 are now in the same mathematical form. Before putting the equivalence into words, we will go on to obtain de Broglie's wave length for a particle. We use Einstein's formula for the momentum of a photon of electromagnetic radiation, and equate this to the momentum of the particle (4.29). Introducing wave length through the standard expression connecting wave length, frequency, and velocity (4.30), we obtain expression 4.31 for the electromagnetic wave length of a particle of mass m moving with velocity v.

The verbal expression for the mathematical content of equations 4.31, 4.28 and 4.25 then would be: A particle of mass m, moving with instantaneous velocity v, and acted upon by a force produced by the potential field V, would follow the same path in going from one point P_1 to another point P_2, as an electromagnetic wave of wavelength $\lambda = \dfrac{h}{mv}$, moving between the same points through a medium of index of refraction $\mu = c\sqrt{2m(E-V)}$.

(A difficulty exists in that the particle moves with a velocity v not equal to the velocity $\nu = \dfrac{c}{\mu}$ of the wave. De Broglie was able to show, however, that the group velocity of the wave could be put equal to the velocity of the particle.)

★ ★ ★

In the case of Black Body Radiation, Photoelectricity, and the Compton Theory, the theoretical work was an attempt at explaining already existing anomalous experimental effects, but de Broglie's work was not in response to any actual observation. In consequence, it was initially considered to be an interesting but entirely mathematical analogy between particle and wave, and some time elapsed before it was experimentally investigated. An experimental difficulty lies, of course, in the fact that the wave lengths of the 'equivalent wave' are very small. As an example, substituting for 'h', 'm', and 'v' for electrons moving with a kinetic energy of 10,000 electron volts, we find a wave length $\lambda = 1.22 \times 10^{-9}$ centimetres, some 50,000 times smaller than that of the wave lengths of electromagnetic waves in the visible part of the spectrum. In the visible region, wave lengths (4×10^{-5} to 7×10^{-5} centimetres) can be measured, and interference and diffraction effects observed, by using gratings consisting of glass plates cut by a diamond stylus with some 10,000 lines to the inch. To produce interference patterns with waves of one one-billionth of a centimetre a grating with a minimum of 10,000,000 lines per inch would be required, a technically impossible construction even today. Fortunately nature provides us with such gratings in the form of certain crystalline structures. Davisson and Germer used a single crystal of nickel as such a natural grating. Electrons at normal incidence were reflected from the crystal, and maxima and minima were observed, located at precisely the places called for by an electromagnetic wave of wave length given by the de Broglie formula. Such interference effects were entirely inexplicable using a purely particle theory of electrons, and these experimental results turned the de Broglie theory from a largely abstract mathematical analogy into a working and necessary physical equivalence.

Electron Gun

Ionization Chamber

Scattering Angle

Nickel Crystal

To complete the equivalence with the electromagnetic wave (corpuscle) picture, let us consider an example of reflection—refraction for material particles.

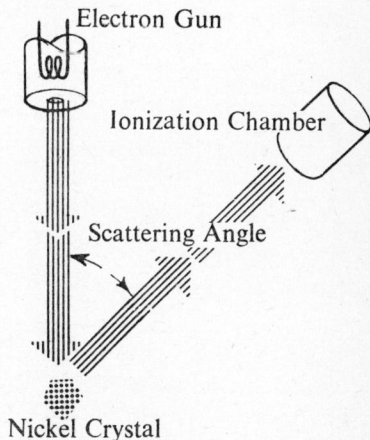

POTENTIAL BARRIERS

At the macroscopic level, particles and waves experience totally different effects when they are incident upon barriers. A bullet striking a tree may be reflected *or* it may penetrate into the tree, moving with decreased velocity. A light wave incident upon a sheet of glass is *partly* reflected *and* partly transmitted.

As an example more pertinent to the phenomenon we are about to discuss, let us consider a ball rolling along a horizontal plane and coming to a hill. (For simplicity we will consider the motion to be frictionless.) If the initial energy possessed by the ball is less than the potential barrier energy, in this case determined by the height of the hill, the ball will roll up to some point below the top of the hill, and, after coming to a stop, roll back down again. If its initial kinetic energy is greater than the potential barrier energy of the hill it will roll to the top, losing kinetic energy all the while, go over the top, and down the other side, regaining its kinetic energy. If the plane is at the same level on both sides, when the ball arrives on the flat on the far side of the hill, it will have as much kinetic energy as that with which it started on the first side.

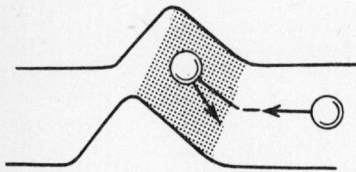

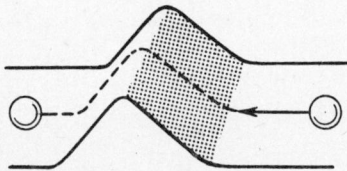

Now this last statement is important. Let us restate it. If we know that the ball has rolled over the top of the hill, then, when we observe it on the other side it must have at least as much energy as the potential barrier energy of the hill. This could even be used as an experimental method of determining the height of the hill. We would measure on the flat the kinetic energy of a number of balls that have come over the hill, and the lowest value we find is an upper limit for the potential barrier energy of the hill.

The phenomenon of alpha 'particle' emission is a microscopic analogue to our billiard ball—hill experiment. The nucleus of an atom is surrounded by a field of force which acts as a potential energy 'hill', and a number of elements are naturally radioactive, giving off α 'particles' which can be observed, and whose energies can be measured. Following our analysis above, we would expect that these energies would be at least as large as the potential barrier energy for any α 'particles' able to escape from inside the nucleus through (over) the barrier into the outside world. There are thus two parts to the experiment. First we determine the height of the barrier energy, E_B, by bombarding the substance with externally produced α 'particles', and increase their energy until they begin to penetrate the barrier and pass into the nucleus, causing nuclear transformations. Next, we measure the energies E_α of the α 'particles' naturally given off by the substance. According to the particle theory E_α should be greater than E_B. In fact it is always less. Unless there are 'tunnels' through the potential barrier this makes no sense according to an α 'particle' theory, but there is no difficulty understanding it on an α 'wave' basis. As a wave incident upon a reflecting barrier, the larger part would be reflected but a small part transmitted. As time went on, more and more of the total 'wave' would be transmitted, until finally 'enough' would be present outside the nucleus for a full-fledged 'α' to exist there. This is of course a very rough verbal presentation of something that can only be understood properly as a mathematical demonstration.

THE PARTICLE NATURE OF PARTICLES

The above are illustrations of phenomena for which a particle theory of material bodies is inadequate to explain what happens at the microscopic level. On the other side of the picture, clicks in Geiger Miller counters, tracks and collisions in Wilson cloud chambers, and the curved motions in electromagnetic fields are equally convincing evidence of the particle nature of the fundamental 'particles'—electrons, protons, alpha particles and the like.

RELATIVITY OF MOTION

We have seen how, at times, phenomena involving 'waves' may only be understood by considering them as 'corpuscles', and how 'particles' may sometimes be visualized as possessing 'wave' characteristics. The same sort of confusion exists for space, time, and velocity. Fundamental to Newton's mechanics was the absolute nature of time and space. Though velocities relative to moving frames were used in certain problems, Newton believed in an absolute system (the fixed ether), with respect to which all accelerations were to be measured, and through which the stars and planets were moving. In 1881 Michelson and Morley undertook to measure the instantaneous velocity of the earth with respect to this fixed sub stratum. This measurement had only become practical for the first time with the invention of the Michelson Interferometer. With this instrument very small distances or times can be measured to a high degree of accuracy. We will make no attempt to describe the actual instrument. The principle is all that is necessary, and this can be easily understood with the help of a considerably idealized version of the experiment.

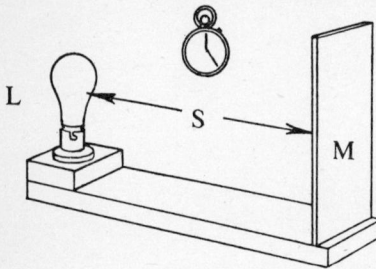

For apparatus we will use a source of light, L, and a mirror, M, mounted on the opposite ends of a rigid bar, and a sensitive clock to measure the time required for the light to travel from L to M and back again. If the bar is not moving in space, the time required for the light trip is obviously the distance, '2s', divided by the velocity of light, 'c' . . . 4.32. Now let us assume the bar is moving to the right at a velocity 'v'. The velocity of light relative to the bar will be 'c−v' as the light makes the first half of the trip, and 'c+v' as it returns. In this case, the time required will be given by equation 4.33. A few mathematical operations reduces 4.33 to equation 4.34. To find how 4.32 and 4.34 differ, we divide the one by the other, and obtain finally equation 4.35. We see that the trip time when the bar is stationary with

$$t_1 = \frac{2s}{c} \quad \dots\dots\dots\dots\dots 4.32$$

$$t_2 = \frac{s}{c-v} + \frac{s}{c+v} \quad \dots\dots\dots 4.33$$

$$\text{or } t_2 = s\left(\frac{c+v+c-v}{(c-v)(c+v)}\right)$$

$$= s\frac{2c}{c^2-v^2}$$

$$= \frac{2s}{c}\frac{1}{1-v^2/c^2} \quad \dots\dots\dots 4.34$$

$$\therefore \frac{t_1}{t_2} = 1-v^2/c^2 \quad \dots\dots\dots\dots 4.35$$

respect to the medium is less than when it is moving by the factor 'v^2/c^2'.

As 'v' is the velocity of the bar, and 'c' the velocity of light (186,000 miles per second), the fraction 'v^2/c^2' is a very small number, and the difference in the two times unnoticeable for most practical problems here on earth. As an example, for the fastest rocket yet built, the difference in the two times is less than one one billionth of one per cent, and no instrument rugged enough to be attached to the rocket could measure such a small time interval. However, the earth itself is in motion around the sun, and, according to classical physics, through the ether. If the bar is attached to the earth it shares the motion of the earth. Thus if the times of the light trip are measured for different orientations of the bar, first pointing east and west, then north and south, the differences in the measured t's should permit a calculation of the velocity of the earth, with respect to which the bar is fixed, relative to the Newtonian fixed ether.

The actual experiment is rather delicate, but Michelson's interferometer is so precise that velocities of the order of the earth about its axis (that is, 25,000 miles per day) should be detectable, and that of the earth in its orbit about the sun ($1\frac{1}{2}$ million miles per day) easily measurable. As it turned out, the experimental result was null, no time difference was found for the various orientations of the bar.

A number of interpretations were possible. The most obvious was that the earth is actually fixed in space and the rest of the universe revolves around it. As a serious assumption this was, of course, unacceptable if one takes into account the enormous body of observation and theory establishing its motion. In a second attempted explanation, it was assumed that the earth dragged the ether along with it so that there was no relative velocity. It is unnecessary to consider those and others in detail. They were all of an ad hoc nature that solved one problem only to introduce others. It was apparent that a re-examination of Newton's fundamental concepts was necessary.

* * *

To quote from Newton: 'I do not define Time, Space, Place, or Motion as being well known to all. Only I must observe that the vulgar conceive these quantities under no other notions but from the relation they bear to sensible objects. And thence arises certain prejudices, for the removing of which it will be convenient to distinguish them into Absolute and Relative, True and Apparent, Mathematical and Common. . . . Absolute,

True, and Mathematical Time, of itself, and from its own nature, flows equably without regard to anything external and by another name is called Duration.' Now it is all very well for Newton to use this 'pure' time, space, and motion in the syntactic part of his system, but, since they bear 'no relation . . . to sensible objects' there is no way in which they may be measured. If the system is to be anything more than a logical exercise there must be some semantic rules. In fact, Newton makes these statements and then promptly violates them by using physical clocks and measuring scales, which of course can only give readings relative to themselves and not to any absolute system. The first experiment—the Michelson-Morley—which had some of the characteristics that Newton desired gave a null result, and seemingly denied the existence of any absolute sub stratum to experience.

* * *

In the twenty years following the Michelson-Morley experiment all attempts to understand its null result within the framework of classical mechanics failed. It was apparent that some major modification of the principles of Newtonian mechanics was necessary, namely, a new theory which would explain the Michelson-Morley (and other) results, but would still reduce to classical mechanics as a valid approximation at the macroscopic level. Einstein did this with his Special Theory of Relativity in 1905. He took over much of the body of ordinary mechanics, but rejected any postulates (such as absolute space, time and motion) which were either devoid of semantic correspondence or were denied by the experimental results.

In particular, he introduced two new postulates. They are straightforward though radical inductions from the experimental fact that all attempts to measure the earth's velocity with respect to an assumed fixed absolute space had failed.

The first: The velocity of light as measured by any observer is a constant, independent of the velocity of the source or observer.

The second: There is no absolute, uniquely defined coordinate system, and thus the equations of motion should be in the same form for all observers.

The operational methods (semantic correlation) of measuring mass, length, and time were taken over from those actually in use in classical physics, but the additional assumption of Newton—that these quantities are constants independent of the motion of the measuring instruments—

was not made. For the rest, the entire body of Newtonian physics and mathematics was examined for consistency with these new assumptions, and if consistent they were incorporated into the new physics.

Among the many changes the new Relativistic Mechanics made, one of the most important was that of changing the constant 'mass' in the fundamental Newtonian equation (f = ma) to a new expression—4.36 which was a function of the velocity of the body relative to the speed of light. For the small values of 'v' occurring in macroscopic terrestrial experience, $\frac{'v'}{c}$ is almost zero, and the equation becomes in practice identical with the classical Newtonian one. This is essential, since Newtonian Physics does work at the macroscopic scale. For the larger values of 'v' that occur in astrophysics and micro-physics the deviation from the classical expression can become large.

$$f = \frac{m}{\sqrt{1-v^2/c^2}}a \quad \ldots\ldots\ldots 4.36$$

If v is small compared with c then $v/c \approx 0$ and:

$$f \approx \frac{m}{\sqrt{1-0}}a$$

or

$$f \approx ma$$

Another important consequence of this theory was the interdependence of length and time and velocity. Thus, if two observers were moving relative to each other they would obtain different answers if they made length or time measurements upon a third object. Even more strange: intervals which have the characteristics of space for one observer might have a time-like nature to the other. That is, the one observer might measure an event with a meter stick, and the other with a clock.

Initially, relativity theory was based upon the result of the Michelson-Morley experiment (and one or two others), but it is now supported by an enormous web of evidence. We will consider here only one of its verified theorems: the essential equivalence of mass and energy as expressed by the now famous equation $E = Mc^2$.

CREATION AND ANNIHILATION OF MATTER

(a) ENERGY INTO MATTER

In the cloud chamber, photographs have been obtained indicating that a photon of radiation has disappeared and a pair of fundamental particles, a positron and an electron, appeared in its place. (The reason that a pair, rather than a single particle, is produced, is that

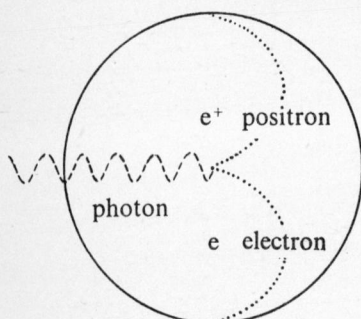

Initial Photon Energy

= The sum of the Kinetic Energies
+the energy needed to produce
their masses

Therefore:

$$h\nu = (\tfrac{1}{2}m_{e+}v_{e+}^2 + \tfrac{1}{2}m_{e-}v_-{}^2)$$

$$+(m_{e+}c^2 + m_{e-}c^2)$$

(e^+ = positron

e^- = electron)

Rewriting the above equation we get:

$$h\nu - (\tfrac{1}{2}m_{e+}v_{e+}^2 + \tfrac{1}{2}m_{e-}v_{e-}{}^2)$$

$$= m_{e+}c^2 + m_{e-}c^2$$

the initial photon carries no electric charge, and thus, taking account of the law of conservation of electric charge, the resulting composite entity must also be without charge. The negative charge on the electron is just cancelled out by the positive charge on the positron.) This qualitative evidence for the mass energy relation can be turned into quantitative corroboration by adding up the energies involved. The initial energy is that possessed by one photon of radiation ($h\nu$). The final energy is the sum of the kinetic energies of the two particles plus whatever energy has had to be used to create the masses of the two particles. We write the difference equation: Initial Energy minus the total Final Energy of the two particles produced, equals the energy converted into mass. The Einstein prediction can be experimentally checked by measuring the frequency of the incident radiation, and the velocities and masses of the resultant electron and positron. The equation has been amply verified.

Here we have had an example of energy in the form of a wave being turned into material particles. The converse can also occur and its consequences are continuously present in the minds of modern-thinking mankind:

(b) MATTER INTO ENERGY

The theory of the atomic bomb and atomic energy is an example on a colossal scale of the conversion of matter into energy.

THE BOHR THEORY OF THE ATOM

As our last example of interphenomena we will consider one in which almost all of the ideas we have been presenting are used: light is considered as both wave and photon; in part of the theory the electron is treated as a particle, while at another stage we think of it as a wave; Classical Mechanics and Electromagnetic Theory, as well as Quantum Mechanics and Special Relativity, are all used.

Early in this chapter we discussed the continuous black body spectrum given off by a radiating solid body. If the atoms are separated from one another, as in a gas, the spectrum is quite different. The simplest of these is the hydrogen spectrum, a section of which is shown here.

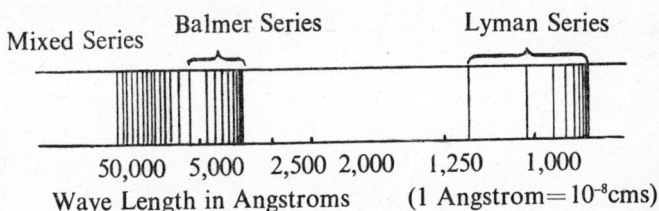

Mixed Series   Balmer Series   Lyman Series

50,000   5,000   2,500 2,000   1,250   1,000
Wave Length in Angstroms   (1 Angstrom $= 10^{-8}$cms)

Many attempts were made towards the end of the last century to write empirical formulae that would locate the lines in this spectrum. The final formula adopted is the Rydberg formula shown in equation 4.38. ('λ', as always, is the wave length, 'R' is a constant called the Rydberg constant, and n and m are integers 1,2,3,4, . . . etc.). Since 'λ' must always be a positive number, 'm' must always be chosen so it is larger than 'n'. It is remarkable that such a simple formula satisfactorily described the many lines of the Hydrogen Spectrum. For more complex elements, variations on the Rydberg formula were needed, but we won't discuss them here. Now it is important to realize that this formula was not a theoretical development. It was obtained entirely by a trial and error empirical procedure.

$$\frac{1}{\lambda} = R\left(\frac{1}{n^2} - \frac{1}{m^2}\right) \dots\dots\dots 4.38$$

Where n and m are integers and m is always greater than n.

(R is a constant called the Rydberg Constant.)

★　★　★

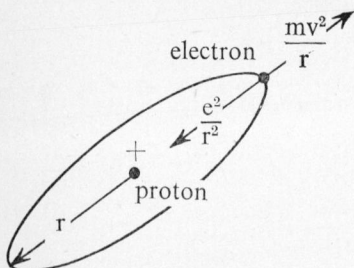

The electrostatic force is: $\dfrac{e^2}{r^2}$

and it must be balanced by the centrifugal force:

$$\dfrac{mv^2}{r}$$

$$\therefore \dfrac{e^2}{r^2} = \dfrac{mv^2}{r} \cdots\cdots\cdots 4.39$$

(e = electron charge
m = electron mass
v = electron speed
r = orbit radius)

★   ★   ★

Energy = Kinetic+Potential

$$\therefore E = \tfrac{1}{2}mv^2 - \dfrac{e^2}{r} \cdots\cdots 4.40$$

Substitute for the v in 4.39 into 4.40 and get:

$$E = -\dfrac{e^2}{2r} \cdots\cdots\cdots 4.41$$

Now:

$$\Delta E = E_1 - E_2$$

$$= -\dfrac{e^2}{2r_1} - \left(-\dfrac{e^2}{2r_2}\right)$$

$$= \dfrac{e^2}{2}\left(\dfrac{1}{r_2} - \dfrac{1}{r_1}\right) \cdots\cdots 4.42$$

In 1913 Bohr published his theoretical derivation of the Rydberg formula from fundamental principles. Bohr made use of the Rutherford atomic model which visualized the atom as a sort of miniature solar system. The nucleus contains most of the mass of the atom and is positively charged. The light negative electron is attracted to it by the electrostatic force between opposite charges, and would move into it except that this force of attraction is balanced by the centrifugal force produced by the electron orbiting about the nucleus sputnik fashion. Equating the two gives us equation 4.39. Next, the energy of the electron is made up of two parts: its potential energy in the field of the nucleus, '$-\dfrac{e^2}{r}$', and its kinetic energy, '$\tfrac{1}{2}mv^2$'. We combine equation 4.39 and 4.40 to get the final expression for the energy, 4.41.

Now if the electron moves from one orbit of radius r_1 to another of radius r_2, its energy will change as shown in 4.42. This energy must appear in some form, and, assuming it is given off as a photon of radiation, we can use the Einstein Planck relation to finally obtain expression 4.44 for the wave length of the radiation produced.

Since nothing in classical theory provides any reason for restricting the electron to particular orbits 4.44 would permit any wave length to be emitted. Classically then the electron would spiral into the nucleus, radiating energy continuously.

It is necessary to impose some limiting conditions (called quantization conditions) restricting the electron to certain specific orbits. We will use the de Broglie theory, treating the electron now as a wave, with wave length given by 4.45. We assume that the electron acts like a standing wave, as in a pipe or on a string, and consequently the circumference of the orbit $(2\pi r)$ must be equal to an integral number (n) of wave lengths. After a little straightforward algebra we obtain 4.48 which gives the allowable orbit radii. Finally, we combine equation 4.44, in which the electron has been treated as a particle, with 4.48, the electron as a wave, and obtain the required equation for the wave lengths that can be produced by the hydrogen atoms . . . 4.49. This is formally the same as the experimentally obtained Rydberg formula. An additional check on the theory was made by checking the value of the theoretical constant $\frac{2\pi^2 me^4}{ch^3}$ with the 'R' of the Rydberg formula. They agreed, and Bohr's radical new theory was justified.

But the energy of a photon is:

$$h\nu = \frac{hc}{\lambda} \quad \dots\dots\dots\dots 4.43$$

If we equate 4.42 4.43:

$$\frac{hc}{\lambda} = \frac{e^2}{2}\left(\frac{1}{r_2} - \frac{1}{r_1}\right)$$

$$\text{or } \frac{1}{\lambda} = \frac{e^2}{2hc}\left(\frac{1}{r_2} - \frac{1}{r_1}\right) \quad \dots\dots 4.44$$

* * *

Now $\lambda_{\text{electron}} = \frac{h}{mv} \quad \dots\dots 4.45$

For a wave of this wave length to fit into the orbit, the circumference must equal an integral number of wave lengths. Thus:

$$2\pi r = n\lambda_e = \frac{nh}{mv} \dots\dots\dots 4.46$$

$$\text{or } r = \frac{nh}{2\pi mv} \dots\dots\dots\dots 4.47$$

Substitute for v from 4.39 into 4.47 and get:

$$r = \frac{n^2 h^2}{4\pi^2 me^2} \dots\dots\dots\dots 4.48$$

* * *

Finally put this r into 4.44 and get:

$$\frac{1}{\lambda} = \frac{2\pi^2 me^4}{ch^3}\left(\frac{1}{n_2^2} - \frac{1}{n_1^2}\right) \quad \dots\dots 4.49$$

A more elaborate analysis, considering the possibility of elliptical orbits, and taking into account the relativistic change in mass the electron experiences because of its high velocity, provided a satisfactory derivation of the fine structure of the spectrum.

★   ★   ★

Two things should now be apparent from our discussions of the 'new experiences' of the twentieth century: First: a concept is not a thing given directly in experience. It is an intimate mixture of sense data and mental operation. Second: the conceptual models that work so well at the macroscopic level—particle or wave, space or time, matter or energy—are completely inadequate at the microscopic and cosmic level which we have now reached as a result of the technological extension of our senses, Despite the work done to integrate the strange new phenomena into the comfortable framework of classical, common-sense, physical theory, the product was such a welter of ad hoc hypotheses that the resultant theory became pragmatically unacceptable. A new approach was needed and this we will go on to describe in the next chapter.

CHAPTER V

The New Physics
of the Twentieth Century

SUMMARY: In Chapter 2 we examined the process by which raw experience is mentally transformed into an organized system of concepts —that is, how it becomes knowledge. In the third chapter we studied the formalization of one part of our common-sense world picture into classical physics. In the language of semiotics we recognized physics as a true system in the three senses of being internally logical, of being consistently correlated with experience and of being pragmatically successful. This success was actually only attained for the less complex phenomena of inanimate nature, and of course only at the macroscopic level observable by man's unaided senses. In Chapter 4 we found that the instrumental extension and enlargement of our sensory experience brought about by our technology, itself developing under the stimulus of classical physics, presented us with a new set of experiences which couldn't be integrated into either the physical or the common sense conceptual scheme.

The revision required in physics was not the simple one of introducing new force terms and energies into Newtonian mechanics, but of a penetrating re-examination of the concepts themselves. This was carried out in two principal theoretical developments: Relativity Theory and Quantum Mechanics. Both of these are fine examples of semiotics. They have clearly expressed pragmatic bases induced from experimental results, well-defined syntactic developments, and semantic correspondence rules which admit only the operationally possible. Both look strange when compared with common-sense classical physics, but this is entirely in keeping with the weirdness of the phenomena they were invented to 'explain'. Though we will make little further use of it in our investigation of determinism, Einstein's Special Theory of Relativity is so conceptually and mathematically simple, that we will begin with it as an example of how a theory evolves in an attempt to explain an experimental result. However there is no reason for carrying Relativity Theory beyond the derivation of the transformation equations. We will go on from this to examine the postulational and syntactical structure of Quantum Mechanics, and apply it to the solution of a problem resembling the potential barrier one of Chapter 4. Finally we will study the predictive mechanism of Quantum Mechanics and compare it with that of the Classical Theory.

Some parts of this and the next chapter involve more difficult mathematics than that which has been used up to now. The author feels that it is essential that these be included so that the reader will gain some understanding of the lively arguments that are currently taking place regarding the function of 'causality' and 'determinism' in physical theory. The mathematics and technical details have been kept as simple as possible so as to encourage the reader to follow them, however those readers who are non-mathematically inclined are reminded that the thread of the argument can be followed in the verbal text, and, as a word of encouragement: the remaining chapters are almost without mathematics at all.

★ ★ ★

RELATIVITY THEORY

The crucial experiment for Relativity Theory is that of Michelson and Morley, already mentioned in Chapter 4. If we refer to the description of the experiment there, we see that the time of light travel, as calculated by classical mechanics, from a source of light to a mirror and back again depends upon the velocity of the bar. The time for a bar motionless with respect to the 'ether' is given by 5.1, for a bar moving with velocity 'v' relative to the 'ether' by 5.2, and the ratio of the two is given by equation 5.3. The Michelson-Morley experiment found this ratio to be 1; i.e. within the limits of experimental error the two times were the same.

(1) Rod still

$$t_1 = \frac{2s}{c} \quad \dots\dots\dots\dots\dots 5.1$$

(2) Rod moving with velocity v

$$t_2 = \frac{2s}{c}\left(\frac{1}{1-v^2/c^2}\right) \quad \dots\dots\dots 5.2$$

$$\therefore \frac{t_1}{t_2} = 1 - \frac{v^2}{c^2} \quad \dots\dots\dots\dots 5.3$$

Now according to 5.3, this ratio could be 1 if:

(1) v is so small relative to the speed of light that v^2/c^2 can be neglected in comparison with 1. This is the case in the usual problems of macroscopic-sized experience where the experimental error is vastly larger than the mathematical error involved in neglecting v^2/c^2. As an example, for a sputnik travelling around the earth in two hours this would amount to an error of less than one ten millionth of one per cent.

(2) v actually is zero. This would mean that the earth is motionless in the ether and all the rest of the universe is rotating about it. This would require such an enormous change in classical science and philosophy that we would use such an interpretation only if all simpler ones failed.

But there is one such simpler explanation:

(3) The transformation equations of classical physics for velocities are wrong; specifically, in calculating the time of light travel in the case where the bar is moving, we must ignore the velocity of the bar itself. This last was Einstein's assumption.

The fundamental hypothesis, then, in his Special Theory of Relativity is: 'All observers, measuring the speed of light (in a vacuum or, to a first approximation in air) relative to their own system, will obtain exactly the same answer, c, regardless of the magnitude of their own velocity'. The second (actually first enunciated by Henri Poincare) is the 'Relativity Principle' and follows closely upon the idea of the first: 'There is no privileged absolute system of coordinates. All observers moving relative to one another with constant velocity are equivalent, and the laws of motion must take the same form for each'. We won't try to be exhaustive in our presentation of Einstein's postulates; let us simply summarize by saying that for the remainder of the postulates he took those of Newtonian Mechanics, making whatever modifications as were necessary to obtain logical consistency with the above. For his syntax he used ordinary logic and mathematics. For observables, he took those actually in use in classical mechanics: position, velocity, mass, momentum, energy, etc., but gave up the assumption of their being absolute quantities independent of the state of the observer.

* * *

We will now derive the transformation equations by which observers moving relative to one another will compare position and time measurements. Our procedure is: first obtain the classical transforms, next show that these violate the Michelson-Morley result, and then show that Einstein's transformation equations do satisfy it.

We consider two observer systems called S and S^1. They are each provided with clocks and measuring rods which have been precisely calibrated against one another when the systems are mutually at rest. Now S^1 is set moving with a velocity 'v' relative to S, and at the instant the origins coincide they both set their clocks to zero. Distances and times measured in S^1 are represented by

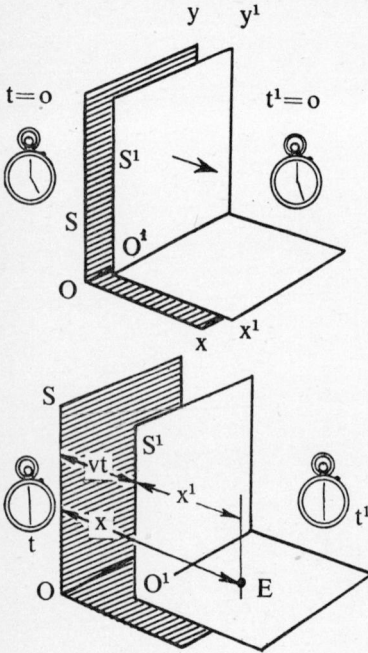

'x^1' and 't^1', those in S by 'x' and 't'. Thus at the instant their origins coincide $t = t^1 = 0$. Let some event occur at time 't^1' and location 'x^1' relative to S^1, and time 't' and location 'x' relative to S. Since S^1 is moving relative to S with velocity 'v', it will have travelled a distance 'vt' as measured in system S by the time event E occurs. In classical physics, if the two clocks are once calibrated against one another and are in good working order, they are assumed to continue to give the same readings. Thus $t = t^1$.

Next it is 'obvious' from the drawing that the equations connecting the distance O^1 to E in S^1 (i.e. x^1) and the distance O to E in S (i.e. x) are related through equation 5.5.

Classically

Our common-sense physics (that is the conceptual scheme we are accustomed to using at the macroscopic level) would affirm that things couldn't be otherwise.

$$t^1 = t \dots\dots\dots\dots\dots 5.4$$

$$x^1 = x - vt \dots\dots\dots\dots 5.5$$

However let us consider for the event E the arrival of a light ray which started out from the coincident orgins at time $t = t^1 = O$. According to the Einstein interpretation of the Michelson-Morley result, the velocity of the ray will be the same, 'c', in both systems. System S^1 will describe the event E by saying that the ray travelled a distance 'x^1' in 't^1' seconds at velocity 'c'. We write the usual equation 5.6, stating that distance travelled equals velocity, times time. System S will describe the event in the same way, but will express it in terms of 'x', 't' and

$$x^1 = ct^1 \dots\dots\dots\dots 5.6$$

$$x = ct \dots\dots\dots\dots 5.7$$

Squaring equation 5.6:

$$(x^1)^2 = c^2(t^1)^2$$

$$\therefore (x^1)^2 - c^2(t^1)^2 = 0 \dots\dots\dots 5.8$$

the same 'c' (equation 5.7). After a few mathematical operations, we obtain equation 5.10, which must be satisfied by our transformation equations. Thus equation 5.10 must be considered to be the symbolic mathematical equivalent of the Michelson-Morley experimental result.

We begin by testing the classical transformation equations. We substitute the expression for 't¹' in terms of 't' (5.4), and 'x¹' in terms of 'x' (5.5), in the right hand side of equation 5.10. If these transformations are correct the right hand side should reduce to the same expression as on the left hand side. We obtain the incorrect result 5.11.

It is apparent that some fundamental modification of the classical theory is required.

The correct transformation equations must do two things: (1) They must satisfy the equality 5.10. (2) Since the classical theory does work at the macroscopic level, the new transforms must reduce to the classical forms, 5.4 and 5.5, in the limit of small relative velocity. Einstein suggested equations 5.12 and 5.13. Putting $v/c = 0$, we see immediately that they satisfy the second requirement. We have still to check if they satisfy the first. We follow the same procedure as with the classical transforms: substitute 5.12

Similarly:

$$x^2 - c^2t^2 = 0 \dots\dots\dots 5.9$$

Equating 5.8 and 5.9:

$$x^2 - c^2t^2 = (x^1)^2 - c^2(t^1)^2 \dots 5.10$$

⋆ ⋆ ⋆

Substitute for t^1 and x^1 in the right hand side of 5.10, using equations 5.4 and 5.5. We get:

$$(x^1)^2 - c^2(t^1)^2 = (x-vt)^2 - c^2t^2$$
$$= x^2 - 2xvt + (v^2 - c^2)t^2 . 5.11$$

which is not equal to the left hand side, $x^2 - c^2t^2$

⋆ ⋆ ⋆

$$t^1 = \frac{t - \frac{vx}{c^2}}{\sqrt{1 - v^2/c^2}} \dots\dots\dots 5.12$$

$$x^1 = \frac{x - vt}{\sqrt{1 - v^2/c^2}} \dots\dots\dots 5.13$$

For $v/c \to 0$, 5.12 and 5.13 reduce to 5.3 and 5.4

Substitute into the R.H.S. of 5.10:

$$(x^1)^2 - c^2(t^1)^2 =$$

$$= \left(\frac{x-vt}{\sqrt{1-v^2/c^2}}\right)^2 - c^2\left(\frac{t-\frac{vx}{c^2}}{\sqrt{1-v^1/c^2}}\right)^2$$

$$= \frac{x^2 - 2xvt + v^2t^2 - c^2t^2 + 2xct - \frac{vx^2}{c^2}}{1 - v^2/c^2}$$

$$= \frac{x^2(1-v^2/c^2)-c^2t^2(1-v^2/c^2)}{1-v^2/c^2}$$

$$= x^2-c^2t^2 \quad \ldots\ldots\ldots\ldots\ldots 5.14$$

as required by 5.10

and 5.13 into the right hand side of 5.10, and see if it reduces to the same expression as on the left. It does, 5.14. Thus the Einstein transforms satisfy all the requirements of classical physics and the additional one at high relativistic velocities: the Michelson-Morley null result.

★ ★ ★

It is not hard to go on from this to the remainder of the Special Relativity Theory and derive the well-known results: the time contraction; the space contraction; the velocity transforms; using the law of conservation of momentum, the increase in mass with increased velocity; the new form of Newton's equations, etc. Since, however, we will make little use of Special Relativity in the remainder of this book the above will suffice as an illustration of the building up of a semiotic from an induced pragmatic base.

QUANTUM MECHANICS

Quantum Mechanics, coming after Relativity Theory by some 20 years, was even more at variance with our common-sense world picture. It took as its experimental foundation the variety of phenomena described in Chapter 4 seemingly implying some wave nature to particles and a corpuscular one for waves. The immediate theoretical stimulus was the work of de Broglie already mentioned previously, but its initial mathematical formulation was due to Heisenberg and Schroedinger. We will make no attempt at an historical presentation, but rather follow the same approach as was used in Special Relativity. We begin by considering a fundamental difficulty in measurement that arises from the particle-wave duality of micro-entities, and then use this as the basis for an exposition of the postulates.

The semantic correlation with experience is obtained through a specification of the observables; and quantum mechanics uses the familiar ones: mass, position, time, momentum, energy, etc. Of course not all of these are independent. Since in the majority of micro-experiments the entities will display both particle and wave aspects—if we apply macroscopic models to these micro-entities—the problem of measuring two or more observables *simultaneously* appears for the first time in physics. (You will remember the need for a simultaneous measurement of position and velocity if Newton's Equations were to be successfully used.) We begin with an analysis of an experiment which attempts to measure simultaneously the position and velocity of an electron.

★ ★ ★

In this experiment, the electron is initially moving from left to right parallel to the x axis as shown in the drawing. Since we know nothing about its y position, the uncertainty in y is infinite ($\Delta y = \infty$). However as it is defined to be moving exactly parallel to the axis its y component of momentum (p_y) is exactly known and its uncertainty is zero ($p_y = 0$ and $\Delta p_y = 0$). Now, in an attempt to measure its y position, a slit of width ab is inserted perpendicular to the x axis. If the electron emerges on the other side of the slit, then its y position at the moment of passing through the slit is known to an accuracy of ab ($\Delta y = $ ab).

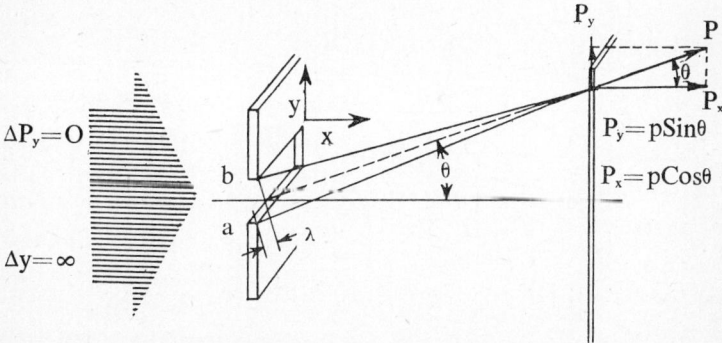

Classically, this uncertainty in y, $\Delta y = $ ab, could be made as small as we like by simply decreasing the size of the slit, and the y momentum of the electron would remain zero unless it actually collided with the slit. Thus, after passing through an infinitesimally narrow slit, y and p_y could be precisely and simultaneously known; $\Delta y = 0$ and $\Delta p_y = 0$.

However, as we have shown in the previous chapter, the actual experimental situation is that the electron is affected by the slit as if it were a classical wave, with wave length given by de Broglie's ex-

$$\frac{\lambda}{ab} = \sin\theta \dots\dots\dots\dots 5.15$$

ab = uncertainty in y = Δy

5.15 becomes:

$$\Delta y = \frac{\lambda}{\text{Sin } \theta} \dots\dots\dots\dots 5.16$$

* * *

If the electron emerges travelling parallel to the x axis (i.e. θ = 0):

$$p_y = 0$$

If it emerges travelling at the angle θ:

$$p_y = p \text{ Sin } \theta \dots\dots\dots 5.17$$

$$\therefore \Delta p_y = p \text{ Sin } \theta \dots\dots 5.18$$

* * *

Now from de Broglie (see previous chapter)

$$\lambda = \frac{h}{mv} = \frac{h}{p}$$

Insert this in 5.16

then: $\Delta y = \dfrac{h}{p \text{ Sin } \theta} \dots\dots 5.19$

* * *

Multiply 5.18 and 5.19 together

$$\Delta y . \Delta p_y = h \dots\dots\dots 5.20$$

* * *

More correctly

$$\Delta y . \Delta p_y > \frac{h}{2\pi} \dots\dots\dots .5.21$$

pression. Now we have all observed the way in which waves (e.g. water waves passing through a gap in a breakwater) diverge in passing through a narrow aperture. The electron will 'diverge' in the same way.

Classical optical theory shows that a light beam passing through a slit spreads out over an angle θ given by equation 5.15. Considering the electron as a wave, this means that instead of continuing to go straight ahead, the electron will emerge from the slit potentially travelling in any direction from its original direction parallel to the x axis up to this angle θ. Thus, the y momentum which was previously known precisely (Δp_y = 0), becomes uncertain by an amount given by 5.18. Inserting the slit has reduced the uncertainty in the electron's y position from ∞ to the Δy of 5.16, but it has increased the uncertainty in its momentum from 0 to that given in 5.18.

In 5.16 we insert the de Broglie wave length for the electron, multiply 5.18 by 5.19, and get equation 5.20. Now actually these are minimal estimates of the uncertainties, so that properly speaking the 'equals' sign must be replaced by the 'greater than' symbol. Also, a more careful calculation shows that instead of 'h' we should have 'h/2π'. The resulting equation, 5.21, is known as Heisenberg's Uncertainty Principle.

★   ★   ★

Since this Uncertainty Principle is of such fundamental importance to this work it is worth looking at another specific example of its appearance. It is an experiment suggested by March in which he considers an attempt to measure the position and simultaneous momentum of a micro-entity by bouncing a pulse of light off it.

The time for the pulse to travel from the observer to the particle and back would locate its position. This is the converse of the technique initially proposed by Galilei to measure the velocity of light. He stationed two observers, equipped with lanterns that could be exposed and blinded very quickly, on two hills a known distance apart. The procedure was: observer A would open his lantern, and as soon as B saw A's lantern he would open his. A would count the number of his heart beats intervening between his first opening his lantern and seeing B's. The velocity of light would then be obtained by dividing twice the distance separating A and B by the time as measured by A's heartbeat. The method failed because of the unexpectedly—to Galilei—high magnitude of the velocity of light, but, in more refined form, it was successfully used two centuries later.

The Doppler change in frequency of the reflected ray would measure the micro-entity's velocity. The same principle applied to sound explains why the pitch of a train's whistle drops as it passes you. When you approach the source of sound the number of pulses passing you per second is greater than when you are still, and when you are receding from the source the number of pulses per second is smaller. The magnitude of the change in pitch depends upon the relative velocity between the train and you.

This method has been successfully used recently to calculate the orbit and velocity of the various sputniks in their motion about the earth. In the case of the micro-entity the experiment is impossibly delicate for the sort of apparatus we possess today, but this is a practical rather than a theoretical difficulty, and the experiment is allowable as a 'thought' experiment. It will serve as a second example of the theoretical impossibility of making a simultaneous precise measurement of position and velocity.

Source   Outgoing wave ν microentity ν

$\rightarrow$

$\mathcal{www} \!\!\rightarrow c$

$c \!\leftarrow\! \mathcal{wwn}$

Detector   Returning wave ν^1

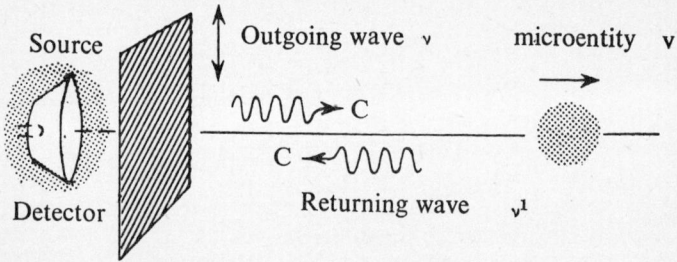

First we consider the light bundle as a group of waves. The standard formula in classical theory for the Doppler change in frequency for a reflected wave is 5.22. In 5.23 we solve this equation for the entity's velocity as a function of outgoing frequency, 'ν', and reflected light frequency, 'ν^1'.

$$\nu^1 = \nu\left(1 - \frac{2v_1}{c}\right) \quad \dots\dots\dots 5.22$$

$$v_1 = \frac{\nu - \nu^1 c}{2\nu} \quad \dots\dots\dots\dots 5.23$$

(c = light velocity
v_1 = particle velocity at the instant of reflection)

★   ★   ★

Initial momentum of photon

$$= \frac{h\nu}{c}$$

Momentum after reflection

$$= -\frac{h\nu^1}{c}$$

Change in momentum

$$\Delta p = \frac{h\nu}{c} - \left(\frac{-h\nu^1}{c}\right)$$

Or, since ν^1 is not too different from ν:

$$\Delta p \approx \frac{2h\nu}{c}$$

$$\Delta(mv) \approx \frac{2h\nu}{c}$$

$$\therefore \Delta v \approx \frac{2h\nu}{mc} \quad \dots\dots\dots\dots 5.24$$

However we have seen that light has also a corpuscular aspect (the Compton effect, the photoelectric effect, etc.) when it strikes a particle. Thus, in rebounding it experiences a change in momentum approximately equal to $\frac{2h\nu}{c}$. Using the law of conservation of momentum, we know that the microentity must receive an equal but opposite change in momentum, and thus experience a velocity change as given by 5.24. The final velocity, 'V_2', of the entity immediately after the reflection of the wave pulse, is obtained by adding 5.23 and 5.24, and the final result is given by 5.25.

The quantities to be measured in 5.25 are 'ν', the initial frequency, and 'ν^1', the reflected frequency. (We assume the mass of the microentity has been obtained in a previous measurement, and that it is moving sufficiently slowly so that we may ignore relativistic effects.) Providing the wave consists of a single initial frequency, 'ν' and 'ν¹' can be measured to any desired accuracy, subject only to experimental error, and the final velocity of the particle can in principle be exactly determined.

Final velocity of micro-entity after the photon has been reflected:

$$v_2 = v_1 + \Delta v$$

Substituting for v_1 and Δv from 5.23 and 5.24:

$$v_2 = \frac{\nu - \nu^1}{2\nu}c + \frac{2h\nu}{mc} \dots\dots 5.25$$

* * *

Now as yet we have not found out anything about the position at the instant of reflection. We will attempt to find this by measuring the time required for the wave to travel from our source to the entity and back. For this we must use a wave pulse of finite length. The shorter the length of the pulse the more accurately we can specify the exact moment of collision. However, it is fundamental in classical optical theory that a short wave train can never consist of a single frequency, but rather of a band of frequencies around some average value. The shorter the wave pulse, the wider the band of frequencies. The exact expression is given by 5.26. We see that pulse duration and spread of frequencies are inversely proportional. To get a short wave pulse (Δt small), in order to measure the position accurately, we are obliged to use a wide band of frequencies.

However this uncertainty in the exact frequency will produce a corresponding uncertainty in our velocity measurement. To obtain an exact expression for this we differentiate 5.25. If we examine the two terms in 5.27 we see that the second, containing 'h' in the numerator (6.6×10^{-27}), and 'c' in the denominator (3×10^{10}), is much smaller than the first, and, to a good approximation can be

$$\Delta t \cdot \Delta \nu = 1 \dots\dots 5.26$$

(Δt = pulse duration

Δν = the band width of frequencies in the pulse)

* * *

Differentiating 5.25 we get:

$$\Delta v_2 = \frac{\Delta\nu}{2\nu}c + \frac{2h\Delta\nu}{mc} \dots\dots 5.27$$

Since h is small and mc a relatively large number:

$$\Delta v_2 \approx \frac{\Delta\nu}{2\nu}c \dots\dots 5.28$$

Put 5.26 into 5.28:

$$\Delta v_2 = \frac{c}{2\nu\Delta t} \quad \dots\dots\dots\dots 5.29$$

* * *

If pulse is reflected at the beginning, the entity moves with velocity v_2 during Δt, and its final position will be:

$$x_1 = x_0 + v_2\Delta t$$

$$= x_0 + \frac{\nu - \nu^1}{2\nu}c\Delta t + \frac{2h\nu}{mc}\Delta t \quad \dots 5.30$$

If reflection occurs at the end of the pulse, at $t_0 + \Delta t$ the particle will be at:

$$x_2 = x_0 + v_1\Delta t$$

$$= x_0 + \frac{\nu - \nu^1}{2\nu}c\Delta t \quad \dots\dots\dots 5.31$$

$$\therefore \Delta x = x_1 - x_2$$

$$= \frac{2h\nu}{mc}\Delta t \quad \dots\dots\dots\dots 5.32$$

* * *

From 5.29 we get:

$$\Delta p \approx \frac{mc}{2\nu\Delta t} \quad \dots\dots\dots\dots 5.33$$

* * *

Multiplying 5.32 and 5.33

$$\Delta x \cdot \Delta p \approx \frac{2h\nu}{mc}\Delta t \cdot \frac{mc}{2\nu\Delta t}$$

$$\approx h \quad \dots\dots\dots\dots 5.34$$

neglected. We get 5.28 as our expression connecting frequency uncertainty with velocity uncertainty, and in 5.29 velocity uncertainty as a function of pulse width, Δt.

We have now to find an expression for the position at the instant of reflection, and the position uncertainty as a function of pulse width. The photon may be reflected either at the beginning or at the end of the wave pulse. If at the beginning, the entity will move with increased velocity 'v_2' during the time 'Δt', and at '$t_0 + \Delta t$' will be at the position shown by equation 5.30. If the photon is reflected at the end of 'Δt,' the micro-entity will have continued to move at its initial velocity 'v_1' during 'Δt', and at '$t_0 + t$' will be at the position shown in 5.31. Thus at the known instant '$t_0 + \Delta t$', the entity has an uncertainty in position given by 5.32.

From our previous result for 'Δv_2' (5.29), it has an uncertainty in momentum given by 5.33.

* * *

In these two expressions 'Δt' occurs in the numerator for 'Δx,' and in the denominator for 'Δp.' Thus, by changing 'Δt,' either 'Δx' or 'Δp' may be made arbitrarily small, but the decrease in the uncertainty in one is balanced by an increase in the uncertainty in the other. Multiplying the two expressions together, we get equation 5.34. This, of course, has been obtained with several approximations, and such a minimal uncertainty product would only be obtainable under ideal circumstances. Closer analysis would again yield the Heisenberg Uncertainty Principle 5.21.

More exactly

$$\Delta x . \Delta p > \frac{h}{2\pi} \quad \dots\dots\dots\dots 5.21$$

* * *

Analysis of a large number of other experiments yields the same results. It seems that at the microscopic level the observables of physics can be arranged in pairs, called conjugate variables, such that the product of their uncertainties satisfy this Heisenberg Principle. For each of these pairs, the more accurately we try to measure the one member, the less accurately we can know the other; and if we set up an experiment to determine the one exactly, the other will become completely undetermined. Now since this 'h' is an extremely small quantity—6.6×10^{-27}—this error, though of considerable importance in microphysics, is entirely negligible at the ordinary macroscopic level of classical physics, and so it is not surprising that it has never been noticed there.

No experiment has as yet been devised which will yield more certain knowledge of conjugate variables than that given by the Heisenberg Uncertainty Principle, so in the same way as the Michelson-Morley experiment is part of the basis for Special Relativity, the notion of conjugate variables is fundamental to Quantum Mechanics. Postulate 3 (see below) embodies this as part of the postulational structure.

Quantum Mechanics

We are now ready to take up the pragmatic structure of Quantum Mechanics: a specification of the postulates. Although we will consider Quantum Mechanics in more detail than Relativity Theory, the same limitation on an exhaustive presentation of all the hypotheses applies as did there. The searching out of all the hidden assumptions, as well as the overt ones special to quantum mechanics, would take us through all of language, mathematics, and logic as well as much of our common-sense world picture, and could never be fully completed. In consequence, we shall restrict our investigation to those postulates which specifically differentiate the new mechanics from the old.

Quantum Mechanics uses the same observables as Classical Mechanics. However, as in Relativity Theory, a thoroughgoing operational approach is used. In this case, this means that it is recognized from the beginning that the observed entity is affected by the observing mechanism, and that the number obtained in a measurement is a combined state of observer and observed. Further, in keeping with the various experiments, already examined, in which the Heisenberg Uncertainty Principle appears, it is recognized that the measuring of one quantity can affect the value of another in an uncontrollable way so that two observables are not necessarily simultaneously knowable.

The first postulate carries out essentially the same semantic task as that which occurs when we name as 'cow' a certain well-recognized type of composite event in our everyday experience.

Postulate 1: *Certain composite percepts will be identified as observables, and to each of these will be associated inside the theory a symbolic mathematical entity called an operator.* (We ask the readers to bear with us for a page or two until the meaning of some of these new terms, such as operator, can be made clearer.)

The first postulate has provided us with building blocks for our mathematical edifice, but we still need mortar and tools to put them together. The second begins the task of doing this.

Postulate 2: *The possible numerical results that can be obtained in a measurement of an observable 'a' will be the solutions of the operator equation 5.35.*

$$A\psi_i = a_i\psi_i \quad \dots \dots \dots \dots \quad 5.35$$

'A' is the mathematical operator associated with the observable, 'a_i' is one of the possible numerical results, and 'ψ_i' (psi) is a mathematical function used to describe the physical system which is under investigation. It will be worth while for the readers to remember that 'ψ_i' is called an eigen function, and 'a_i' the corresponding eigen value.

Now, of course, this operator equation cannot be solved to find the various possible values of 'a_i' until we have adopted specific mathematical forms for the operator 'A'. In the corresponding problem in Newtonian Mechanics, the equation 'f = ma' could only be solved when we had expressions for 'f'. These were found on a purely pragmatic basis by picking out those mathematical functions which, when substituted into 'f = ma', gave results agreeing with observation. Similarly, in Quantum Mechanics, the first—pragmatic—restriction is: that the operators 'A' be so chosen that the resultant answers 'a_i', obtained by solving the operator equation, will agree with the actual experimental results.

This is a pragmatically necessary condition for a satisfactory theory, but is obviously not sufficient to determine the quantum operators. The next postulate incorporates into the theory the Heisenberg Uncertainty Principle, which thus becomes fundamental to Quantum Mechanics just as the Michelson-Morley result was to Relativity Theory. (The Uncertainty Principle will not be immediately recognizable but we will show later that it is deducible from this postulate.) At the same time, this third postulate establishes a connection with Classical Mechanics which is essential since Quantum Mechanics must give the same answers as Classical Mechanics for large enough bodies.

Postulate 3: *If 'A' and 'B' are two quantum mechanical operators corresponding respectively to the two observables 'a' and 'b', then 'A' and 'B' must be so chosen that they satisfy equation 5.36.* 'AB—BA' is called the commutator of 'A' and 'B', and '[a, b]' the 'Poisson Bracket' of 'a' and 'b'.

To a non-physicist this appears to be a strange and formidable equation. In ordinary mathematics, if 'A' is the number '2', and 'B' the number '3', the left hand side of 5.36 would come out to be 0, and this would hold true for any pair of numbers or ordinary algebraic functions. However 'A' and 'B' are quite different entities: Operators. An expression like 'AB' means that first we operate upon some mathematical quantity with 'B', and then operate upon the result with 'A'; while 'BA'

$$AB - BA = \frac{jh}{2\pi}[a,b] \quad \ldots \ldots 5.36$$

* * *

e.g. Let A and B be the operators shown below and let them operate upon a square, □

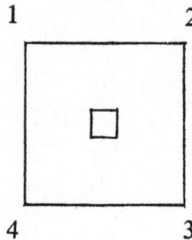

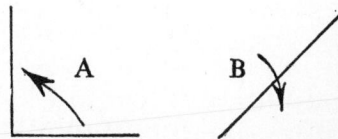

E

Then AB□ and BA□ are:

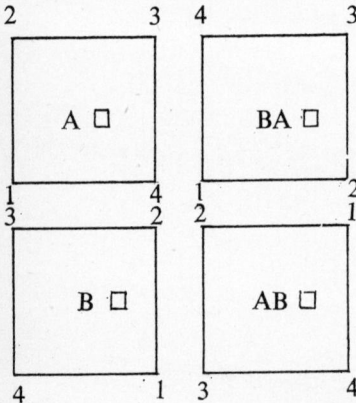

Thus AB□−BA□

   = (AB−BA)□

   ≠ 0□

and AB≠BA

        *   *   *

$$[a,b] = \frac{\partial a}{\partial x}\cdot\frac{\partial b}{\partial p} - \frac{\partial a}{\partial p}\cdot\frac{\partial b}{\partial x} \quad \dots 5.37$$

        *   *   *

For example, if $a=x$, and $b=p$:

$$[x,p] = \frac{\partial x}{\partial x}\cdot\frac{\partial p}{\partial p} - \frac{\partial x}{\partial p}\cdot\frac{\partial p}{\partial x}$$

   $$= 1\times1 - 0\times0$$

   $$= 1$$

means we first operate upon it with 'A', and then with 'B'. When we consider the more general class of operators used in Quantum Mechanics, 'AB' will not usually be equal to 'BA'. As a simple example let us take for the entity to be operated on, the operand, the square with vertices identified by the numbers 1,2,3,4, and take as our operators, 'A', a 90° rotation as shown, and 'B' a mirror reflection about a diagonal. If the reader carried these out as an exercise, he will see that 'AB' carries the vertices into a different final position from 'BA', and thus 'AB' is not equal to 'BA'. This holds true for a very large class of mathematical quantities, including derivatives and matrices.

The Poisson Bracket, '[a,b]', is an expression that comes up in more advanced treatments of Classical Mechanics. It is calculated using partial differentiation as shown in equation 5.37.

Equation 5.36, then, makes the statement that the Quantum Operators must be so chosen that their commutator equals a constant times the classically computed Poisson Bracket of the corresponding variables.

We can gain some understanding of this equation, and move a step further into Quantum Mechanics, by working out the Poisson Bracket for the particular pair of variables: position, 'X', and momentum, 'P'.

We obtain the result 5.38. In words this would read: The Quantum operators for position and momentum, 'X' and 'P',

$$\therefore XP - PX = \frac{jh}{2\pi} \ldots \ldots \ldots 5.38$$

must be so chosen that:—The result of operating upon some function with 'P', and then operating upon the result with 'X', minus the result obtained by operating upon the function with 'X', and then by 'P', is the same as would be obtained by multiplying the function by the number $\frac{'jh'}{2\pi}$. Though this does not give us final exact expressions for 'X' and 'P', at least it does serve as a test to see if a particular pair of expressions are suitable.

If 'AB−BA = 0' so that 'AB = BA' we say that the operators commute, otherwise they are called non-commuting. Since commuting operators can operate in any order upon a function and the same result will be obtained, they can have simultaneous eigen functions. Conversely, if two operators do not commute they cannot hold eigen functions in common. As we will see at the end of this chapter, this means that if we begin with two identical systems and in one case first measure 'X' and then 'P', we will obtain a different answer than for the second system where we first measure 'P' and then 'X'. This is why in Quantum Mechanics it makes no sense to speak of simultaneous values of X and P. This has no analogue in Classical Mechanics, where, at least in principle, two measurements can be made in any order, or simultaneously.

Next, we must impose some restrictions upon the eigen functions 'ψ_i'.

Postulate 4: *The 'ψ_i' must be 'well behaved'.*

Properly speaking this should be followed by a comprehensive spelling out of what constitutes 'good behaviour'. Rather than try to do this in general, we will content ourselves with describing it below for the special case of Schroedinger Quantum Mechanics.

$\star$ $\quad$ $\star$ $\quad$ $\star$

The choice of operator form depends upon the particular kind of quantum mechanics used. In symbolic mechanics, by far the most elegant but not generally the most useful, the operators are left purely as symbols and problems are solved without ever specifying their form, or even solving for the 'ψ_i'. All effort is directed towards obtaining the 'a_i', which, of course, are the only real observables. In Matrix (Heisenberg) mechanics the operators and eigen functions are matrices. In Wave (Schroedinger) mechanics, the operators are mathematical quantities corresponding to multiplication, differentiation, and integration, and the eigen functions are ordinary algebraic functions of position. Since all recent arguments about determinism in Quantum Mechanics have used the Schroedinger form, it will suffice to restrict ourselves to it. In it, well-behaviour of the 'ψ_i' consists in the function being continuous, its first derivative being continuous, and its integral over all space being finite.

$$X \longleftrightarrow x \dots\dots\dots 5.39$$

$$P \longleftrightarrow -\frac{jh}{2\pi}\frac{\partial}{\partial x} \dots\dots 5.40$$

$$\left\{XP-PX\right\}\psi$$

$$= \left\{x\left(-\frac{jh}{2\pi}\frac{\partial}{\partial x}\right)-\left(-\frac{jh}{2\pi}\frac{\partial}{\partial x}\right)x\right\}\psi$$

$$= \frac{jh}{2\pi}\left\{-x\frac{\partial\psi}{\partial x}+\psi+x\frac{\partial\psi}{\partial x}\right\}$$

$$= \frac{jh\psi}{2\pi}$$

$$\therefore XP-PX = \frac{jh}{2\pi} \text{ as required}$$
by 5.38

$$\star \quad \star \quad \star$$

Total Energy =

Kinetic + Potential

$$\therefore H = \frac{1}{2}mv^2 + V$$

$$= \frac{1}{2m}(mv)^2 + V$$

In Schroedinger Mechanics the operators used for position and momentum are as shown in 5.39 and 5.40. These must satisfy the third postulate. We can check the proposed operators by letting them work on some function ψ, and we find that they are indeed suitable.

The fundamental equation in Wave Mechanics is Schroedinger's Equation. To write it, it is first necessary to obtain the operator for the energy of a particle. Since the energy is calculable from the position and momentum of a particle, we can obtain this operator by building it up from the position and momentum operators already written in 5.39 and 5.40. For the energy operator we use the symbol 'H', (The Hamiltonian), and for its numerical values E_i. The operators for other observables which are functions of position and momentum are found in the same way.

The energy eigen function equation (refer to postulate 2 and equation 5.35) written out in its explicit form, 5.42, is Schroedinger's Equation. 'V' is the potential energy function which specifies the physical restrictions imposed upon the motion in a particular case. To solve a quantum mechanical problem, the 'V' function appropriate to the problem is substituted and the equation is solved for those 'ψ' functions that are well behaved. Each 'ψ' function 'ψ_i' will correspond to a particular value for 'E_i', and the ensemble of these 'E_i's' constitutes the set of possible values that may be obtained in an energy measurement. In general, in Quantum Mechanics it is impossible to predict precisely what particular E_i will be obtained in a given measurement.

$$= \frac{1}{2m}P^2 + V$$

$$= \frac{1}{2m}\left(-\frac{jh}{2\pi}\frac{d}{dx}\right)^2 + V$$

$$= -\frac{h^2}{8\pi^2 m}\frac{d^2}{dx^2} + V \quad \ldots \ldots 5.41$$

Since the operator equation is:

$$H\psi_i = E_i\psi_i,$$

substituting for H, we get:

$$-\frac{h^2}{8\pi^2 m}\frac{d^2\psi_i}{dx^2} + V\psi_i = E_i\psi_i$$

or, as it is usually written:

$$\frac{h^2}{8\pi^2 m}\frac{d^2\psi_i}{dx^2} + (E_i - V)\psi = 0 \quad \ldots 5.42$$

*   *   *

Before going on in our exposition of the postulates of Quantum Mechanics, it is worthwhile taking time out to examine a particular example of the way the predictions of that theory differ from those of Classical Mechanics. The problem we will consider, corresponds, at the microscopic level, to the barrier-hill problem discussed in the previous chapter. The micro-entity will be an electron moving inside an arrangement of charged plates producing a potential field of the shape represented in the

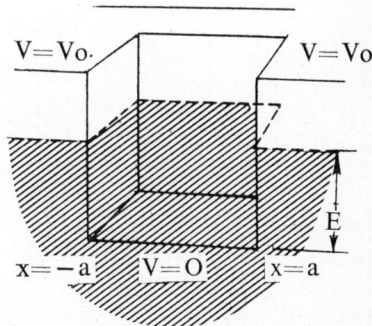

The total electron energy is represented by the dotted line of height E

E = Kinetic+Potential

$= \frac{1}{2}mv^2+V$

In the central regions

$V = 0$

$\therefore E = (\frac{1}{2}mv^2)_c +0$

and $v_c = \sqrt{\dfrac{2E}{m}}$

$\star \quad \star \quad \star$

In the outer regions

$V(x) = V_0$

$\therefore E = (\frac{1}{2}mv^2)_0+V_0$

but $E < V_0$

$\therefore (\frac{1}{2}mv^2)_0$ is negative and v_0 is imaginary.

$\therefore$ Classically, the electron is trapped inside the well, moving back and forth with velocity v_c and period:

$$T = \dfrac{4a}{\sqrt{\dfrac{2E}{m}}}$$

$\star \quad \star \quad \star$

drawing. We will consider the case where the energy of the electron (E) is less than the height of the potential barrier.

As we have seen in our previous discussion, Classical Physics would predict that the electron would be restricted to move back and forth in the hole indefinitely; that it could have any value of E; and that the time for one complete trip from one wall to the other and back to the first, i.e. the period, is found by dividing the total distance travelled, 4a, by the electron velocity, $v_c = \sqrt{\dfrac{2E}{m}}$. Classically the electron could never escape through the walls to the outside.

$\star \quad \star \quad \star$

Now let us solve the problem using Quantum Mechanics. It is unfortunate that we must use calculus, but this is unavoidable. For those not familiar with this branch of mathematics some understanding of the method of solution can still be obtained by following the verbal exposition. In any event it is the final conclusion which is of principal importance, the rest is only technical detail. The conclusions are on pages 136 and 137.

$\star \quad \star \quad \star$

The Schroedinger Equation (5.42) is solved by substituting into it the appropriate expression for 'V', the potential field applicable to the particular problem. In this physical situation, since 'V' has different constant values in the three regions, the Schroedinger equation can be solved most easily if we break it up into three separate parts, putting 'V = V_O' in the first, 'V = 0' in the second, and 'V = V_O' in the third, solve each equation separately, and then join the three solutions together. We write Schroedinger's equation for each of the three regions with appropriate 'V's' (5.44). The resulting three differential equations are of a standard, easily solved type. Among the set of possible solutions the well-behaved ones are given in equations 5.45. Now since the three 'ψ's': '$ψ_L$', '$ψ_C$' and '$ψ_R$' represent in reality only one function, the three must join together smoothly. '$ψ_L$', and '$ψ_C$' and their first derivatives must be continuous at 'x = −a', and similarly '$ψ_C$' and '$ψ_R$' at 'x = a'. These four conditions, written out mathematically, give us the four continuity equations. When we add the requirement that the total '$ψ_L$' be normalized, i.e. have an integral which is finite over all of space, we get a total of five equations, 5.46. Since we are solving for only the four quantities 'A_1', 'B_1',

$$V = \begin{cases} V_0 \text{ for } x \leqslant -a \\ 0 \text{ for } -a \leqslant x \leqslant a \\ V_0 \text{ for } a \leqslant x \end{cases}$$

$$ψ_i = \begin{cases} ψ_L \text{ for } x \leqslant -a \\ ψ_c \text{ for } -a \leqslant x \leqslant a \\ ψ_R \text{ for } a \leqslant x \end{cases}$$

$$-\frac{h^2}{8π^2 m}\frac{d^2 ψ_i}{dx^2} + Vψ_i = E_i ψ_i \quad .. 5.43$$

Put $K = \frac{8π^2 m}{h^2}$ and split 5.43 into

3 equations:

$$\begin{cases} \frac{d^2 ψ_i}{dx^2} + K(E_i - V_0)ψ_L = 0 \\ \frac{d^2 ψ_c}{dx^2} + KE_i ψ_c = 0 \\ \frac{d^2 ψ_R}{dx^2} + K(E_i - V_0)ψ_R = 0 \end{cases}$$
$$.. 5.44$$

These are standard differential equations with solutions expressible as sines or cosines, or more generally as:

$$ψ_i = \begin{cases} ψ_L = A_1 e^{\sqrt{K(V_0 - Ei)}x} \\ ψ_c = B_1 e^{j\sqrt{KEi}x} + B_2 e^{j\sqrt{KEi}x} \\ ψ_R = C_1 e^{-\sqrt{K(V_0 - Ei)}x} \end{cases}$$
$$\ldots\ldots\ldots 5.45$$

$(\psi_L)_{x=-a} = (\psi_c)_{x=-a}$

$(\psi_c)_{x=a} = (\psi_R)_{x=a}$

$\left(\dfrac{d\psi_L}{dx}\right)_{x=-a} = \left(\dfrac{d\psi_c}{dx}\right)_{x=-a}$

$\left(\dfrac{d\psi_c}{dx}\right)_{x=a} = \left(\dfrac{d\psi_R}{dx}\right)_{x=a}$

$\int \psi_i^2 dx = 1$ 5.46

★   ★   ★

$$\sqrt{\dfrac{E_i(V_0-E_i)}{2E_i-V_0}} = \tfrac{1}{2}\tan 2a\sqrt{KE_i}$$
. . . . 5.47

★   ★   ★

$E_1 \longleftrightarrow \psi_1$

$E_2 \longleftarrow\!\!<\psi_2$

. . .

. . .

$E_i \longleftrightarrow \psi_i$

'B_2', and 'C_1' they are over-determined, and in general the five equations can only have a unique set of solutions if 'E_i', the remaining unknown quantity, is restricted in some way. If we now solve the five equations in 5.46 for 'A_1', 'B_1' 'B_2', 'C_1' and 'E_i', we find that 'E_i' is given by equation 5.47. This rather cumbersome equation can most easily be solved graphically, where it gives a discrete set of values for 'E_i'. Each of these values—identified by a subscript, i.e. 'E_1', 'E_2', 'E_3', . . . —is called an eigen value of 'E_i'. To each one of these 'E_i's' will correspond a set of values for 'A_1', 'B_1', 'B_2', and 'C_1', and consequently one particular expression for 'ψ_i', which will be identified by giving it the same subscript as on the E_i. Thus our solution of the potential barrier problem yields us a set of eigen values for the Energy 'E_i', each with a corresponding eigen function 'ψ_i'. If we insert numerical values for the barrier height 'V_o', the hole width '$2a$', the mass of the electron 'm', and the other constants in equation 5.47, we obtain specific numbers for the 'E_i's', and analytic expres- s for the 'ψ_i's'.

★   ★   ★

In what ways do these results differ from those of Classical Mechanics? First, the ψ function which represents the electron has a value not only inside the potential hole but outside as well. This means that there is a possibility of 'finding' the electron in the region excluded by Classical Mechanics. We have already mentioned in Chapter 4 that this prediction has been verified for the case of alpha particles. Second, the electron is not permitted to have any arbitrary value of energy. Only a certain set (eigen values) of energies are allowed. This 'quantization' is characteristic of Quantum Mechanics and is experimentally confirmed in spectrum analysis. Third, we are not able to predict exactly what energy will be found in any particular observation.

If we actually make a measurement on the electron and obtain some particular value, say E_5, then we know that the electron is in the state ψ_5. Conversely, if in some way we know the electron is in state ψ_5, then we would know that a measurement of energy is bound to yield E_5 as a result.

This holds for any observable in any quantum problem. If a measurement yields a certain eigen value, then the system is in the corresponding eigen state, and conversely if by some means we know it is in a certain eigen state, then we know that a measurement of the observable will necessarily yield the corresponding eigen value.

* * *

This all falls within the set of postulates already introduced. However there is another problem yet to be considered. If all the information that we have about a system under study is expressed by a function which is *not* an eigen function for the observable 'a' we are interested in, what predictions can be made as to the result of a measurement of 'a'? This requires an addition to our set of postulates and a little more syntactical development. We begin with postulate 5. To emphasize that the state of the system is not an eigen function for our observable 'a', we will label this state by 'φ' (phi), rather than the symbol 'ψ', which we will reserve to stand for an eigen function of 'a'.

Postulate 5: *If a system is in the state specified by the state function φ₅ then the average value that will be obtained in a large number of measurements of any observable 'a' is given by equation 5.48.*

$$a_{avg} = \int \varphi(A\varphi)dx \ldots\ldots\ldots 5.48$$

Equation 5.48 requires the mathematical operations of first operating upon φ by A, multiplying this result by φ, and then integrating over the

$$x_{avg} = \int \varphi(x\varphi)dx$$

$$= \int x\varphi^2 dx \quad \ldots \ldots \ldots \ldots 5.49$$

entire region of space in which the φ function has some value. As an example of what this means, we will consider the particularly simple case where the operator A is position, x. Now 'x' operating upon a function gives simply the algebraic product of x and the function. The final result is given in 5.49.

If we compare this result with the ordinary formula of probability theory we can obtain an interesting interpretation (first noticed by Born) for the state function φ. Probability theory states that the average value of a set of measurements of any quantity can be obtained by multiplying each of the possible values by the probability of its occurring, and then adding them all up (5.50). Thus,

$$\text{avg } a = \Sigma a_i P_i \quad \ldots \ldots \ldots \ldots 5.50$$

*   *   *

$$\text{avg } N = 1 \times \tfrac{1}{6} + 2 \times \tfrac{1}{6} + \ldots + 3 \times \tfrac{1}{6}$$

$$= \frac{1+2+3+4+5+6}{6}$$

$$= \frac{21}{6}$$

$$= 3\tfrac{1}{2}$$

*   *   *

$$\text{avg } x = \int x P_x dx \quad \ldots \ldots \ldots 5.51$$

Comparing 5.49 and 5.51:

$$\varphi^2 \longleftrightarrow P_x$$

in flipping a die we may turn up 1, 2, 3, 4, 5, or 6, each with a probability of $\tfrac{1}{6}$. The average number of spots that will be obtained over a large number of flips, as shown by our calculations on the left, is $3\tfrac{1}{2}$. If we have some quantity which is continuously variable we must replace the summation by an integral. $P_x dx$ replaces P_i in 5.50, and gives the probability of the value x occurring in any observation. We multiply x by the probability of its occurring, and integrate over all the x's and their probabilities (5.51). We see that 5.49 and 5.51 are formally the same, where the 'φ^2' in 5.49 replaces the P_x in 5.51. Thus, a model interpretation for 'φ^2' is that it gives the probability of finding the 'particle' at a given location x.

In the same way as we obtained

an expression for 'average x' we get 'average p', 5.52. However the operator for p is $-\dfrac{jh}{2\pi}\dfrac{d}{dx}$, a differentiation performed upon the function, and no such simple model interpretation is possible.

$$\text{avg p} = \int\varphi\left(-\frac{jh}{2\pi}\frac{d}{dx}\right)\varphi dx \ldots 5.52$$

* * *

Equation 5.48 only gives the average value that will be obtained in a large number of measurements of some observable. Each time it is measured some particular value will be found, and in general it will be different from this average. To obtain a measure of the spread of these values around the average we define in 5.53 a quantity called the inexactitude. For a verbal description of 'Δa' we can say that: in a measurement of an observable 'a' the majority of the results will lie between: 'average a minus Δa', and, 'average a plus Δa'.

$$(\Delta a)^2 = \int(a-\text{avg a})^2\varphi^2 dx \ldots 5.53$$

* * *

Thus:

$$(\Delta x)^2 = \int(x-\text{avg x})^2\varphi^2 dx$$
$$(\Delta p)^2 = \int(p-\text{avg p})^2\varphi^2 dx \ldots 5.54$$

If we insert the values for 'average x' and 'average p' from equations 5.49 and 5.52 into equations of the form of 5.54, and use equation 5.38 relating 'X' and 'P',

$$\Delta x \cdot \Delta p > \frac{h}{2\pi} \ldots\ldots\ldots\ldots 5.21$$

a rather involved mathematical procedure leads to an equation already found earlier in the chapter—Heisenberg's Uncertainty Principle. There is however a vital difference. In the earlier instances it was obtained by analysing the problems of measurement in particular experimental situations, while now it is found as a perfectly general deduction from the postulates of quantum mechanics.

In consequence of this, the Uncertainty Principle is applicable to every physical problem which is analysed in quantum terms. Despite this apparently inescapable conclusion a number of authors, most prominent of these being Einstein, have attempted to develop experiments specially planned to obtain a simultaneous measurement of conjugate variables. We will discuss one of the subtlest of these in the next chapter.

★   ★   ★

Before closing this chapter, it is important to state a theorem which is of major importance in the quantum theory of measurement. An application of it will be made in the next chapter when we discuss a theorem of Von Neumann which has figured prominently in recent discussions about determinism in physics.

So far we have learned how to make the following predictions:

(1) The set of possible results of a measurement of an observable 'a'. This is done by solving the eigen equation 5.35 or, more specifically, the Schroedinger equation 5.42 for the eigen values of 'a'.

(2) If the system is in a state 'ψ_i' which is an eigen function for an observable 'a', then a measurement of 'a' will yield the eigen value 'a_i' corresponding to 'ψ_i'.

(3) If the system is in a state φ which is not an eigen function for 'a', the average value that will be obtained in a large number of measurements of 'a' is found from 5.48 . . . 'avg a $= \int\varphi(A\varphi)dx$.'

The present theorem permits one to calculate the probability of obtaining any particular value 'a_i' of 'a' when the system is in a state 'φ' which is not an eigen function of 'a'. We will not deduce the theorem from the basic postulates, but instead content ourselves by showing that it is consistent with Postulates 2 and 5.

System is in state 'φ'

Problem: to find the probability of obtaining any particular valve 'a_i' in a measurement of 'a'.

The procedure required in calculating the probability is as follows:

Solution: Expand φ in a series of eigen functions of a, ψ_i.

$$\varphi = \Sigma C_i\psi_i \quad \dots\dots\dots\dots 5.55$$

Step 1. The known state of the system, 'φ' is expanded in a series made up of the eigen functions of the observable whose values we are to predict (5.55). It is shown in the mathematical theory of series that this series has a unique set of coefficients 'C_i'.

Step 2. This done, the probability that any particular (eigen) value 'a_i' will be obtained in a measurement is obtained by squaring the coefficient 'C_i' of the corresponding eigen function 'ψ_i'.

First we show it is consistent with postulate 2: If 'φ' is actually one of the eigen functions of 'a', say ψ_R, then the series expansion 5.55 will have only one term. All the 'C_i's will be 0 but 'C_r' and this will be 1. Thus, in this case, the result of a measurement of 'a' is a certainty, 'a_r', as required.

Next we show it is consistent with Postulate 5, equation 5.48: Using our theorem, if the probabilities of getting the various values of 'a' is given by 5.56, then the average value is obtained by multiplying each of the 'a_i' by its probability, and adding them up as shown in 5.57. This result should be the same as using 5.48. Using this latter, we substitute into it the expansion 5.55 for φ. After a few mathematical manipulations, as shown on the right side of the page, 5.58 is obtained, which is seen to be identical with the result 5.57 using the theorem.

This of course does not constitute a full-fledged deduction of the expansion theorem. For this the reader can consult some of the

Then the probability of obtaining a_i in a measurement of a is given by:

$$P(a_i) = 1C_i1^2 \dots\dots\dots\dots 5.56$$

$\star \quad \star \quad \star$

If $\varphi = \psi_R$

Then all the C_i will be zero except C_R which will be 1. Thus the probability of obtaining C_r is 1, certainty.

$\star \quad \star \quad \star$

By the theorem:

$$\text{avg } a = \Sigma P(a_j) \cdot a_j$$

$$= \Sigma |C_j|^2 \cdot a_j \dots\dots 5.57$$

$\star \quad \star \quad \star$

Using Postulate 5:

$$\text{avg } a = \int \varphi(A\varphi)dx$$

$$= \int (\Sigma C_j \psi_j) \cdot A(\Sigma C_r \psi_r)dx$$

$$= \int (\Sigma C_j \psi_j) \cdot (\Sigma C_r A \psi_r)dx$$

$$= \int (\Sigma C_j \psi_j) \cdot (\Sigma C_r a_r \psi_r)dx$$

But if the ψ_i are orthogonal as required in Q.M.

$$\int \psi_j \psi_r dx = \begin{cases} 0 \text{ if } j \neq r \\ 1 \text{ if } j = r \end{cases}$$

$$\therefore \text{ avg } a = \int \Sigma C_j^2 a_j \psi_j^2 dx$$

$$= \Sigma C_j^2 a_j \dots\dots 5.58$$

Let the result of a position measurement be: x_j

∴ The state of the system is: ψ_j

* * *

Expand ψ_j in terms of θ_r:

$$\psi_j = \Sigma C_r \theta_r \dots\dots\dots\dots 5.59$$

∴ The probability of observing p_r in a momentum measurement is $|C_r|^2$

* * *

Suppose the result of a momentum measurement is p_s, then the state of the system is the corresponding eigen function θ_s

Now expand θ_s in terms of ψ_u:

$$\theta_s = \Sigma d_u \psi_u \dots\dots\dots\dots 5.60$$

∴ Probability of getting x_u in a remeasurement of it is now: $|d_u|^2$

Quantum Mechanics texts mentioned in the bibliography. In particular, see that of Von Neumann.

* * *

We now go on to consider the case where we first make a measurement of a variable, say position 'x', and then make a measurement of a second variable, such as momentum. Assume that the position measurement gives a result 'x_j'. We now know that at this instant the system is in the corresponding position eigen state 'ψ_j'.

Since position and momentum are conjugate variables they have no common eigen states, and to make a prediction for the result which will be found in a momentum measurement made after the position measurement has been completed we must use the above expansion theorem: 5.55 and 5.56. We expand 'ψ_j' in terms of momentum eigen functions (call these 'θ_r') (5.59). Any one of the momentum eigen values is a possible result and the probability of getting any value 'p_r' is 'C_r^2'.

If we now actually measure the momentum and obtain the particular result 'p_s', we know, according to postulate 2, that the system is in the corresponding momentum eigen state 'φ_s'.

Thus the result of the second measurement is to abruptly throw the system from state 'ψ_j' into

'θ_s'. However, something even more important now appears. Knowing the system is in state 'θ_s', we want to predict the result of a position measurement that will now be made. This is calculated by expanding 'θ_s' in a series of position eigen functions, 5.60. Any value 'x_u' of 'x' is now a possibility, with probability given by $(d_u)^2$. Thus, the intervention of the momentum measurement has changed the position state of the system in an entirely unpredictable way. The second measurement of position will, in general, give a different result from the first, no matter how short the time interval.

★ ★ ★

This result holds for all sets of conjugate, non-commuting variables. The results of a set of measurements depend upon the order in which they are made. This is in contrast to the classical theory, where, so long as the time interval is sufficiently short, measurements can be made in any order and the same results will be obtained. This situation only exists in Quantum Mechanics when the observables commute with one another.

CHAPTER VI

The New Conceptualization
Required in the New Physics

SUMMARY : We have seen that classical physics, by developing a method of describing (a part of) experience quantitatively, improved upon our common-sense world picture, but remained closely linked with it conceptually. Now while success over the millennia guarantees the essential adequacy of this conceptualization scheme at the macroscopic level, there is no a priori reason for it being equally successful in dealing with phenomena outside the regions accessible to man's unaided senses. In Chapter 4 we investigated a number of these phenomena that were contradictory and inexplicable in Newtonian Mechanics and in the next chapter we examined part of the semiotic of the new theories, Relativity Theory and Quantum Mechanics, developed to cope with this new experience. Both of these theories use the same observables as those of the classical theory: position, momentum, energy, etc. In contrast, however, to the classical theory whose structure is such that (in principle) its predictions are of the form: at time 't', the value of the observable quantity 'a' will be 'a_1'; we have seen that a typical Quantum Mechanics prediction would be: at time 't', the possible values that will be obtained in a measurement of 'a' are 'a_1', 'a_2', 'a_3' . . . etc., and the probability of getting 'a_1' is 'P_1', of getting 'a_2' is 'P_2', etc. (The sum of the probabilities, ΣP_i, must of course be 1, because, if a measurement is carried out, some answer 'a_i' must be obtained.) Since no mechanism exists inside Quantum Mechanics permitting unique predictions of the classical deterministic type, we are up against a radically new sort of physical theory and a new conceptual world picture seems to be required.

The rather ascetic nature of Quantum Mechanics and its 'renunciation of a more complete and precise description of experience' has rendered it unpalatable to a number of physicists and philosophers. These feel that the essence of a satisfactory scientific theory lies in its ability to make deterministic predictions. For them, any theory unable to do this is of only interim value, and is due for revision as our knowledge and techniques advance. The psychological origin of their beliefs, rooted in the up-to-yesterday successful common-sense—classical physics world picture, is obvious, but this in no way invalidates the desirability of the development of a deterministic theory. In this chapter we will discuss the principal interpretations of Quantum Mechanics, and consider some of the attacks upon the theory, and the attempts to reintroduce determinism into microscopic physics.

★   ★   ★

In its purely mathematical-symbolic aspect quantum mechanics necessarily takes no stand on the 'wave or/and particle' nature of micro-entities. It is just a set of mathematical operations on paper. Of course the same holds true for the mathematical part of classical physics. But a scientific theory is more than an exercise in logic plus a set of semantic correspondence rules relating certain of its symbols with operations in our physical experience. If it is successful in its fundamental aim it tends to take on a conceptual superstructure, and, by incorporating additional linguistic and philosophical elements, builds up into something approaching a universal world picture. Though such a conceptual interpretation of the symbols is not logically essential to the minimal physical theory, it is necessary if the theory, as incorporated into the broader picture, is to prove intellectually satisfying and fertile.

In developing a consistent interpretation of Quantum Mechanics, it is necessary to be very much on guard against believing that because we can measure a certain quantity in an experiment, there exists some entity possessing this as a property. Instruments are designed to give answers and this they will do. The interpretation of the results obtained is up to us. Let us begin with examples of this at the macroscopic level where interpretation, because of long familiarity, is easy. We first consider a case where objectification is reasonable, and then two where it is not:

(1) A thermometer is inserted into a block of melting ice. If it is a good instrument, after a while it will read 0°. In this instance it does make sense inside our conceptual picture to say there is an object, the ice, possessing the property of being at a temperature of 0°C.

(2) The same thermometer is mounted by means of insulating blocks on the outer skin of a satellite orbiting about the earth several thousand miles above the surface. Again it will come to read some temperature, say 0° again, but, with the exception of the thermometer itself, there is now no object with a corresponding temperature, and a differently shaped thermometer would, in general, give a quite different reading. The thermometer is in a complex radiation equilibrium with the sun, earth,

satellite, the few bombarding molecules left of the earth's atmosphere at this height, and the rest of the universe. It is entirely senseless to say it is measuring the 'temperature of space' at this point.

(3) As another example let us consider an experiment in which a sensitive balance with one pan blackened and the other polished is placed in a vacuum vessel. If an intense light floods the enclosure the side of the balance bearing the polished pan is depressed, because of the unequal reflection of the radiation, and balance can only be restored by adding weights to the blackened pan. It is not a legitimate interpretation of this result to assert the existence of some invisible object sitting on the polished pan, and growing and shrinking according to the light intensity.

Experiments of this kind are not likely to cause any real confusion in objectification at the macroscopic level, where we have developed a consistent, and commonly agreed upon, conceptual world picture, but we must be very much on our guard at the microscopic. Thus, if we examine an electron in a grating spectroscope we will obtain a certain wave length, λ_1. If we measure the 'curvature of its path' in a magnetic field we obtain a number for mass, m_1. If the electron falls upon a photographic plate the emulsion will be sensitized at one location only, s_1. The total result of these and other experiments does not mean that the electron is a ' ' possessing the simultaneous (and contradictory) properties λ_1, m_1, s_1, v_1, etc.

* * *

The Quantum Mechanical interpretation that came to be held by a majority of physicists was developed by Bohr and is called his Principle of Complementarity. It emphasizes the dual nature of fundamental experience, and renounces any attempt to give the continuous description of events that was used in the classical theory. Complementarity is best described by Niels Bohr himself. We quote from his essay in the book *Albert Einstein, Philosopher Scientist* (Library of Living Philosophers Series):

'The individuality of the typical quantum effects finds its proper expression in the circumstance that any attempt of subdividing the phenomena will demand a change in the experimental arrangements introducing new possibilities of interaction between objects and measuring instruments which in principle cannot be controlled. Consequently, evidence obtained under different experimental conditions cannot be comprehended within a single picture, but must be regarded as complementary in the sense that only the totality of the phenomena exhausts the possible information about the objects. . . .

'The finite interaction between objects and measuring agencies, conditioned by the very existence of the quantum of action entails—because of the impossibility of controlling the reaction of the object on the measuring instruments, if they are to serve their purpose—the necessity of a final renunciation of the classical ideal of causality and a radical revision of our attitude towards the problem of physical reality.'

It is evident that Bohr's principle of complementarity sticks very closely both to the experimental possibilities, and to the minimum implications of Quantum Mechanical Theory. As such it implies the impossibility of a deterministic treatment of microscopic phenomena.

There are several ways in which determinism might be re-established in microscopic physics:

The first and most obvious would be to decide that Quantum Mechanics is an 'incorrect' theory, and that a more general and deterministic theory will eventually be developed which will cover the microscopic, now more or less adequately handled by quantum mechanics, as well as the macroscopic and the cosmic. Des Touches has endeavoured to show that any more complete theory must still be indeterministic in that part which it explains in common with Q.M. However it seems to be impossible to demonstrate that Des Touches' results would hold for every possible variation in logic and mathematics that the human mind might devise in the future. It must remain a possibility that a deterministic theory will be developed which will supersede Q.M. However this doesn't really concern us in this book. We do not (and never can) make statements about 'absolute reality', nor can we expect to foretell the nature of all possible future theories. (Though we will permit ourselves a cautious extrapolation into the sort of short range developments that might occur.) For micro-phenomena the only workable theory existing today is Quantum Mechanics and this is what we must study.

A second possibility is that Quantum Mechanics is 'correct' but that (a) either the conventional Bohr interpretation is wrong, or (b) although Q.M. is indeterministic in the variables as used, it is a covering theory (like the example discussed in an earlier chapter of Thermodynamics and the Kinetic Theory of Gases) whose predictions are statistical averages over a set of non-measured but determined quantities. In the first of these, the aim would be to develop a consistent interpretation in which micro-entities are considered as particles *or* as waves. For (b) we must see if any of our known present-day observables could function as a set of hidden parameters and also to predict the possibility of finding such a set at some time in the future.

*   *   *

Einstein has been one of the more important of the anti-Bohr protagonists, so we will begin by listening to his arguments and examine in some detail a thought experiment set-up designed to avoid the limitation of complementarity. (A thought experiment is frequently used in physical discussions to turn difficult mathematical or philosophical arguments into concrete models easier to understand and analyse. It is obviously essential that the experiment violate no theoretical principles, but usually it is not actually carried out for a variety of practical reasons. These latter are such things as—the necessity for a perfect vacuum, a perfect physical black body, a perfectly round sphere. . . . None are 'theoretical' impossibilities but in practice they could never be achieved.)

For Einstein 'There is a real state of a physical system which exists objectively, independently of all observations or measure'. Otherwise '. . . a free body in space has no position until it is observed', and, 'this is absurd'. Now if we are talking about a billiard ball we can, at least in principle, observe at any instant its position and momentum simultaneously to any order of accuracy that might be desired. As any additional assumption we might say that even when it is not being observed it is located at every instant at some specific point and is moving with some specific momentum. However this is an additional assumption that adds nothing to the theory and is unnecessary. (Notice that we can postulate anything we like about its properties when we are not observing it and no one can ever prove us wrong . . . or right.) To do the same for electrons is much more dangerous, particularly when we are introducing properties that can never be observed. The application of Occam's Razor, which is fundamental in scientific theory, would demand the elimination of such postulates. Now while we agree with Einstein that it is an entirely reasonable *assumption* that 'There is a real state . . . measure' we take violent exception to the second part of his remark. It is apparent that Einstein confuses 'reality' or what we have called the 'source of experience' with our physical picture of it. That something exists 'external' to 'ourselves' is most certainly a reasonable assumption and one that is regularly made at both the common-sense and the philosophical level. But that this 'externality' must consist of particles moving about in a classically describable manner 'possessing' position and momentum at all instants, is another thing altogether.

About this 'reality' he says: 'If, without in any way disturbing a system, we can predict with certainty the value of a physical quantity, then there exists an element of physical reality corresponding to this physical quantity'. Now his initial criterion, 'without in any way disturbing a system', if taken at its face value of referring to an actual measurement, is such a strong one that nothing would be left of 'physical reality' if it were applied. Even at the macroscopic level of classical physics we recognize that every act of measurement disturbs a system to some extent, and one of the prime jobs of standards laboratories is to reduce this interference to a minimum. As one example, take the apparently simple operation of placing a meter stick alongside an object whose length is to be measured. If the meter stick is at a different temperature from the object, it will change the latter's temperature and hence its length. This could be avoided if the meter stick were at the same temperature as the object, but to ascertain this it would be necessary to take the temperature of the object, and this measurement in turn would affect the object. If we interpret his criterion more weakly, as he presumably intended it to be, we come up against the more serious objection: We have already considered examples—the thermometer attached to a sputnik, and the balance— where a certain measurement was being successfully carried out and yet there was no 'element of physical reality corresponding to the physical quantity'.

★   ★   ★

Rather than continue with the general discussion we now examine one of Einstein's more specific attacks on the adequancy of quantum mechanics. In the Physical Review (May 15, 1935, p. 777) Einstein, Podolsky and Rosen (henceforth abbreviated as E.P.R.) proposed a situation in which, apparently contradicting Heisenberg's Uncertainty Principle, the simultaneous momentum and position of a micro-entity could be measured. Instead of considering it as it was originally presented and discussed as a mathematical argument, we will look at it in the more concrete experimental form suggested by Bohr.

In the initial part of this 'experiment', a strip containing two slits is suspended from a solid support by means of a spring. A pointer is attached to the strip in such a way that any momentum

$\eta = x_1 - x_2$

$p = p_1 + p_2$

$$AB - BA = \frac{jh}{2\pi}[a,b] \quad \ldots 6.1 \; (5.36)$$

$$NP - PN = \frac{jh}{2\pi}[\eta,p]$$

but $[\eta,p] = 0$

$$\therefore NP - PN = 0 \quad \ldots\ldots\ldots 6.2$$

$\therefore$ η and p are simultaneously measurable to (theoretically) any desired degree of accuracy and $\Delta\eta$ and Δp can be simultaneously 0

imparted to the strip can be measured by the displacement of the pointer over an adjoining scale. If two electrons now pass through the two slits, we know at the instant of passage that they are separated by the distance, '$\eta = x_1-x_2$', between the two slits. In addition, by the law of conservation of momentum, the change in momentum of the electrons in passing through the slits, 'p = p_1+p_2', is equal and opposite to the measured momentum change of the strip. Thus we apparently have a simultaneous measurement of η and p. We must check to see that this is theoretically possible.

Quantum Mechanically these quantities are representable by operators that must satisfy the fundamental operator condition (Chapter 5 (5.36).) Unless the right hand side of this equation is zero, the operators do not commute, and the observables are not simultaneously precisely measurable. We have previously seen that in the case of the position and momentum of a single particle this results in the Uncertainty Principle. In the E.P.R.—Bohr experiment now being considered the observables are 'η' and 'p'. If we compute the Poisson bracket '[ηp]' we find it comes out to zero. This means that 'η' and 'p' can be simultaneously measured, according to quantum mechanics, with errors limited only by experimental difficulties, and, at least theoretically, reducible to zero. Experimentally, this would be done by making the strip infinitesimally light, $\Delta p = 0$, and the two slits infinitesimally narrow, $\Delta \eta = 0$. We will ignore the practical problems involved and consider that this has been done. Thus in equations 6.3 we will assume that 'η' and 'p' have been precisely measured.

Since these are two equations with four unknowns we cannot solve them for the four desired quantities 'x_1', 'p_1'; 'x_2', 'p_2'. This can only be done if we can obtain two more equations containing these variables. E.P.R. propose the following method of doing this:

Once the particles have passed through the double slit frame they are now separated from one another (?) and any further measurement performed upon the one will not affect the other. Thus for example we might measure the position 'x_1^1' of the first particle, and the momentum of the second 'p_2^1'. This can be done by inserting two more single slit strips as shown in the diagram. The first is solidly attached to the basic frame so as to give an accurate position measurement, and the second is spring mounted, so as to provide a momentum measurement.

$$\eta = x_1 - x_1$$

$$p = p_1 + p_2 \quad \dots \dots \dots \dots \quad 6.3$$

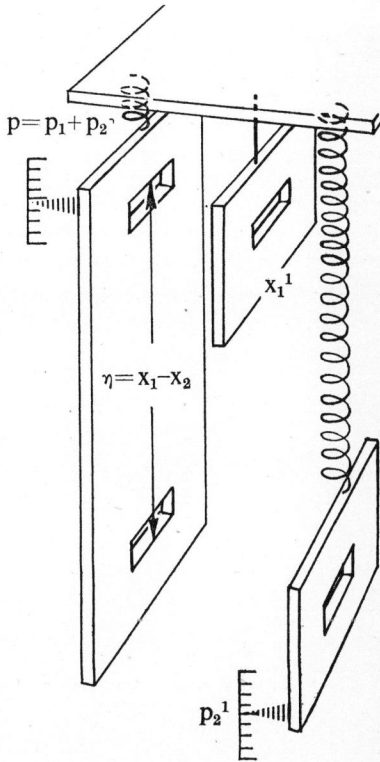

x_1^1 and p_2^1 can be measured to any degree of accuracy without violating the Uncertainty Principle.

$$\therefore \Delta x_1^1 = 0 \quad \Delta p_2^1 = 0$$

$$\overset{\smile}{\eta} = x_1 - x_2$$

$$\overset{\smile}{p} = p_1 + p_2$$

$$x_1 \approx \overset{\smile}{x_1}{}^1$$

$$p_2 \approx \overset{\smile}{p_2}{}^1 \quad \ldots\ldots\ldots\ldots\ 6.4$$

Now, following the argument in a simplified version of the way E.P.R. might present it, if the second pair of measurements are performed as closely in time as is possible after the first, '$x_1{}^1$' will be almost the same as 'x_1', and '$p_2{}^1$' will be almost equal to 'p_2'. In the limit, as the time interval approaches zero, they will become equal. We have now measured the four quantities checked in equations 6.4. These four equations can be easily solved for the four unknowns 'x_1', 'p_1', 'x_2', 'p_2', once we replace the 'approximately equal' sign with the 'equals' sign. We now appear to have determined the simultaneous position and momentum, x_1, p_1; x_2, p_2, of each particle in contradiction to the Uncertainty Principle.

*   *   *

Cooper and others have discussed this experiment in rigorous detail

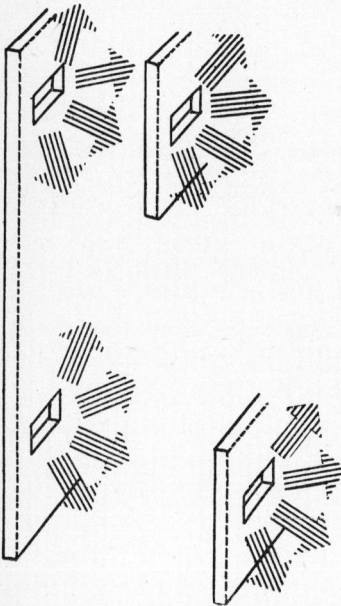

and exposed the errors involved. Although their analyses are too advanced to present here we can achieve the same result in two more elementary ways.

In the first, we will use a particle language, which we do not ourselves endorse but presumably is acceptable to E.P.R. In this interpretation, the electrons possess a position and momentum at each point along a determined trajectory, and the impossibility of a simultaneous measurement is due to our instrumental limitations. To obtain 'η' and 'p' exactly in the first measurement it was essential that the slits be infinitesimally thin. Now it is a demonstrated experimental fact that a slit acts upon an electron in such a way that the set of its possible paths diverge on the other side of the slit. For an infinitesimally thin slit, the divergence, and consequently the range of possible momenta, is infinite. In a particle theory this would hold true whether or not we carry out a measurement of the slit position and/or momentum of the particle at the slit. This means that no matter how closely the second measurement follows the first, the position '$x_1{}^1$' obtained can be different from 'x_1' by any amount. Exactly the same argument applies to the second momentum measurement '$p_2{}^1$'. Thus in the second pair of equations in 6.4 the 'approximately equal' signs must be replaced by simply 'unequal', and no simultaneous solution exists.

The next form of the argument that is about to be presented uses the language of complementarity and is probably much more acceptable to physicists. It has already been shown by experiments such as those of Davisson and Germer (Chapter 4) that electrons in inter-action with slits behave as waves. Thus, it is incorrect to say that one particular electron passed through slit 1 and later through slit 1^1, and the other electron passed through slit 2 and later through 2^1. More correctly both electrons pass through all four slits, and the second assumption of E.P.R. — that after passing through the first double slit there is no correlation between electrons—is invalid. Thus the second pair of measurements bears no relation to the first, and again it is illegitimate to solve equations 6.4. This latter result is the same as Cooper obtained in a much more elegant way: namely, that in fact the two systems are not separate in the second stage of the measurements.

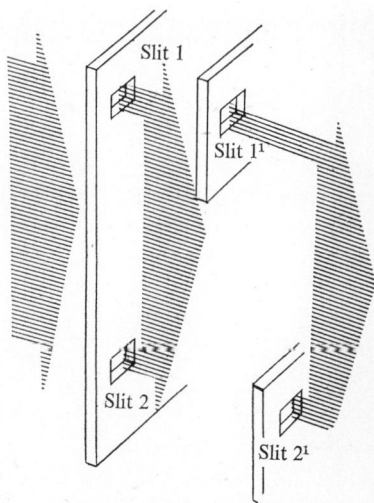

*   *   *

This has been the universal fate of all set-ups designed to get around the Uncertainty Principle. Of course our general theoretical consideration of the preceding chapter has already guaranteed this in so far as Quantum Mechanics is a semiotically true system, but confirmation of the Uncertainty Principle in particular instances increases its reliability as a universal principle.

★ ★ ★

Later in the chapter we will consider other attempts to interpret micro-entities as exclusively particles or waves. For the moment let us go on to consider the second possibility mentioned earlier: assuming it is established that Quantum Mechanics is indeterministic when it makes use of the traditional observables of physics—position, momentum, energy, etc.—would it still be indeterministic if some new variables were used?

Let us remind ourselves of the example of this in the Kinetic Theory of Gases discussed in an earlier chapter. Thermodynamically, the macroscopic behaviour of a gas is described in terms of the variables: pressure, temperature, volume, etc., and for large quantities of gases or bodies immersed in the gases these variables follow deterministic laws. For small volumes of gases, or Brownian sized particles, these variables fluctuate in an indeterministic and unpredictable way around the macroscopic averages, and there is no mechanism inside thermodynamics for providing a deterministic theory of this fluctuation. However determinism was restored to this branch of physics by developing a new theory, the Kinetic Theory of Gases, using a new set of variables: the positions, momenta, and kinetic energies of the myriads of molecules assumed to make up the gas. A thermodynamic variable describing the gross macroscopic behaviour of the gas is evaluated by a summation over the microscopic mechanical variables describing the behaviour of all the individual molecules. Thus, as one example, the macroscopic variable pressure (the force per unit area of wall surface) is equated to the total change of momentum experienced by all the molecules striking that area per unit of time. For a sufficiently large surface, the number of molecules striking it is so huge that, using the same principle as an insurance company in calculating its premium, the percentage variation is very small and the pressure remains essentially constant. Therefore this pressure can be quite simply calculated by multiplying the average momentum of the molecules by the average number striking unit area per second. For small areas this procedure will still give the average pressure, but the percentage fluctuation in number and momentum is now large enough to give observable changes in pressure. In principle, though in practice it would be a most difficult operation, we could follow the motion of all the individual molecules of the gas and predict the way in which the force on a Brownian particle would fluctuate with time, and from this predict its motion in detail. Thus we have a theory which is statistical and indeterministic for a certain set of observables (pressure, temperature), based upon a set of determined but unobserved parameters (position, momentum and energy).

The formal resemblance with quantum mechanics is striking, although in it we are dealing with a single entity rather than a gas made up of molecules. By analogy, we could consider that the conventional observables—position, momentum, energy—which are only statistically predictable in quantum mechanics, are, in actuality, averages over a set of unobserved but determined quantities, the hidden parameters.

It will be clearer if we put this in mathematical form. For simplicity we will consider only a single parameter, 'u', whose behaviour follows strict deterministic laws, but for some reasons, either theoretical or practical, it cannot be directly measured. The observables, position and momentum, are functions of this 'u', and could be obtained by substitution into these equations, if 'u' were known.

Thus a number of systems which appear to be in identical states, or to have undergone the same experiences, could actually be in completely different states as far as the parameter 'u' is concerned. A measurement of 'x' performed on system 1 would give the value corresponding to the 'u' value of that system, say 'u_1'. A measurement on system 2 would, in general, give the different value 'x_2' corresponding to 'u_2' . . . and so on. Therefore the dispersion in the values of 'x' that results in a set of measurements on micro-entities could result from our present inability to fix 'u'. For the same reason we could not obtain a simultaneous pair of values for

$$x = f_1(t,u)$$

$$p = g_1(t,u) \dots\dots\dots\dots\dots 6.5$$

'x' and 'p'. The best that could be done would be to make probabilistic predictions for 'x' and 'p' by averaging over all possible values of 'u', the hidden parameter. Naturally if some method were devised to measure the 'u', this situation would promptly change. The same 'u' would enter into each of equations 6.5, and a simultaneous measurement of 'p' and 'x' would become possible.

* * *

$$P_x = (\psi)^2 \ \dots\dots\dots\dots 6.6$$

$$P_p = (\varphi)^2 \ \dots\dots\dots\dots 6.7$$

(P_x = probability of finding the micro-entity at x

P_p = probability of finding the micro-entity with momentum p)

Solving 6.6 and 6.7 for 'x' and 'p':

$$x = f_2(t, P_x)$$

$$p = g_2(t, P_p) \ \dots\dots\dots\dots 6.8$$

$$\varphi(p,t) = \sqrt{\frac{m}{h}}\int e^{2\pi i p x/h}\psi(x,t)dx$$

$$\psi(x,t) = \sqrt{\frac{1}{mh}}\int e^{-2\pi i p x/h}\varphi(p,t)dp$$

$$\dots 6.9$$

In Quantum Mechanics we can set up equations resembling those in 6.5. In Chapter 5 we have obtained an expression giving the probability of 'finding the micro-entity at any point "x"' (6.6). An exactly similar expression can be set up for the probability of finding the micro-entity with any particular value of momentum (6.7). Now the 'ψ' is a function of position 'x', and 'φ' a function of momentum 'p'. Thus equations 6.6 and 6.7 can be turned backwards and solved for 'x' in terms of 'P_x', and 'p' in terms of 'P_p'. The resulting equations 6.8 are analogous to 6.5 with 'P_x', and 'P_p' replacing the hidden parameter 'u'.

If 'P_x' and 'P_p' could be measured in some way and a definite number assigned to each, 'x' and 'p' would be simultaneously found by substituting these numbers into equation 6.8.

Now, 'P_x' (ψ^2) and 'P_p' (φ^2) are not independent functions. They are inter-related according to equations 6.9. However, the general characteristic of these equations is that if 'ψ' is concentrated (i.e. only large for a small value of x and small outside this), 'φ' is diffuse, and vice versa. Thus it is impossible that precise values could be assigned to each, and 'x' and 'p' determined.

In fact, we can use these equations to calculate 'average x', and 'average p', the inexactitude in 'x', 'Δx', and the inexactitude in 'p', 'Δp', and finally derive the familiar Heisenberg Uncertainty Relation. This is not surprising, since these

$$\Delta x \cdot \Delta p > h/2\pi$$

equations are straightforward deductions from the axioms of Q.M. It does mean however that 'ψ', the wave function, can never be considered as a hidden parameter.

⋆ ⋆ ⋆

We have still to consider the possibility of discovering some other observables that might function as hidden parameters. It is instructive to approach this by comparing classical with quantum statistics. (The following argument comes from Reichenbach.)

In the first instance we consider the case in Classical Physics where it is possible to measure the simultaneous initial position, 'x_1', and momentum, 'p_1'.

Given:

(1) The values of 'x_1' and 'p_1' at the initial time.

(2) The physical laws (as an example: Newton's Equation, and a knowledge of the forces entering into a given situation).

Then:

The values of 'x' and 'p', and any other entity formed from them, are determined for all future time. This is represented symbolically in equation 6.10.

$$x_t = f(t, x_1, p_1)$$
$$p_t = g(t, x_1, p_1) \quad \dots\dots\dots\dots 6.10$$

In the next instance, we assume that for some reason of an experimental practical nature, the initial values of 'x_1' and 'p_1' are not known exactly, and we have available only their probability distributions. There are three of these latter: 'P_{x1}', the probability distribution in the initial values of 'x_1'; 'P_{p1}', the same for initial values of 'p_1'; and '$P_{x1,p1}$', the distribution function that gives the probability that certain pairs of values of 'x_1' and 'p_1' will occur.

$$P_{x1} = \int P_{x1,p1} dp$$

$$P_{p1} = \int P_{x1,p1} dx \quad \ldots\ldots\ldots 6.11$$

$$P_{t,x,p} = f(P_{x1,p1} st) \ldots\ldots\ldots 6.12$$

then:

$$P_{t,x} = \int P_{t,x,p} dp$$

$$P_{t,p} = \int P_{t,x,p} dx \quad \ldots\ldots\ldots 6.13$$

. * * *

Given $\psi(x_1)$, then:

$$P_{x1} = |\psi(x_1)|^2$$

$$P_{p1} = |\varphi(p_1)|^2 \quad \ldots\ldots\ldots\ldots 6.14$$

$$\psi(t,x) = f(\psi(x_1),t) \quad \ldots\ldots\ldots 6.15$$

then:

$$P_{t,x} = |\psi(t,x)|^2$$

$$P_{t,p} = |\varphi(t,p)|^2$$

Of these three distributions the last one is the one needed. Knowing it, the individual probability distributions of 'x_1' and 'p_1' can be found as in equations 6.11, but in general the converse is not true.

We are now ready to proceed.

Given:

(1) The probability distribution $P_{x1,p1}$, at the initial time.

(2) The Physical laws.

Then:

The initial distribution in 'x_1' and in 'p_1' is obtained as in 6.11. The future probability distribution of pairs of 'x' and 'p' is calculated from the physical laws, and is represented symbolically in 6.12. From this last the future probability distribution in 'x', '$P_{t,x}$', and in 'p', '$P_{t,p}$', is calculated by integrating as in 6.13 over the joint distribution found in 6.12.

* * *

The situation in Quantum Statistics is quite different from the above classical case.

Given:

(1) The state function ψ (x_1) at the initial time.

(2) The physical laws.

Then:

The initial probability distributions in 'x_1' and 'p_1' are obtained as we have seen earlier, and are shown in 6.14. The future ψ

functions is found from Schroedinger's Equation. This is represented symbolically in 6.15. The future probability distributions in 'x' and 'p' are then found from the future 'ψ' function . . . 6.16.

where

$$\varphi(t,p) = \sqrt{\frac{m}{h}} \int e^{2\pi i p x/h} \psi(t,x)dx$$

. . . 6.16

The essential basis for predictions in the classical statistical case is the joint probability distribution in position and momentum '$P_{t,x,p}$'. When this distribution becomes concentrated, so that in effect only one pair of values of 'x' and 'p' exists, the calculations in 6.11, 6.12, and 6.13, easily reduce to the exact causal case.

Since there is no equivalent in Quantum Mechanics of this reducible joint probability distribution, no similar reduction to a causal theory is possible.

* * *

Von Neumann in his *Mathematical Foundations of Quantum Mechanics* has carried out a rigorous analysis of the question of hidden parameters in Q.M. which serves as the basis for many of the present-day arguments on the subject. It is beyond the mathematics of this book to follow his reasoning in any detail, but it is not too hard to understand his line of argument.

In Q.M. a system is described by the 'ψ' function. Consider an ensemble of systems all described by the same 'ψ' function and thus quantum mechanically all in the same state. As has been demonstrated previously, if a set of conjugate observables is measured in each of these systems, many different answers are obtained. In a deterministic theory, this result would be interpreted to mean that the systems in the ensemble had not really been in the same state to begin with. The question is then:

Can the state of a system be specified more completely than is done by the 'ψ' function, so that it will become possible to produce an ensemble of systems such that no matter how, or in what order, measurements are made on different systems in the ensemble, the same results will always be obtained. In Von Neumann's terminology—Is it possible to set up an ensemble of systems such that the set of all measurements carried out upon them is dispersion-free? The conclusion of his theorem is in the negative.

What follows constitutes an elementary proof of this theorem.

We begin with an arbitrary ensemble of physical systems and carry out a series of measurements of each system in the ensemble for the observables 'a', 'b', 'c', . . . etc. This set of observables can include both the ordinary ones in use now in Q.M. as well as any number of additional (hidden parameter) ones. Now, in general, each of these observables will have a set of different eigen values, a_1', 'a_2', 'a_3' . . . ; 'b_1', 'b_2', 'b_3', . . . etc. We examine the results of our measurements and collect into sub-ensembles all those systems which have the same set of observed values. Thus the first sub-ensemble would include those for which the results 'a_1', 'b_1', 'c_1' . . . were obtained. The second, those with the measurement results 'a_2', 'b_1', 'c_1' . . . The third, 'a_2', 'b_2', 'c_1', . . . etc. Then the question asked above becomes: does each of these sub-ensembles represent a pure state, such that the set of measurements specifying it can be carried out in any order without changing the results and carrying systems out of the sub-ensemble? To anticipate—if the set of variables commute, the sub-ensemble is pure, but if some do not commute, then it is not.

We can show this quite simply by referring to our results of Chapter 5. Let the first two of our variables 'a' and 'b' be known quantum mechanical ones. If a measurement of 'a' results in the value 'a_1', then we know that the system is in the corresponding eigen state ψ_1'. Now if a measurement of 'b' is carried out and the result 'b_1' is obtained, the system must be in the corresponding 'b' eigen state 'φ_1'. If 'a' and 'b' commute, 'ψ_1' and 'φ_1' will be identical functions, and any succession of remeasurements will continue to give the same results 'a_1' and 'b_1'. However if 'a' and 'b' do not commute, then 'ψ_1' and 'φ_1' will be different functions, and the measurement producing the result 'b_1' will throw the system from its initial state 'ψ_1' into the new state 'φ_1'. If measurement 'a' is now repeated then any one of the eigen values of 'a' can be obtained, 'a_1', 'a_2', 'a_3' . . . (with probabilities obtained by expanding 'φ_1' in a series of eigen functions of a: $\varphi_1 = \Sigma_1 C_i \psi_i$). Thus, in general, the remeasurement of 'a' following the measurement of the non-commuting variable 'b' will not result in the original value being obtained. This holds true no matter how many additional hidden parameters are introduced.

Thus the final conclusion is: So long as all the traditional observables of physics are used, including the conjugate variable pairs, position and momentum, energy and time, etc., no hidden variable theory will make microscopic physics causal without in the process contradicting some of the results of Q.M. as it exists today. There still remains the possibility of giving up some or all of the traditional observables and introducing a set of new variables, and, providing the resulting set as a whole commutes, obtain a causal theory. The problem, of course, is how to find such a set, and as of the present time this remains unsolved.

⋆ ⋆ ⋆

Pauli has raised another even more general consideration. Much of quantum statistical thermodynamics depends upon the qualitative identity or difference among various states. Here's a simple example. The various ways in which two men and one woman can be arranged in a row is $M_1. M_2W; M_1.W.M_2; W.M_1.M_2; M_2M_1.W; M_2W.M_1; W.M_2.M_1$. Now, if the two men are identically dressed identical twins, so that there is no way of distinguishing between them, each of the last three arrangements are respectively identical with the first three. We have six different arrangements in case one, but only three if the men are identical. In a hidden parameter theory these new variables would provide additional means of distinguishing among states and would change the probability calculations. Since quantum statistics are in remarkably good agreement with experimental fact this would again tend to rule out a hidden parameter theory.

⋆ ⋆ ⋆

Despite the above considerations various authors have attempted to find a causal formulation. De Broglie's original 'Pilot Wave Theory' was such an attempt, but he gave it up in 1927 as a result of objections raised at the Solway Conference by Bohr, Pauli and Von Neumann. A development of this theory was presented by David Bohm in 1952. The general arguments presented above would seem to guarantee the failure of any such theory, but it is still interesting to look at it in some detail to find its specific shortcoming.

In this 'causal' theory, the Q.M. Schroedinger equation, in the time dependent form 6.17, is converted into a pair of differential equations, which are immediately recognized as identical with ones used in the solution of certain problems in classical physics. Thus the electron can be apparently treated entirely as a particle.

$$-\frac{h^2}{8\pi^2 m}\frac{\partial^2 \psi}{\partial x^2}+V(x)\psi = \frac{jh}{2\pi}\frac{\partial \psi}{\partial t} . \quad 6.17$$

Try a solution:

$$\psi = R(x)e^{jS(x)/t} \quad\ldots\ldots\ldots 6.18$$

Insert into 6.17 and, after separating reals and imaginaries, we get the two equations:

F

$$\frac{\partial R}{\partial t} = -\frac{1}{2m}\left[R\frac{\partial^2 S}{\partial x^2}+2\frac{\partial R}{\partial x}\frac{\partial S}{\partial x}\right]$$

$$\frac{\partial S}{\partial t} = -\left[\frac{1}{2m}\left(\frac{\partial S}{\partial x}\right)^2+V(x)-\right.$$
$$\left.\frac{h^2}{8\pi^2 m}\frac{1}{R}\frac{\partial^2 R}{\partial x^2}\right] \quad \dots\dots 6.19$$

Put $P(x) = R^2(x)$ and get:

$$\frac{\partial P}{\partial t}+\frac{\partial}{\partial x}\left(P\frac{1}{m}\frac{\partial S}{\partial x}\right) = 0$$

$$\frac{\partial S}{\partial t}+\frac{1}{2m}\left(\frac{\partial S}{\partial x}\right)^2+V(x)-$$
$$\frac{h^2}{8\pi^2 m}\left[\frac{1}{P}\frac{\partial^2 P}{\partial x^2}-\frac{1}{2P^2}\left(\frac{\partial P}{\partial x}\right)\right] = 0$$
$$\dots\dots\dots 6.20$$

Put $\dfrac{1}{m}\dfrac{\partial s}{\partial x} = v$

and
$$-\frac{h^2}{8\pi^2 m}\left\{\frac{1}{P}\frac{\partial^2 P}{\partial x^2}-\frac{1}{2P^2}\left(\frac{\partial P}{\partial x}\right)^2\right\}=U(x)$$

then we get:

$$\frac{\partial P}{\partial t}+\frac{\partial}{\partial x}(Pv) = 0$$

$$\frac{\partial s}{\partial t}+\frac{1}{2}mv^2+\left\{V(x)+U(x)\right\} = 0$$
$$\dots\dots\dots 6.21$$

The non-mathematician can skip to the final result on page 163.

For the ψ function in 6.17 we make the substitution shown in 6.18, where $R(x)$ and $S(x)$ are two real functions of x. After a little mathematics, including the separation of the real and imaginary parts of the equation, the two interdependent equations 6.19 are obtained. These are changed to the form shown in 6.20 by writing $P(x) = R^2(x)$. (This $P(x)$ is thus equal to '$|\psi|^2$', our previously obtained probability distribution for position.) Finally if we put '$\frac{1}{m}\frac{\partial s}{\partial x}$' equal to the 'velocity of the particle' 'v', and for the last term,'$-\frac{h^2}{8\pi^2 m}\left\{\frac{1}{p}\frac{\partial^2 P}{\partial x^2}-\frac{1}{2P^2}\left(\frac{\partial P}{\partial x}\right)^2\right\}$' write '$U(x)$', a new 'quantum potential energy', we get equations 6.21. The first of these is the standard Equation of Continuity, and the second, the Hamilton-Jacobi Equation of Classical Mechanics.

The continuity equation appears in many classical problems—the flow of fluids, the flow of electric charge, the diffusion of one gas through another, etc. In words, it states that the rate of increase of the probability of finding an entity in a given region, equals the rate of influx of probability over the borders of the region. The second equation will also be familiar to the physicist. It is one used in the solution of more advanced problems in the mechanics of the motion of a particle (particularly in electromagnetism and astronomy). It can be derived from Newton's equations (to which, in consequence, it is mathematically equivalent), but since the proof involves a rather extended mathematical argument we will not carry it out here. We will content ourselves with the simpler task of show-

ing that it is reducible to the familiar law of conservation of energy
for the special case where S = Ct
('C' is a constant, and 't' the time.)

$$S = Ct$$

Substituting for '$\frac{\partial s}{\partial t}$' *into 6.21*

$$\frac{\partial S}{\partial t} = -C$$

we get the energy equation 6.22.
(The sum of the kinetic energy of
the particle and its potential energy
is a constant.)

Insert this into 6.21 and get

$$\frac{1}{2}mv^2 + V(x) + U(x) = C \ldots 6.22$$

Thus we have converted Schroedinger's equation 6.17 into a pair of
deterministic classical physics equations 6.21 which contain a new
quantum mechanical potential energy term (U) in addition to the
ordinary potential energy term (V). To make precise predictions
for future position and momentum measurements all that is needed
is to integrate 6.21, or simply the equivalent Newtonian equation 6.23,

where we have written for 'f' the
customary negative gradient of
the potential energy. Since at the
macroscopic level Newton's equations work satisfactorily without
any quantum mechanical potential,
this 'U' should vanish for problems
involving masses large as compared with that of an electron, and
velocities small as compared with
that of light. When we examine the
expression defining 'U', we see that
this criterion is satisfied through

$$f = ma$$

$$-\frac{\partial}{\partial x}\Big\{V(x) + U(x)\Big\} = m d\frac{^2x}{dt^2}$$
$$\ldots 6.23$$

Where U is the new quantum
potential energy term introduced
by Bohm to restore determinism
to Quantum Physics.

the occurrence of h² (h = 6.6×10^{-27}) in the numerator.

Since the Bohm theory is directly derived from quantum mechanics it
is bound to agree with it under reasonable assumptions, but is it truly a
causal theory? Consider first this 'quantum mechanical potential'. 'P'
simultaneously determines both it and the probability distribution of
position of the particle through the continuity equation, or, alternatively, if one has a large number of particles, the relative number of
particles at any given position. This dual significance bothers some critics
of the theory but it does not seem to be a valid objection. In fact the
usual way in which a potential function is determined in classical
mechanics is to observe the behaviour of particles at different locations

in the field, and then use Newton's laws to calculate the appropriate potential function. We can easily think of macroscopic-sized experiments in which a particle would enter an electromagnetic field with some range of arbitrary initial positions and momenta, and the resultant probability distribution of particles would be directly related to the form of the field potential. The new quantum potential has certain weird characteristics, but not particularly more so than some others in use in classical physics, and the addition of a new potential energy term is always justifiable as we have seen in earlier chapters.

Since Bohm's Theory is simply a variation of ordinary quantum mechanics it is open to all the general criticism that we have recorded above, and we move on to what is the particular and serious objection: despite its title it is not a hidden variable theory at all. The introduction of a new type of potential energy term does not constitute finding a new parameter. In classical physics the constant task was the finding of new potential energy or force terms suitable to new physical situations. Bohm's observables continue to be position and momentum since his object was to put Q.M. in the form of deterministic classical mechanics. The solution of any classical mechanics equation requires a knowledge of the instantaneous and simultaneous position and momentum of the particle (or its equivalent), and Bohm has not been able to show any way of escaping the uncertainty principle in the obtaining of these. The fact of his being able to reduce the Schroedinger Equation to the classical Hamilton Jacobi Equation is without any particular significance. We have seen in Postulate 3 that Q.M. has been set up deliberately to be asymptotic and reducible to the classical theory in certain limiting cases. Conclusion: the theory is only an interesting mathematical exercise.

★   ★   ★

Schroedinger has never approved of the indeterministic interpretation of Quantum Mechanics. Since he accepts the indeterminacy principle and recognizes the impossibility of a deterministic theory of the motion of micro-entities so long as they continue to be considered as particles, he takes a different tack. He focuses his attention on the wave function 'ψ', whose behaviour is rigorously specified in its space-time evolution by the Schroedinger wave equation. Thus if the micro-entity is simply the 'ψ' we would have a deterministic theory.

For Schroedinger, an example of the deficiency of the Bohr atomic theory lies in its inability to deal with the transition periods between the stationary energy states. 'Since all intermediate states are forbidden, the "quantum jumps" must be instantaneous. But if this is the case how can coherent wave trains be produced which are several metres long' . . . 'Alternatively, if one assumes the jumps are not instantaneous, the time for producing such wave groups would be so long that the atom would be left with almost no time to spend in the "stationary states".'

To meet this difficulty, Schroedinger suggests shifting, at the microscopic level, entirely over to a wave theory. Thus an atom would be treated in a manner analogous to a vibrating bell, if the physical bell were removed while the vibrations and possibility of different modes of vibration remained. Although there is an infinite variety of these vibrations, they can all be mathematically analysed as a superposition of a discrete set of (eigen) modes characteristic of the bell. As the atom changed from one characteristic mode to another, it would emit the energy difference as a wave. Similarly an electron would be treated entirely as a wave group, with principal wave length given by de Broglie's formula, and travelling with a certain group velocity and path governed by the refractive index of the medium it is moving through. (We have seen how this can be done in Chapter 4.) The interaction between two systems would be described as a gradual change in the amplitudes of the characteristic vibrations of each.

Let us see how Schroedinger would interpret an experiment ordinarily described by conventional theory. A beam of electrons is shot into a region containing sodium vapour. If the initial energy is low, the only result is a scattering of the electrons. As the energy is increased, a new phenomena appears. Some of the scattered electrons appear with decreased energy and the sodium vapour glows, giving off electromagnetic radiation.

The particle explanation is that as an electron strikes an atom some of the kinetic energy is transformed into excitation energy of the atom. An orbital electron in the atom jumps to a new energy level, a little later drops back to its rest level, and in the process gives off a wave group of characteristic frequency. The balance equations are given by equating the change

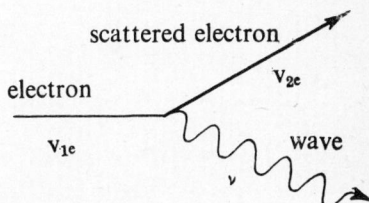

Using the energy equations:

$$\frac{1}{2}mv_{1e}^2 - \frac{1}{2}mv_{2e}^2 = E_2 - E_1 \quad ..\,6.24$$

But:

$$E_2 - E_1 = \Delta E = h\nu$$

$$\therefore \tfrac{1}{2}mv_{1e}^2 - \tfrac{1}{2}mv_{2e}^2 = h\nu \quad \ldots 6.25$$

where: ν = The frequency of the light emitted.

* * *

If we consider the interaction as a resonance phenomenon:

$$\nu_{1e} - \nu_{2e} = \nu_2 - \nu_1 \ldots\ldots\ldots 6.26$$

(where:
ν_{1e} = initial electron frequency
ν_{2e} = final electron frequency
ν_2 = final atom frequency
ν_1 = initial atom frequency)

Multiply 6.26 by h and get:

$$h\nu_{1e} - h\nu_{2e} = h(\nu_2 - \nu_1) \ldots .. 6.27$$

$$= h\nu \ldots\ldots\ldots 6.28$$

* * *

Now $\nu_{1e} = \dfrac{v_{1wave}}{\lambda_{1e}}$

$$\nu_{2e} = \dfrac{v_{2wave}}{\lambda_{2e}} \ldots\ldots\ldots\ldots 6.29$$

If we write $v_{wave} = kv_{group}$

Then $\nu_{1e} = \dfrac{kv_1}{\lambda_{1e}}$

$$\nu_{2e} = \dfrac{kv_2}{\lambda_{2e}} \ldots\ldots\ldots\ldots 6.30$$

in electron energy to the change in energy of the atom 6.24. In turn, this change in atom energy is equated to that possessed by the emitted photon, Planck's constant times frequency. Substituting, we obtain equation 6.25.

Now Schroedinger treats this phenomenon as a simple resonance phenomenon between two interacting wave systems, the one being the electron and the other, the atom. He would solve the problem mathematically by equating the change in frequency in the one to the change in the other as shown in 6.26. We will now show that 6.26, (the wave interpretation), and 6.25, (the conventional interpretation), can become quantitatively equivalent by making a few reasonable assumptions. First, multiply the frequency equation 6.26 on both sides by 'h', thus changing it to an energy equation. The right hand side immediately reduces to the same expression as on the right hand side of 6.25. Now we must go to work on the left of 6.28. 'ν_{1e}' and 'ν_{2e}' (the frequencies of the electron before and after interaction) must be converted into electron velocities. First, we use the standard equation connecting frequency, wave-length, and wave velocity, 6.29. However, this wave velocity is not usually equal to the velocity with which the wave group travels, which, in the de

Broglie Theory, is the velocity of the electron. Having nothing else to guide us, we will put the wave velocity equal to a constant, 'k', times the group velocity, and choose the 'k' later so as to get agreement between the Schroedinger picture and the conventional one. (In water waves, for example, the wave velocity is twice the group velocity.) For the wavelength we use the standard formula developed by de Broglie 6.31. Substituting 6.31 into 6.30 we get 6.32 and putting this into 6.26 we obtain finally 6.33. We see that 6.33 becomes identical with 6.25 by choosing the value $\frac{1}{2}$ for k.

But from de Broglie's theory:

$$\lambda_{1e} = \frac{h}{mv_{1e}}, \lambda_2 = \frac{h}{mv_{2e}} \ldots \ldots 6.31$$

Substituting 6.31 in 6.30:

$$\nu_{1e} = \frac{kmv_{1e}^2}{h}, \nu_{2e} = \frac{kmv_{2e}^2}{h} \ . \ 6.32$$

Substitute 6.32 into 6.26 and get:

$$k(mv_{1e}^2 - kmv_{2e}^2) = h\nu \ \ldots . 6.33$$

for $k = \frac{1}{2}$ this becomes identical with 6.25.

In this way the conventional particle-wave picture of this phenomena can, by making certain not unreasonable assumptions, be replaced by an entirely wave picture. The question remains, is there any advantage in doing so? Schroedinger sees two. The first, is that the wave (the ψ function) is governed and determined precisely by the Schroedinger wave equation. Thus, if the microscopic systems are treated as waves, physics would retain its classical deterministic nature, which for Schroedinger, as for Einstein, is the only valid form of scientific explanation. The second advantage, is that a number of phenomena can be understood much more easily by a wave theory than by a particle theory. As an example of the latter, Schroedinger suggests the photo-electric effect. Considered on the basis of a resonance phenomenon, an incident wave (light) strikes a surface, is swallowed up (experiencing a change in wave length), and another wave (electron) is emitted. There is no uncertainty, as with the particle theory, as to how a light photon can be localized at one particular point of the guiding wave, and why an electron is emitted at one point rather than another.

The Schroedinger picture, as presented in the best possible light, is very attractive. But now let us look at its shortcomings. Although certain phenomena can best be described by a wave theory, the same holds for a particle theory. Thus, while a particle explanation of electron interference, barrier penetration, . . . etc., seems impossible, a wave explanation (as Schroedinger admits) of tracks, collisions, and stars in cloud chambers and photographic emulsions, of the randomly developed grains at low intensity for photographic plates registering interference phenomena, seems equally impossible. Even if we consider one of the very phenomena Schroedinger uses as an example of the power of the purely wave theory—the photo-electric effect—we run into the problem insoluble by wave theory of why a geiger counter will give random clicks for the electrons emitted from a surface, rather than a continuous regular response as presumably would be produced by a wave. The fact is, that neither a purely particle nor a purely wave theory can serve as a universal model for all microscopic phenomena. Now, in the wave theory, placing the emphasis upon the 'ψ' function amounts to treating it as a variable, a hidden variable, since it itself is not observable, and we have already seen in our earlier analysis of hidden parameters that the 'ψ' is not acceptable as a hidden variable if significance is to be given to position and momentum measurements.

In addition to these objections we have the further difficulty that any wave packet inevitably spreads with time. With sufficient time, a wave spreads throughout all space and there is no possibility of such a theory representing the observed 'particularity' (in some instances) of nature. De Broglie developed, and has recently returned, to a 'Theory of the Double Solution' which meets this objection by introducing an additional mathematical function as a solution to the wave equation. This is a singular solution, a wave with amplitude concentrated at one point. As such it would not spread in time but the 'particle' is now concentrated in a region of zero dimension. At the time of writing this book, his theory has not been successfully completed.

*   *   *

Before closing, it is necessary to mention that Bohm, Vigier, and others are hard at work in an attempt to derive a deterministic theory which would give the usual Q.M. results by a statistical averaging process over the set of hidden variables in a causal substratum. In the analysis of this chapter we have seen that the possibility of this is not ruled out by Von Neumann's Theorem providing that the new total set of observables does not include conjugate pairs. However a usable theory making predictions different from those of ordinary Q.M. does not as yet exist, and we are forced to consider present-day Quantum Mechanics Theory to be a theory indeterministic in principle as well as practice.

CHAPTER VII

Indeterminism in Man

SUMMARY: The last several chapters have shown that microscopic-sized phenomena, as described by Quantum Mechanics in terms of the customary mechanical observables—position, momentum, energy, time, etc.—are indeterministic for individual events. However when large numbers of micro-entities combine to produce some effect, this quantum indeterminism is swallowed up in a statistically predictable behaviour; and, at the macroscopic level, Classical Mechanics, an entirely deterministic theory, has proven itself to be the most successful universal theory of historical time judged by its ability to make verifiable predictions.

As an example of this, take the familiar phenomenon of a cube of sugar dissolving and diffusing throughout a cup of hot coffee. If one wanted to study this event in detail it would be necessary to follow the behaviour of each molecule as it moved through the potential field set up by all the other molecules. The complete analysis of this would require the solution of a set of simultaneous Quantum Mechanical equations, and, in consequence, each of the individual motions would be subject to the usual quantum uncertainty, and only a probabilistic description would be possible. Finally, the macroscopic density of the sugar would be calculated by a complicated statistical summation over all the molecules and all their individual possible locations. Now in fact no one would ever attempt, or need, to handle the problem in this way. The motion of individual molecules is ignored, and the diffusion is described by working directly with the solute density 'ρ'. (This

$$\frac{\partial \rho}{\partial t} = D\Delta^2\rho \quad \dots\dots\dots\dots\ 7.1$$

is defined as the number of grams of solute per unit volume of solvent, in this case grams of sugar per cubic centimetre of coffee.) To find 'ρ' as a function of position and time we solve the diffusion equation of classical physics (7.1). In non-mathematical terms this equation states that the rate at which the amount of substance inside a given boundary is changing is equal to the rate of diffusion of outside substance over the boundary into the region. This equation is entirely deterministic, in terms of our earlier definition, and its predictions have been consistently verified in practice.

We can say quite generally that classical thermodynamics which doesn't concern itself in the slightest with the behaviour of molecules is reliable for describing most macroscopic phenomena, as, for example, in analysing the operations of an automobile engine. The unpredictable irregularities which are of the essence in understanding Brownian Motion are cancelled out in the predictable average motion of the tremendous numbers of molecules (one cubic foot contains some 700,000,000,000,000,000,000,000 of them) entering into the functioning of the engine.

This statistical regularity, which appears when large numbers of entities are concerned, can be better understood if we express it quantitatively. The mathematical theory of statistics tells us that if the average number of molecules bombarding a surface per second is 'N', we can anticipate a variation about 'N' equal to the 'square root of N'. That is, we expect the number arriving per second to vary between 'N$-\sqrt{N}$' and 'N$+\sqrt{N}$', but only rarely outside these limits. If 'N' is small, then, although the 'square root of N' is also small, percentage-wise this variation is very large as compared with 'N' (7.2). As N becomes large, then although $\sqrt{N}$ also grows, its size compared to N becomes progressively smaller, and the percentage variation eventually becomes unmeasurably small. In our example of the number of molecules in one cubic foot of a gas, we can see this—the absolute value of the fluctuation ($8\cdot4\times10^{11}$) is a very large number, but the percentage variation when compared with the

If N = 100

$$\sqrt{N} = 10$$

Expected variation:

100$-$10 to 100$+$10

i.e. 90 to 110

i.e. $\pm10\%$ 7.2

If N = 7×10^{23}

$$\sqrt{N} = 8\cdot4\times10^{11}$$

% variation is:

$$\pm\frac{\sqrt{N}}{N}\times100 = \frac{1}{8\cdot4\times10^9}$$

approximately

$$\frac{1}{10,000,000,000} \text{ of } 1\%$$

average (7×10^{23}) is only one ten billionth of one per cent. If one set up an experiment to measure the masses of different equal-volumed samples drawn from a gas which was in a uniform state of temperature and pressure such a variation would be entirely undetectable.

Although this is the usual situation at the macroscopic level, it is possible to find instances where microscopic uncertainty does have a large-scale effect. Later on we will be examining instances of this in living bodies, but for the moment we will consider a possible example in inorganic nature. One of the world's fairs was officially opened in an exciting way which was presented as an illustration of the precision and determinacy of science. A telescope was pointed at a region of the sky where it had been predicted that Arcturus would be at the specified desired time. The light coming from the telescope, when Arcturus appeared duly on time, was focused on a photo cell. The current generated actuated a relay, which in turn closed a giant switch, turning on all the lights of the fair simultaneously. Now in the actual case the light was sufficiently intense that any quantum uncertainty could be ignored and an exact prediction of the lighting-up time could be made. However it would have been possible, by using a suitably weak star and a small objective telescope, to have a light of such a feeble intensity that only a few dozen photons would be arriving per minute. In this instance (we would have to substitute a more sensitive device for the photo tube) it would have been impossible to predict more closely than within a few seconds the exact time all the lights would go on. Here we are dealing with a divergent chain reaction having its origin in a microscopic event.

Our particular concern in this book is the human being, and in his case huge numbers of molecules are co-operating in the production of even the smallest motion. In addition, we have to take into account a new phenomenon not found in inorganic nature but very definitely characteristic of life—homesostasis. This is the name for phenomena in which changes in the environment stimulate compensating processes in the body which work to oppose the effect of the altered surroundings. Some familiar examples are: the sun-tanning reaction of the human skin to protect the body from sunburn; sweating to cool the body, shivering to warm it; the narrowing of the eye's pupil in a bright light, and its widening in a weak light. (It is interesting to note here that man has no similar reaction to protect himself against atomic radiation, although medical men are working to develop one artificially. The reason is our old familiar one that man as he developed had no need in the past to protect himself

against large doses of radiation. It was not a survival factor. Will it
become one?) Nevertheless we intend to show in this chapter that quantum uncertainty does have a role to play in the human body—small but
unavoidable—and the end result is necessarily indeterminism for man.

* * *

It is inevitable that when we shift our attention from the inorganic
world to man we come up against the emotionally loaded mind-body
problem. Any attempt to carry out a detailed study of this subject would
lead us far astray from the main theme of this book, so, as with many
others of the topics encountered in this investigation, we must restrict
ourselves to little more than an exposition of our point of view. However
this latter is essential, and we can at least take the time to give some of our
reasons for adhering to our particular position.

Chapters 1 and 2 have indicated that any attempted organization of our
immediately apprehended experiences into a conceptual world picture
seems to lead inevitably (with certain exceptions, especially in Eastern
philosophies and religions) to the assumption of an 'I' that experiences
and a set of other 'things' that are experienced. It is also common to
subdivide the 'I' into two parts: a body, which is considered to be part of
the physical world, though much more under our immediate control than
external things; and a non-physical mind which is more or less co-
extensive with the body, but still distinct from it. Viewed in this way,
a person has two simultaneous histories, one consisting of events happening to and in his body, and the other consisting of what happens in his
mind. The relation of the two, mind and body, has been under continuous
speculation since earliest times, but the problem has become more acute
in the last several centuries when the success of the mechanical theory of
space and time seemed to void the possibility of free will unless the mind
(or 'soul') of man were distinct from his mechanically determined body.
Of course this led to the question: If the mind is totally non-material,
how can mental processes, such as deciding to do a certain act, bring about
spatial movements; and conversely, how can a physical change in the
inner ear bring about the mind's perception of sound, an electromagnetic
stimulation of the retina of the eye—produce a perception of light . . .
etc.?

The question of the interconnection has never been satisfactorily
solved, and, although we will look at a recent attempt to do this later on
in the chapter, the only alternative to an entirely material theory seems

to be some form of picture of the two, mind and body, moving along separate but parallel paths in pre-established harmony. This could certainly be taken as a postulate, but then it runs foul of one of our criteria for a choice of postulates forming the basis of a semiotic: namely, succinctness. If the 'mind' as distinct from 'body' can never be directly observed, and its behaviour is exactly parallel to the body's behaviour, the semiotic will be syntactically and semantically exactly the same whether the 'separate mind' assumption is made or not. If this is the case our rules would require us to eliminate it, and this we shall do.

Just for a moment again let us go over our guiding pattern of thought. By the above we do not say that 'in reality' there is or there is not a separate mind. Our job is only to set up a symbolic system of thought which will be maximally pragmatically successful in organizing our experiences, and this semiotic system does not include a non-material mind. Therefore from now on when we say that people are thinking in such and such a way we are not referring to 'some mysterious and un-approachable events of which their overt behaviours are the effects, but we are talking about whatever behaviour we can in fact observe'. As Ryle put it: 'In making sense of what you say, in appreciating your jokes, in unmasking your chess strategisms, in following your arguments and in hearing you pick holes in mine, I am not inferring the workings of your mind, I am following them'. In terms suitable to the external observer this amounts to a definition of the class of phenomena constituting 'mind'.

Thus in this chapter, which is devoted to the study of indeterminism in man, we will concern ourselves only with the physical, observable man; our postulates do not include a ghostly, non-observable, spirit either in some peculiar non-physical interaction with man or moving parallel with him. When we are talking about any aspect of man's behaviour, whether it is the easily examined macroscopic motions of his body, the responses of his senses, or (as yet mostly not understood) brain mechanisms, we will use only what has been 'established' scientifically. (We will admit introspection in its proper role as providing an entirely different brand of evidence in the next chapter, when we are considering man from the 'inside' out.) This should not be taken to imply that science has all or even a large part of the answers to the how's and why's of the enormous com-plexities of man's behaviour, but it has some, they are rationally demon-strable and confirmable by anyone willing to take the trouble to examine and check them, and no other system has had any appreciable, consistent success.

★   ★   ★

When we look at a man's actions we are seeing phenomena belonging almost entirely to the macroscopic world. Even for those aspects only visible under the magnifying glass—spermatozoa and ova, neural structure, etc.—huge numbers of molecules are involved. Thus it might seem that he can be adequately described by classical physics which we have classified as a deterministic theory. Now there is no doubt that the bulk of his actions are determined. If any indeterminism, any variation from a pattern of behaviour laid down far in advance of any particular action, is to be found, there must be situations in which the execution of one or an alternate course of action hinges upon an event of microscopic size. As in the case of the single photon (potentially) triggering off all the lights at the world's fair, we must find divergent chains in man. We will consider three examples of these: the first of these occurs in the theory of genes and their mutations; the second, researches into the amount of energy required to stimulate a response in the eye; and for the third, a study of neural circuitry in the brain. The first two of these are on reasonably firm experimental ground, but in the last we will be making a considerable extrapolation from what is actually known about neurons and their interconnections to hypothetical circuits for such mental phenomena as the conditioned reflex and decision making. More of this later.

GENETIC UNCERTAINTY

We begin with a discussion of the applicability of quantum uncertainty in the theory of genes and mutations. It is unfortunate but inevitable that little of the experimental work has been done on man himself, but there is every reason to believe that the results obtained with other animals are generally applicable to man. A very popular animal for research in genetic theory has been the Drosophila (fruit fly). There are a number of reasons for this. Among them: as an experimental animal it is small, easy to house, cheap to feed; in a short space of time it goes through many generations, so the inheritance of certain characteristics can be followed; the individual cells in the fruit fly's salivary glands are large enough to be studied in some detail.

It is of course not possible to recount the enormous amount of research that has led in little over half a century from practically no knowledge about the mechanism of inheritance to the present state of genetic theory. A bald statement of the results must suffice: The four-dimensional (space and time) ontogenetic development from the initial fertilized egg to the mature adult seems to be specified, subject of course to the continuing effect of environment, by the structure of the nucleus of that initial egg. This nucleus contains a set of chromosomes (8 in the case of Drosophila; 46 or 48 for man; the exact number seems to be in doubt) which duplicate themselves on division, carrying the initial pattern into both of the resulting cells. This process is repeated in successive division, and in this way the initial code pattern is carried over into every cell, with certain exceptions, of the mature body.

These 'certain exceptions' include the processes connected with reproduction. In a special kind of division, called reduction division, the number of chromosomes contributed to each of the newly formed cells is cut in half. These resulting incomplete cells ('gametes') are called egg cells or ova if produced by a female, and sperm if by a male. In reproduction, an ovum and a sperm unite, forming a composite cell containing a complete set of chromosomes, one half being supplied by the male and one half by the female parent. The animal which will develop from this fertilized egg will thus contain a composite of characteristics of the mother and the father.

Now all this is the usual state of affairs. However from time to time offspring appear, containing characteristics present neither in the immediate mother and father nor in the preceding ancestry. Such an event is called a mutation and the resultant product, a mutant. Although experiments have shown that the general rate of mutation can be increased by raising the temperature or by increasing the radiation to which the gametes are subject, it has not been possible as yet to induce or predict a particular mutation. The progeny of the mutants retain the new characteristic of their parents, so it must be assumed that the mutation represents a permanent alteration in one or more of the chromosomes. The locus of particular chromosomal changes has been found for many of the mutations in fruit flies.

These and the results of other investigations, aided enormously by the relatively recent development of high magnification electron microscopes, have permitted a linear mapping along the various chromosomes of the determining factors for the macroscopic characteristics of the mature fruit fly. Each of the regions where one of these property specifiers is concentrated is called a gene. The accompanying sketch shows such a gene-property chart for Drosophila.

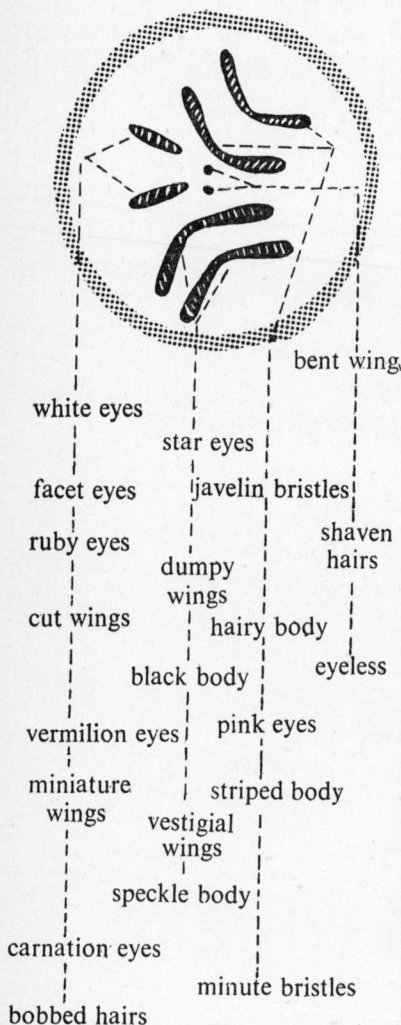

An individual gene would appear to be a giant protein molecule containing something between 1,000 and 1,000,000 atoms. Following an argument given by Schroedinger it is assured that such a molecule can exist in a number of different isomeric configurations, each presumably corresponding to a different characteristic of the adult. According to quantum mechanics these different configurations would be separated from each other by discrete energy differences. We can make an estimate of the magnitude of these differences by comparison with other organic molecules, and a good estimate for the energy interval between the ground level and the next energy level would seem to be about 1·8 electron volts (about three trillionths of an

bent wing

white eyes

star eyes

facet eyes

javelin bristles

ruby eyes

shaven hairs

dumpy wings

cut wings

hairy body

black body

eyeless

vermilion eyes

pink eyes

miniature wings

striped body

vestigial wings

speckle body

carnation eyes

minute bristles

bobbed hairs

erg, 3×10^{-12} ergs). It seems reasonable to assume that a mutation occurs when, by some means or other, a gene acquires this amount of energy and abruptly changes its molecular state from one level to another.

There are many ways in which this energy may be gained. For example, except at absolute zero every molecule possesses some energy which fluctuates as it gains or loses energy in exchanges with other molecules. This is analogous to the kinetic energy possessed by molecules of a gas, although in the case of the gene the molecule is more or less fixed in position. The average value of this energy is a function of temperature, increasing with rising temperature. Now, although the energy difference between two isomeric levels is considerably larger than the average 'temperature energy' of the molecules, over a long enough period of time there is a possibility that the molecule will momentarily pick up sufficient energy to make the transition. Statistical theory gives expression 7.4 for the average time 't' a molecule will spend in one energy state before jumping to the next higher isomeric energy level. This time is a function of the energy difference and the temperature.

$$t = \tau e^{E/kT} \quad \dots\dots\dots\dots\dots 7.4$$

$$
\left\{
\begin{aligned}
t &= \text{time} \\
\tau &= \text{a constant} \\
E &= \text{Energy difference between} \\
&\quad \text{the ground state and the} \\
&\quad \text{stable level} \\
k &= \text{the Boltzmann Constant} \\
T &= \text{Temperature}
\end{aligned}
\right.
$$

Inserting the value of $E = 1 \cdot 8$ electron volts and choosing the usual value, 10^{-13} seconds, for τ we find that at ordinary temperatures 't' is of the order of 30,000 years. If this analysis, then, can be applied to genes it would explain simultaneously two aspects of genetic behaviour: (1) the fact that ordinarily genetic transmission is regular, and (2) the fact that from time to time mutations do occur.

Experimental checks are in order and they have been made. (1) Since T enters into the exponential in the denominator, a lowering of the temperature should decrease the mutation rate and a rise in temperature increase it. This has been experimentally observed for Drosophila. (2) Any method of providing energy should be effective so long as it supplies sufficient energy. This has been verified in artificial mutations produced both chemically and by X-rays. It is found that the mutation rate is directly proportional to the X-ray dosage, and is independent of the X-ray wavelength, providing only the ion density produced (dosage) remains constant.

It seems then that for a human being his having blue or brown eyes, his susceptibility to cancer, haemophilia, . . . and in general a majority of the mature characteristics that differentiate him from his fellows, are dependent upon the stability of genes of microscopic size, which are subject to bombardment by cosmic rays and general radiation from terrestrial objects, occasional stimulation by chemical agents, and, as an irreducible minimum, their own 'temperature energy', fluctuating in interchanges with other molecules, and only vanishing at absolute zero.

To talk about the stability of these genes we must decide upon an appropriate theory. Since they are intermediate in size between the micro-entities which can only be dealt with by Quantum Mechanical methods and those bodies for which classical physics is an entirely adequate theory, there is a momentary hesitation between the two. However, of the two Q.M. is the more general. It can be shown (see Chapter 6—the theory of Bohm) to approach the classical theory asymptotically under appropriate limiting conditions, while the converse is not true. Thus we use Quantum Mechanics, but at the same time we must realize that we are working in a region close to the asymptotic point where the gene's behaviour becomes classically determinate.

* * *

First, consider that we are confronted with the problem of predicting the physiology of the mature adult, assuming that we have all the knowledge which is possible of the state of the universe, and of the egg and the fertilizing sperm. Once we are committed to using Quantum Theory we know that even assuming we have this maximal knowledge the best we can do is to give a list of possible sets of characteristics with their attendant probabilities. Now this probability distribution will be enormously concentrated. It will be very close

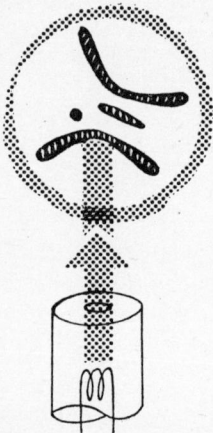

to 1 for that set that would be obtained by a straightforward use of the classical theory; however there will be finite, although very small, probabilities for a number of other sets of variant characteristics.

If, instead of passively attempting to predict what characteristics will result from a given initial state, it becomes a question of deliberately introducing a certain characteristic by a specific genetic change, we are subject to the same limitation as above. For instance, if we attempt to bring one about by shooting an electron at one particular gene in the chromosome, an accuracy of about 10^{-10} square centimetre would be required. Such an experiment is entirely governed by the indeterministic laws of Quantum Mechanics, and we could never be certain of producing exactly the desired result. The best we could do would be to ensure a maximum of probability that the change would be the desired one.

SENSORY UNCERTAINTY

As our next example of the way in which quantum indeterminism can enter into man's affairs we consider the response of the eye to light of feeble intensity. If the threshold of sensitivity (the minimum amount of light to which the eye will respond and a signal will be transmitted and perceived in the brain) is of the order of some billions of photons (still a very weak light) then any indeterminism in the arrival of individual photons would have essentially no effect. On the other hand, if the threshold is as little as 10 photons, then the indeterminate fluctuations in the number arriving per unit time could produce an unpredictability in response which in certain situations could have large-scale consequences. We begin by discussing some of the investigations which have led to an estimation of the value of this threshold.

Experiments have been done upon the eye both in and out of the body. Dewar and McKendrick have been able to remove the eye of the frog, cut it open, and, with the exercise of suitable precautions, keep it alive for several hours. To study the eye's response, electrodes were applied to the retinal surface and to the back of the eye, and the amplified signal observed on an oscilloscope. Flashes of light of known intensity were focused upon the eye and the resulting electric potential was measured. In another experiment (Hartline and Graham) connections were made to individual nerve fibres coming from the various components of the compound eye of the crab and the voltage pulses

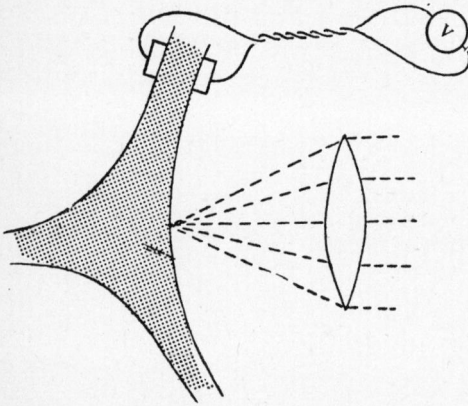

were measured. Hecht was able to measure induced voltages for the human eye *in situ*. In this case the electrodes consisted of wet cotton pads, one applied to the front of the eyeball and the other to some other part of the body.

The results are as follows: If a light of constant intensity falls upon the eye a stream of identical impulses is transmitted along the nerve fibres. If the light intensity is increased, or if the eye is sensitized by being left in the dark for some hours before the experiment, a more rapid barrage is produce. However, for weak individual flashes of light, single voltage pulses are induced. The size of these pulses is found to be proportional to the logarithm of the quantity of light above a certain threshold value. The exact value of this threshold varies with the experimental arrangements, but the best estimate seems to be that a light pulse containing some 25 photons, incident upon the eye, is sufficiently intense to stimulate a response in the retina and induce a pulse travelling along the nerve fibre. If we use a figure of 0·1 for the eye efficiency (the fraction of photons that arrive at the outer corneal surface and are subsequently effectively absorbed by the retinal rods) we find the retina capable of responding to a pulse containing something of the order of 2 or 3 photons. For a number as small as this, quantum uncertainty is of major importance, both in the exact number of photons arriving in the pulse, and in the exact point at which the retinal stimulation is registered. (This is very much analogous to the electron-slit experiment examined in Chapter 4.)

* * *

It is of course quite feasible to carry out the direct experiment in which a light is flashed on the eye of a human subject and increased in intensity until the subject reports seeing it. Any such highly subjective experiment has its disadvantages, particularly when quantitative results are wanted, but there is the overwhelming advantage of the immediate pertinacy of the results. After all, what we are really trying to discover is when a man is or is not *consciously* aware of a certain visual situation, and such an experiment provides this. It takes into account the entire visual apparatus rather than just one small part of it at a time.

Some 100 years ago Fechner summarized the results of such experiments in what came to be known as the Fechner-Weber law; If I is the background illumination in a certain region, and ΔI the additional intensity in an independent signal which is just visible against this background, then the ratio ΔI to I is a constant for different values of I. Unfortunately this general law was quickly shown to be incorrect. The actual curve flattens out asymptotically at low intensities and for some signals, particularly small area ones of short duration, is flatter than that predicted by this law.

To have a specific situation to talk about, let us consider the sort of experiment recently performed by Barlow in which, under carefully controlled conditions, the incremental threshold of the eye is measured. Left eye closed, the subject is confronted with a picture like that shown in the sketch at the right. The subject fixes his attention at X. A certain field is switched on over F, and a gradually increasing signal is applied in S until the subject announces he can just distinguish the boundary between S and F. The results are shown in the graph, where the Fechner theoretical curve and another about to be described are included for comparison. (For convenience, instead of plotting ΔI (the just visible signal) against I (the background intensity) the log of ΔI is plotted against log I. This permits more of the curve to be shown in a small space.) The Fechner-Weber and the other curve can be arbitrarily shifted. It is their shape which is to be compared with the

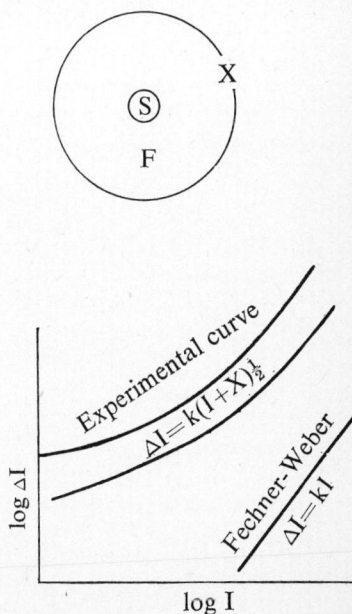

experimentally-obtained curve. It is seen that the theoretical curve provides a good fit over a wide range of intensity. The Weber-Fechner is only adequate for high intensitities.

Such experiments give results for the absolute threshold of the same order as that already given above. However it is important to examine the theory that has been developed to account for the shape of the curve. If we consider light in terms of the Quantum Theory, we recognize that the light intensity will not remain constant, with a certain number, 'N', of quantum arriving per second, but rather will fluctuate around this number with an expectable fluctuation equal to the 'square root of N'. Thus, any signal applied on top of a given ground can only become visible if in average magnitude it exceeds this fluctuation. If we relate 'ΔI' (the just visible change in the light intensity) to '$\sqrt{N}$' and 'I' (the background average intensity) to 'N' we obtain an equation for the relation between 'ΔI' and 'I' as shown in 7.3 where 'k' is an adjustable constant. Now such an equation would produce a curve passing through the origin. This is corrected by assuming that even in the absence of any external illumination there is a certain internally produced background, with a quantum fluctuation, $\sqrt{X}$, which ΔI must exceed before it can be observed. (This 'black-light' can result from a number of causes. As example: The spontaneous breakdown of the photosensitive substances in the retinal substances.) The corrected equation, 7.4, does not entirely satisfy the experimental results but it fits sufficiently well to justify our using it.

$$\therefore \Delta I = k(I)^{\frac{1}{2}} \dots\dots\dots 7.3$$

$$\Delta I = k(I+X)^{\frac{1}{2}} \dots\dots\dots 7.4$$

For large values of I and ΔI the number of quanta involved becomes so huge that any quantum uncertainty plays no role. However when ΔI is small, fluctuations in N and ΔN can become increasingly important. This is a phenomenon similar to that of Brownian Motion discussed earlier. There is however a vital difference. In the classical theory, at least in theory, determinism could be restored in Brownian Motion by simply carrying out a detailed analysis of the motions of the molecules which make up the containing fluid. Such a procedure is not permitted in the modern theory. The behaviour of individual quanta is governed by Quantum Mechanics, with, as we have seen, its essential and irreducible uncertainty, and the seeing or not seeing of light signals of feeble intensity is indeterministic in principle. That it is also so in practice, Barlow's and others' experiments clearly show in the varying responses of the subjects. Only the average visibility is given by the equation and curve.

* * *

Now let us set up a situation in which this quantum uncertainty can have a macroscopic effect. A man is awakened in the middle of the night by the sound of a burglar downstairs. He grabs his gun, creeps out of the bedroom, and looks down from the balcony into the living room. No lights are on and the only illumination is the extremely feeble light coming in through the windows. We assume that it is a moonless and cloudy night with only a few of the brightest stars showing through. If the average level of light intensity is of the order of a few photons (per unit of retinal sensitive area and unit response time) it is apparent that whether the home-owner sees the burglar and shoots first or vice versa is theoretically indeterminate and unpredictable. In this case microscopic indeterminism could make the difference between the death of the burglar or of the householder.

NEURAL UNCERTAINTY

We have been on relatively firm theoretical and experimental ground in these first two instances of microscopic events inducing macroscopic effects. In our next example—thought processes in the human brain—the evidence is not nearly so well established. At the level of immediate introspective awareness, on occasions we have all been self-consciously aware of almost remembering something: 'It's on the tip of my tongue', and frequently a decision may depend upon this remembering. We struggle hard for a while, give up, and then suddenly for no apparent reason the desired knowledge pops into consciousness (Proust's 'involuntary memory'). This all has a superficial resemblance to probabilistic chance mechanisms and we must now see if there is any justification for applying microscopic indeterminism here. Naturally it will not be possible to state quantitatively the exact number of ergs of energy involved in remembering or in making a decision, nor would such a confusion of scientific and introspective evidence be permissible, but the all or none characteristic of nervous response suggests that a sharp split in being conscious or of not being conscious of something may be dependent upon microscopically tiny differences in energy.

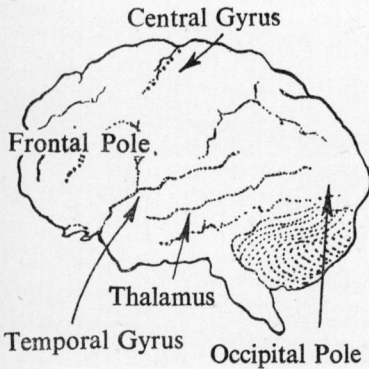

The human brain consists of two large oval masses (the cerebral hemispheres) linked together by a bridge of nerve cells. The total weight averages about 1,400 grams. From the middle of the base there extends the brain stem which serves as the principal neural switchboard with the remainder of the body. The surface of the cortex is convoluted and fissured, resulting in a surface area estimated to average some 2,300 square centimetres. There is a distinguishable thin surface layer, having a variable thickness ranging in the neighbourhood of ·25 centimetres, which is densely packed with nerves. An estimated average number of these nerves for man is 5,000,000,000. Impulses come from the sense organs and other organs to a mass of fibres at the brain base known as the thalamus which seems to act as a sort of relay station passing impulses on to the cortex and finally to the surface layer.

The first thing that must be done is the identification of the brain, and more particularly the brain surface, henceforth simply called the 'cortex', as the principal organic centre concerned for the functions grouped together under the single concept '(physical) mind'. Here the weight of evidence is clearest. As a result of a host of experiments carried out on animals, and extensive clinical studies of man, much is known about the effect of anatomical disorders in the cortex upon the overt sensory and motor behaviour of living beings. Thus destruction of one area results in blindness in man, destruction of another seriously impairs his ability to carry on a logical conversation, while the remainder of the intellectual apparatus seems to be largely unaffected . . . etc. A series of very interesting experiments have been performed by Penfield on living and 'conscious' beings in which a weakly stimulating electrode is moved over an exposed area of the cortex, called the central gyrus, from top to bottom. As the electrode moves from one part to another, a succession of move-

The following labels appear on the brain diagram: Central Gyrus, Frontal Pole, Thalamus, Temporal Gyrus, Occipital Pole.

ments is observed at the knee, the hip, trunk, shoulder, arm, finger, neck, face, in that order; and at any one time an area of the cortex can be mapped out for a specific movement. (A hard-to-understand feature of this is that these foci shift with time, and even reverse their function depending upon the state of the body.) Stimulation of other regions can cause a subject to feel tingles in arms or legs, 'see' lights, 'hear' sounds, 'smell' odours. . . . (An interesting problem in determinism and free-will is provided by the particular situation where the subject's arm starts to move and he can only prevent the motion by seizing it with the other hand.) In the temporal lobe, 'forgotten' memories may be re-awakened, and the subject may experience dream-like sequences while remaining simultaneously fully conscious. It does appear, however, that there is a large part of the cortex in the fore part for which there is no specific function, and large sections of it can be removed with little or no observable diminution of intellectual powers or sensory or motor ability. (An example of this is the recently current practice of lobotomy for otherwise apparently intractable mental patients.)

Let us agree then that the brain cortex is the seat of much of our 'mental' operations. The question is now: how are they carried out? Now we are really in trouble. From the above it is apparent that this relatively enormous sheet of nerves making up the cortex has something to do with 'mind', but despite the wealth of theories dealing with the subject none has been really satisfactory in accounting for more than a small fraction of the phenomena, and then usually in a way that is largely speculative and not open to experimental verification or rejection. There are two principal categories of these theories: 'switchboard' theories and 'field' theories. Each type is partially successful and partially not. Hebb has produced a theory that, to some extent, combines the best features of both; and, despite its shortcomings, it will serve as the basis for our discussion. Before proceeding any further with it and applying it to the particular problem we are considering in this section, we must learn something about the physiology of nerves, their form of interaction, and their topological distribution in the cortex.

* * *

An individual unexcited nerve is in a precarious electrical-chemical balance with its environment. Some success had been attained in understanding the mechanism of this balance, but it is not necessary to go into any detail here. The important result is that the effect of any electrochemical impulse applied to a nerve ending is cancelled out by a migration of ions unless this impulse is larger than a critical size called the threshold. If an impulse of more than this magnitude is applied, regenerative action occurs, the potential difference between the interior of the nerve and its exterior builds up to a value of the order of one tenth of a volt, and a full-sized pulse is generated and travels along the nerve. The size of this pulse is independent of the magnitude of the initial impulse provided only it is above the threshold.

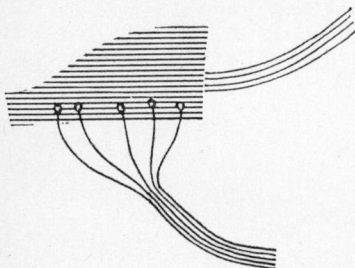

Now one nerve does not directly contact the next. At the ends they branch off into a number of smaller dendritic fibres with bulbs on their ends, called synaptic knobs. Two nerve cells interact through many of these knobs. Each knob will contribute to the depolarization at a synapse, and if this depolarization reaches the critical threshold value an impulse is transmitted along the second nerve. If no impulse is generated the depolarization dies away, and the synapse gradually returns to its former state; though there appears to be some evidence for cumulative changes at synapses, in which the ease of excitation is increased by usage and depressed by disuse. This all applies to a single impulse. A continuous stimulus causes a series of excitation pulses all of the same fixed intensity and following one another at regular intervals. In this case the frequency varies with the stimulus.

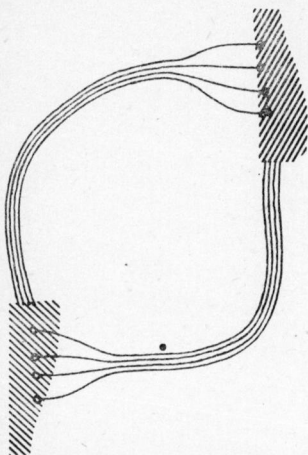

To avoid making the situation intolerably difficult for discussion, we will talk in what follows as if the transmission of an impulse at a synapse is entirely a function of the initial impulse strength and the number of contacting synaptic knobs.

It two nerves form a closed circuit as shown in the diagram, once a pulse has been induced in the circuit, it will continue to circulate until enough terminal bulbs fail simultaneously at one of the synapses so that the integrated impulse does not reach the threshold for excitation. The probability of this happening will be a rapidly decreasing function of the number of functioning bulbs in excess of the threshold. Thus if the threshold is 100 and there are 125 bulbs the circuit may fail relatively quickly, while if there are 500 bulbs the circuit will be for all practical purposes permanent.

It two or more neurons end at the same synapse, and if impulses arrive within the period of latent addition (about two one-thousandths of a second), their effects may be added together or they may partly cancel each other. In the first instance we say they are mutually excitatory and in the second inhibitory.

Now such simple circuitry as that shown above, while holding true in the spinal cord and many other parts of the body, does not exist in anything so straightforward a manner in the cortex. It is important to realize the enormous complexity of the neuron structure in a section of the cortex, where any one neuron is potentially able to act upon some thousands of others directly, and indirectly without limit upon many more

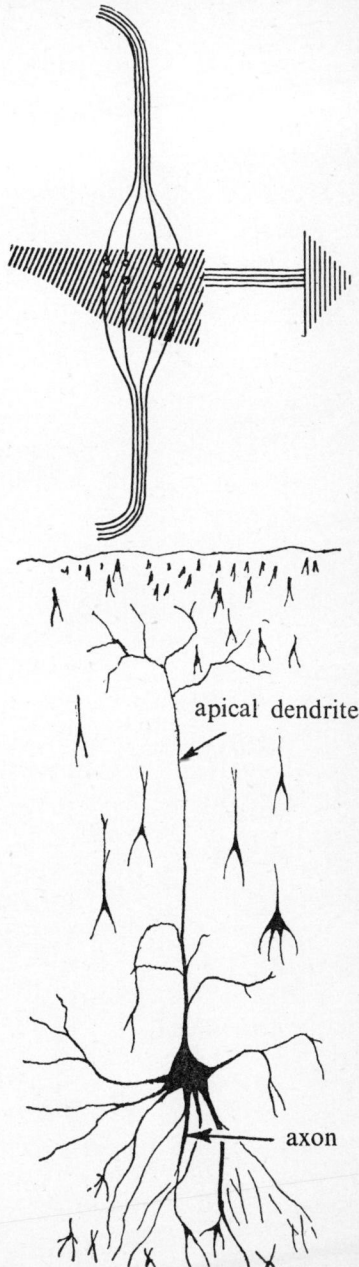

apical dendrite

axon

through neural chains. An added complication is that there are no longer any obvious terminal bulbs for the locus of interaction as was the case in the spinal nerves. Certain types of stains produce pictures showing club-like endings, but whether these are part of the neural structure or local concentrations of stain deposits is unknown. However the axon of any one cell passes close enough to the dendrites of others for interaction to take place, and it is usually assumed that the general details of the interaction are the same. The drawing at the bottom of page 187 shows a typical pyramidal cortex cell, displayed against the cortex section background.

★   ★   ★

Now to take up once again our earlier discussion on cortex neural circuitry. To summarize: The main objection to a 'switchboard' theory is that it fails to explain the relatively minor effects resulting from major brain damage. Its advantage is that it affords, as we shall see, a ready explanation for memory and other typical mental phenomena. The converse set of advantages and disadvantages holds for a theory that ignores individual nerves and their interconnections, and instead treats the cortex as if it were an isotropic and homogeneous medium, with mental phenomena explained in terms of widespread domains or fields. Intellectual behaviour would then not be qualitatively affected by many types of brain damage. Such a theory, however, offers no satisfactory explanation of the long-time persistence of memory, nor would the information-carrying capacity of such a system seem adequate for the enormous amount stored and operative in the brain. It is also difficult to understand why such a set of fields would not be seriously and irreversibly affected by the shock treatment extensively used in treating certain mental disorders.

Hebb uses a 'switchboard' theory, without insisting there is a simple one to one relation between circuits and individual mental operations. To appreciate his approach fully, it is necessary to read his book where he treats his theory in detail. He shows in it that it is possible for many neurons to combine into quite complex circuits, and for each neuron to enter into many different circuits while still keeping individual mental 'entities' distinct. It is apparent that this meets much of the objection mentioned above to the simpler form of switchboard theory. He explains memory by assuming that it is carried for a short time by a set of reverberating neuronal circuits, that 'harden' into longer lasting ones as growth or other processes take place that permit the various neurons in the chains to affect one another more easily. The principal objection to the theory is that no such growth processes have been experimentally observed, although there is some evidence that an elaboration of the dendritic processes after birth does take place.

In any event the precise details of what actually happens is not of the essence in our discussion. All that is necessary is that 'all or none' impulse transmission at synapses is in some way important in any correct theory. We will now give some simple circuits that illustrate the ideas we have been discussing.

To be fully rigorous in what follows no introspective language should be used and we should discuss the circuits entirely in physical terms. However, since their purpose is to provide a satisfactory physical analogue to 'mental' phenomena, we can make their operations more understandable if we simultaneously interpret them introspectively.

In these we will make use of established information on the stimulation, transmission, and transfer of nervous impulses at synapses. Any of these circuits could actually be constructed as part of an electrical brain (as for example some of Grey Walter's 'animals') and would exhibit the behaviour described.

★   ★   ★

We begin with a circuit which, although simple, can still demonstrate most of the phenomena of the conditioned reflex. The various nerves interact with one another at the various synaptic junctions marked J_1, J_2, J_3, J_4.

S_1 will be a certain stimulus (with a nod towards Pavlov, let it be the presentation of food to a dog) which is strong enough to act through J_1 and stimulate pulses in nerves 1 and 2. The pulse in 2 goes on through J_2 to elicit a particular response R (say the watering of the dog's mouth). The pulse in 1 is too weak to cause any effect at J_3.

S_2 (say the ringing of a bell) is another stimulus which travels as a pulse along nerve 4, but, like the pulse in 1, is not strong enough when acting alone to actuate junction J_3. We assume, however, that if S_1 and S_2 are applied simultaneously they are sufficiently strong to actuate J_3 and induce a pulse along 3 and a circulating pulse around the reverberating circuit 5-6. This pulse will continue to travel around C until it decays so much that it is unable to energize one of the synapses, J_3 or J_4.

In the first instance the application of stimulus S_2 was without any effect. However, suppose we apply S_1 and S_2 simultaneously a few times until a

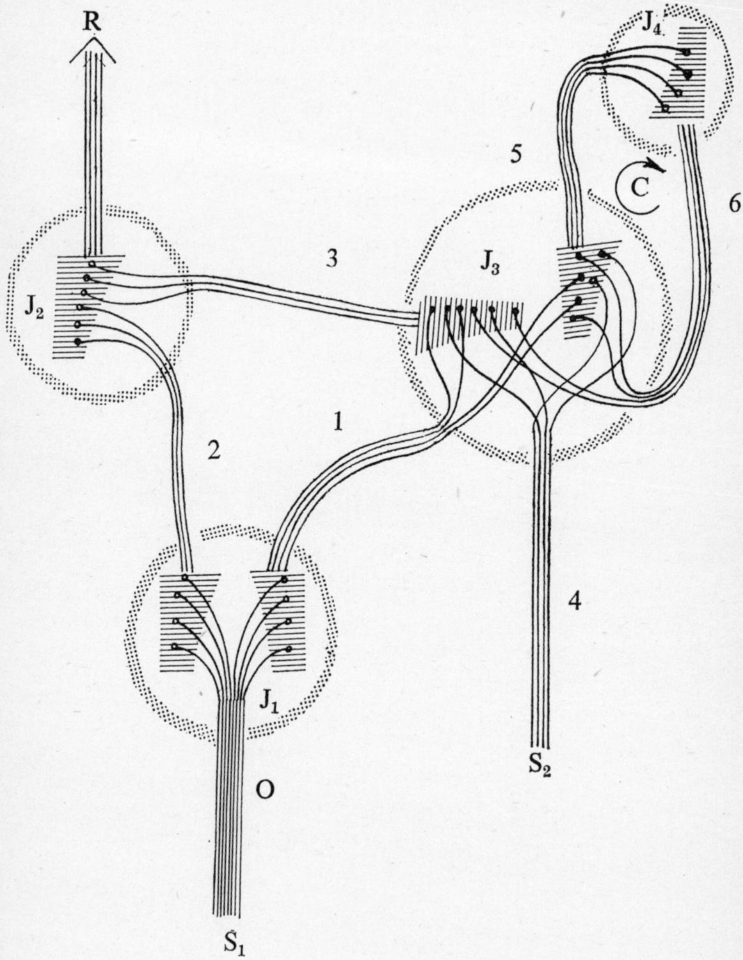
R
J$_4$
5
C
6
3
J$_3$
J$_2$
1
2
4
J$_1$
S$_2$
O
S$_1$

strong circulating pulse is built up in C. Now if S_2 is applied alone, its pulse travelling up 4 is able to combine at J_3 with the circulating pulse in C and actuate nerve 3 and through J_2 induce the same response R as initially was produced only by S_1. (The ringing of the bell now will cause the salivation that was formerly only produced by the presence of food.) Here is much of the typical phenomenon of the conditioned reflex: its being produced by an initially unrelated side stimulus; the decrease with time of the effect of the side stimulus (as the pulse in 5-6 decays and fluctuates with time); and the relative permanence of the conditioning if the primary and the secondary stimulus are applied together often enough.

* * *

In the next case we will set up a circuit which, in physical terms, displays some of the characteristics of the introspective situation in which we are endeavouring to decide between two conflicting patterns of action. Circuits C_1 and C_2 correspond to the two alternative behaviours. Instead of, as in the first case, having the various nerves add to one another's effect at junctions, we assume that C_1 inhibits C_2 at J_2 and C_2 inhibits C_1 at J_1. Introspectively, we would be aware of the two thought patterns and the responses appropriate to them, R_1 and R_2, but are unable to 'decide' which response must be made. In this we resemble the fabled donkey standing starving but immobile exactly half way between two equally attractive bales of hay. If due to some momentary fluctuation of impulse rate or to a 'remembering' of some auxiliary information M, C_2 overpowers C_1, then response R_2 will be elicited, or alternatively C_1 might overpower C_2 and R_1 would result. Thus both the typical qualitative aspects of decision making are present in even this simple circuit: the vacillation between several different choices, the introducing of additional information, and the final, often abrupt decision with a 'Well, something's got to be done'. The built-in (conscious) pathways C_1 and C_2 and information M (partly subconscious, partly conscious) correspond to influencing factors (partial causes) from genetic and earlier environmental influences.

* * *

It is not difficult to build up other circuits that would duplicate other typically mental phenomena, but the above two are sufficient to illustrate the technique required. Again we repeat that it is not pretended that the circuits correspond in any other than the most descriptive way to the

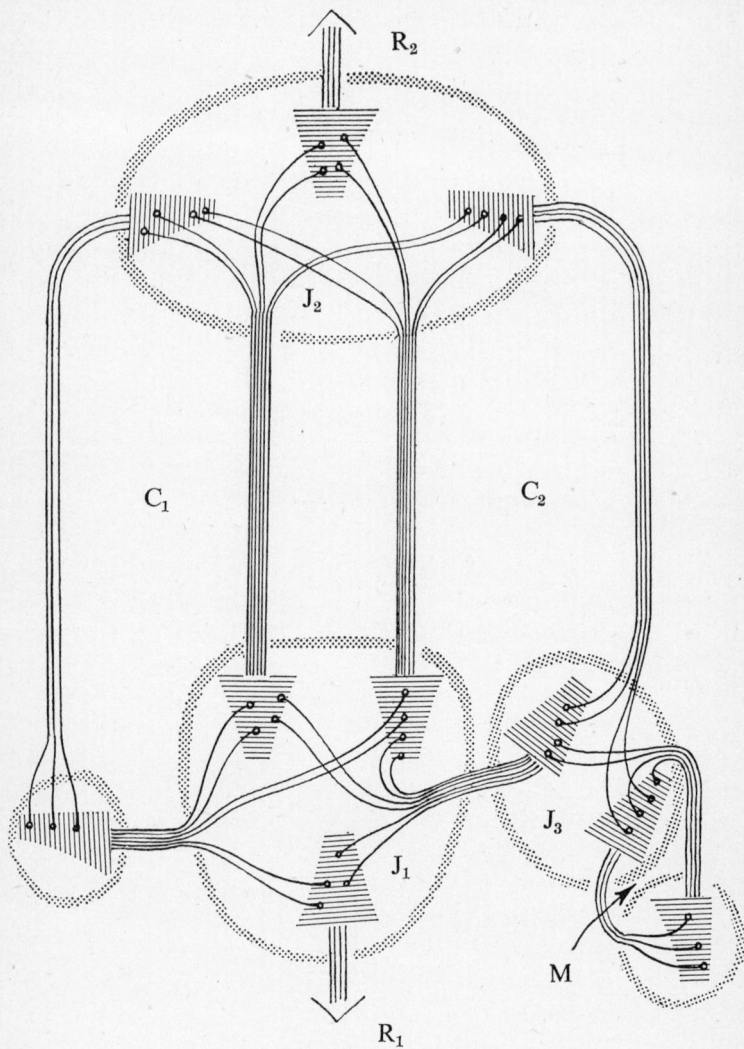

actual neural circuits involved in mental processes. However the above analysis is in keeping with what is known and scientifically demonstrable, and with our introspective appreciation of what seems to be going on when we think.

★ ★ ★

Now where does quantum uncertainty fit into all this? We have already described the stimulation of mental phenomena by the introduction of minute electrical voltages at various points in the brain. Conversely if passive pick-up probes are used, or, even more simply, electrodes connected to the skin of the head and then connected through a suitable amplifier to a cathode ray oscilloscope, they show that the brain is very active electrically. Analysis of the brain pattern produced shows that there is a basic frequency of about 10 cycles per second with a complex superimposed set of other frequencies. The very large-scale circulaing currents producing the fundamental frequency require the co-operation of vast numbers of nerves acting in concert, and the power concerned is so large that classical physics would appear to be entirely adequate for their description. In consequence, the human functions corresponding to these must be entirely determinate. Even when some special problem is being considered, and smaller groups of nerve circuits are carrying on semi-independent activities, the amount of circulating power is intermediate between the microscopic and the macroscopic, and huge numbers of ions are oscillating back and forth. It would seem then that if quantum uncertainty has any part to play it is a small one. This is undoubtedly true, the question being: does it have any role at all? The key lies in the nature of the synaptic mechanism, in the all or none nature of the response. Remember that the size of the transmitted pulse is independent of the stimulating pulse, providing only the latter is in excess of the threshold. Thus even though the absolute threshold of response is very high in comparison with the energy carried by single ions, the relative threshold must be very much smaller; and consequently when the initial pulses are of the approximate size of the threshold the response can become minutely critical as to their exact size. Small fluctuations up and down about the mean (absolute threshold) value can make the difference between a pulse being transferred or not. For the small number of microscopic entities involved in such fluctuations, Quantum Mechanics with its indeterminism is the only working theory.

Now we have restricted ourselves to extremely simple circuits that do

G

not at all do justice to Hebb's theory. However, when the systems become more complicated and more neurons are interacting the situation becomes in fact more favourable to our argument. In his book, Eccles shows how a minuscule effect at one synapse can expand to enormous dimensions. He obtains a figure of 100,000 neurons being affected in 20/1000's of a second by one such quantum uncertainty. (He goes on to apply this to a theory of a brain—immaterial mind interaction that can take place at the synapses with only an infinitesimal consumption of energy. We cannot endorse such an argument. The question is a qualitative one rather than quantitative, and a small interaction energy is no different in principle from a large one. If there is any physical interaction at all between 'mind' and body it must be accounted for inside physical theory.)

*   *   *

Thus although man is a being of macroscopic size and in consequence the majority of his actions, sensory responses, and mental decisions are largely determined by his existing physical structure and environment, there remains an irreducible residue of indeterminism. Granted it is small, but as time goes on the accumulation of indetermined aspects affect his whole structure. Thus, through strict physical control and brain-washing it may be possible to so shape a man's total being that his immediate subsequent behaviour is almost entirely predictable. Given time, however, these almost eliminated neural circuits and almost minuscule indeterminisms assume an increasingly important role. This is well known to both dictators and head-shrinkers and, by both, put to practical use.

CHAPTER VIII

The Relation between Free-will and Determinism

WE ARE at last ready to apply the analysis and the results obtained in the preceding chapters to the eternally vexing question of 'free will'. What does the term mean, and, once defined, does it 'exist'? Now although we have been able to develop a definition of 'determinism' satisfactory to a modern operationalist, one for 'free will' is much more elusive. As the words stand they seem to suggest that there should be some identifiable 'will' about which freedom might or might not be attributed. A search for any such hypothetical entity would prove to be fruitless. This is in much the same way as: though we may speak of a 'school spirit', we do not actually expect to find one roaming the corridors of the school; when we say 'I don't know what possessed him', we (that is, at least most of us) no longer believe there is a real physical possession; nor when the psychoanalyst speaks of a mental censor, is he suggesting that there is a little man hidden inside the brain inspecting all ingoing and outgoing messages. Thus, just as in the last chapter we decided against consideration of a mind which was non-material and distinct from the physically observable brain (plus nervous system, etc.), similarly we will not concern ourself with a will which is assumed to be an entity in itself. Despite the apparent obviousness of this it has not always been realized, and it has been the source of much confusion in past and even in some contemporary discussions. (As an example of this, Eccles speaks of a 'will' acting upon the brain at the synaptic junctions.)

The coupling of the expression 'free-will' with that of 'determinism' in the title to this book indicates that we consider the two to be concepts of the same functional type. Now the work of the earlier chapters has shown that 'determinism' or 'cause' is not something which is to be directly sought for and identified in immediate perceptual experience itself. If present at all, it is to be found inside the pragmatic postulational structure of a world-picture, specifying the kinds of relations that we are permitting to hold among elements of our representation of experience. When a person affirms his belief in 'determinism' what he actually means is that his semiotic world picture is structured in such a way that it is theoretically possible to make such a set of physical observations at one time, and to execute such a set of syntactic operations, that a single-valued prediction can be made for the result which would be obtained if some quantity were observed at any other time. The converse of this, 'indeterminism', denies that this can be done. In the latter system there are certain quantities, recognized as legitimate observables, for which single-valued predictions are impossible. As we have seen, Classical Physics is a system of the first, deterministic, sort, and Quantum Mechanics, the system under particular scrutiny in this book, is an example of the latter. (To complete the picture, there remains one more logical possibility for a system, namely, that no predictions whatsoever can be made, but such a system would possess no syntactic development and would be without value.) Thus, if 'free will' is a concept of the same type as 'determinism', the assertion that: 'man has "free will"' is a statement about the postulational structure of the particular semiotic in terms of which the remark is being made. We intend to show that a postulate of 'determinism' and one of 'free will' are contradictory and cannot be simultaneously part of the same total semiotic. Since there is no separate 'will' but only 'free-will' the words must always appear as a pair and we emphasize this with the hyphen.

This understood, we must move on to investigating what kind of a postulate it is. A satisfactory definition is difficult to find. So difficult in fact that some authors have been led to advocate eliminating the word 'free-will' from respectable philosophical discourse; and others have defined it in such a way that, although clear and comprehensible, it has had its meaning stretched so far from its street usage that the ordinary man would hardly recognize it. Neither of these courses is acceptable. 'Free-will' is a part of our language at all levels from the street to the pulpit and will continue to be used. It is the necessary job of the philosopher to make its meaning clear. Next, where it is possible, a term should be defined in a way in keeping with its common-sense significance and this we must try to do with 'free-will'. Now, though the average man would have some considerable difficulty if asked to define the term in itself, he and his fellows understand what is meant when he says that he did something 'of my own free-will', particularly when this is asserted rather than its contrary: 'I did it, but it wasn't of my own free-will'. If we investigate, we will find that in instances of the first type there were a number of alternative decisions that the performer of the action considers are possible ones that he might have done instead of the actual one selected, and he, in consequence, accepts some measure of personal responsibility for the particular one chosen. In the second type there were no alternatives he recognizes as feasible and he refuses responsibility. We see in this opposition between multiple and single choice at least a superficial resemblance to the contrast between the indeterminism of Quantum Mechanics and the determinism of Classical Physics.

*   *   *

Before going any further it is necessary to split the field of investigation into two distinct but interrelated parts: (1) 'I', as a thinking, feeling, being, introspectively directly aware of my own thoughts and decisions, and (2) the Universe minus 'I', the external world looking at the being from the outside and in continuous interaction with him through his physical body and sense organs. Each of these parts must be considered separately, and in the study of free-will quite a different brand of evidence must be considered in the two cases. Thus, in the last chapter, when we were studying man biologically, we were looking at him from the outside. We were trying to decide if Laplace's Omniscient God, with complete knowledge of all the laws of the Universe and maximal knowledge of the state of the environment and of the physically observable man, could exactly predict every aspect of his development. This is a quite different situation from the individual looking out at the world and wondering to what extent he is correct in believing that he is 'free'.

When we are considering man from the point of view of the external observer we will be using his terms: the language of science. In this latter we have the benefit of an extreme precision that permits us to be most clear in our analysis. This however must not be allowed to blind us to the fact that analysis using only science tends to deprive man of much that is uniquely his as a living and self-conscious being. The point of view of the self-conscious individual is essential and complementary to that of the scientist, although when we use it nothing like the same precision of analysis is possible. Words have to be used in an implicatory, almost poetic way, and it is hopeless to aim at equivalent exactitude. Here we are using the language of 'introspection'.

Much discusssion has taken place during the first half of this century about the acceptability of introspective 'evidence'. Some schools of psychology have exalted it above all other and have developed very precise methods of obtaining reliable results using introspection. Other schools have denied that there is any value in it at all and turned all their attention to observation of 'external' behaviour. Now the work we have been doing throughout this book shows that there is no real difference between the two kinds. They are both part of our continuum of experience and there is no absolute way of drawing a line between them. It happens that physical science has concentrated its attention on the one kind and has achieved spectacular success with it but only at the expense of ignoring an enormous part of our experience. We will consider the two as equally valid, but hold in mind the extreme difficulty in establishing criteria of reliability for the personal kind of evidence.

★   ★   ★

We turn for awhile to the introspective 'I'. It is immediately evident that this 'I' of considerations and decisions, of desires, compulsions and duties, of things remembered and things forgotten, is made up of two components. There is the component of which I am consciously aware, in which pros and cons are being argued, and in which decisions are being made. But this is only a very small part of the total 'I'. There is another much vaster subconscious 'I' from which memories and ideas emerge, and into which they disappear. To some extent, material present in this second part is available to the conscious 'I', and with an effort, sometimes small, sometimes large, information can be extracted for inspection and use. However it is never totally under 'my' conscious control, and the inability to call up a certain item can be most tantalizing: 'It's just on the tip of my tongue'. However it is all very much part of the total 'I', and twentieth-century psychoanalysis has revealed the enormous influence of the subconscious upon decisions arrived at in the surface, conscious 'I'. An illuminating analogy can be made with a pool of dark water. From outside only the constantly changing surface is evident, but little currents and bubbles keep disturbing the surface, and a vigorous stirring will dredge up long-forgotten things.

When 'I' am confronted with a decision-requiring situation 'I' can only work with whatever is present in the conscious and what can be readily brought there and continuously 'kept in mind'. When I examine the components making up many such situations 'I' feel that only one choice is a real possibility. 'I' want to play with the moon but all my efforts or tears are of no avail. 'I' cannot have my cake and eat it too. 'I' want to go swimming but my mother tells me and insists that the garden must be weeded. 'I' must write 'A noun is the name of a person, place, or thing' one hundred times on the blackboard before going home. 'I' have no money; 'I' want to eat; the only job available is ditch-digging;

therefore 'I' shall dig ditches. 'I' am vitally concerned about whether 'I' am a mechanical automaton following a preordained path through my space-time future, or whether 'I' possess some measure of self-origination, so 'I' must read, study, and write this book to clarify my thoughts.

There is another large class of situations in which the nature of my decision does not appear nearly so inevitable, and the more 'I' dig into the pros and cons of the various alternatives the more difficult the choice becomes. ('Decisions, decisions, always decisions'.) Do 'I' read my newly bought Theodore Sturgeon's *E Pluribus Unicorn*, or bicycle to the beach for a swim?—

Sturgeon is my favourite science fiction author.

Lorna will probably be at the beach in her much talked about bikini.

The house is cool and it is hot outside.

But the lake will be cool.

It will be hot riding back home at 5 in the afternoon when the sun will be in my face.

But anyway the house will have become unbearably stuffy by 5.

. . . .

If I stay home I may get one of these boring house jobs to do.

. . . .

. . . .

The advantages and disadvantages on each side can be so extensive that in many instances there is no immediately obvious relative preponderance, and the process of arriving at a decision can be drawn out and even painful; so much so, that in some cases it can result in a truly neurotic state. However, a decision must be made, additional factors are taken into account. The old ones are re-examined and new relative weighting factors are introduced. If all this fails to decide the issue I may actually or 'mentally' flip a coin. My actual decision seems to be dictated neither by external influences nor internal predisposition, and certainly the process of decision-making does not resemble what we ordinarily associate with that of a machine, no matter how complicated.

Instead of a conflict of desires there may be one of duties. Take Sartre's man of the French Resistance: Should he stay home to look after his mother, for whom he was the sole support and who would undoubtably perish if he left her, or should he join the underground and fight for the liberation of France? He finds it difficult to decide which is his higher duty, and neither decision will completely satisfy his conscience. For the existentialists it is important for man to seize mental hold of such decision-requiring situations, to recognize the possibility of making any one of a set of alternate choices, rather than simply blindly following behaviour patterns imposed upon him by his immediate or previous environment. The more this is done in the 'despair and anguish of searching for the truly "right" choice', the more man is becoming truly 'sapiens'. This notion of taking over into consciousness a large part of our behaviour which is normally reflex and involuntary is contemporarily being exalted by some groups into a full-fledged philosophy of action. They devise methods of exercising their sense of 'free-choice' analogous to the ways physiotherapists exercise muscles.

It is doubtful that most of us would feel inclined to go so far but it does seem to be true, at least for the majority, that there occur many situations in which we feel it legitimate to say not only that 'I' am making the decision, but that my decision is, within certain limitations, a 'free' one. Though my decision is restricted by the state of my present external surroundings, and though my desires and sense of duty have been developed under the influence of all my past environment, my decision is not totally dictated by them. That if several identical 'I's' with identical previous histories had arrived at the same situation, in general they would make different decisions. In looking back over instances of past alternative choice situations 'I' feel that it would have been entirely possible for me to have chosen differently, and that an advance prediction of the actual decision would have been impossible for me or for any outside observer no matter how omniscient he might have been. The unpredictability and the freedom of choice is the important aspect, even if it is only the freedom to choose to flip a coin and abide by the result.

When there is a question of responsibility, of guilt, of blame or praise, 'I' differentiate sharply between the two classes of situation. In the first class, such as deciding between digging ditches or starving, 'I' admit that it was 'I' who 'decided' to carry out a certain behaviour but insist that there was no real choice. If ditch-digging coarsens my hands so that 'I' become unable to perform an emergency operation which 'I' otherwise could have done and 'I' am accused, 'I' shrug my shoulders—'What else could I do?' 'I' would give the same response if 'I' am praised for taking the menial job of ditch-digging. In the second, on the other hand, where there is the possibility of choosing one from a number of real alternatives, 'I' feel liable to praise or blame. If 'I' go to the beach and develop a bad sun burn on the way home 'I have only myself to blame'. Sartre's hero is excruciatingly aware of his responsibility and will never be satisfied with his choice, no matter which one he makes, whether in favour of filial fidelity or of patriotism. If there is a conflict between desires and legal or moral duty, 'I' admit personal responsibility and the reasonableness of punishment or commendation if 'I' make the wrong decision. Now, particularly in cases where there was a lack of sufficient information which would have aided in making the 'right' choice, the situation can become vastly more complicated than this; but in essence it remains the same: Is more than one choice a real possibility?

*   *   *

The two classes really merge rather smoothly, and whereas at the extremes it is easy to separate decision situations into one or the other, there is a large middle area where differentiation is very difficult. In attempting to analyse the distinguishing characteristics we recognize a number of limitations upon real choice. The most obvious ones are logical ones. Thus 'I' cannot 'decide' to be in Montreal for Christmas dinner with my parents and also be in Toronto with my wife's parents (although it is possible for me to be present symbolically through a telegram). Next there are physical restrictions. 'I' cannot be tall and wear standard size clothes. 'I' cannot 'decide' to swim under water for an hour without any artificial breathing equipment. 'I' cannot 'decide' to jump over the moon. There is no sense in my 'deciding' to clear by hand a 100 acre farm of stumps this afternoon. There are further physiological restrictions peculiar to the individual. The blind man cannot 'decide' to see a movie, the deaf man to listen to David Oistrakh playing the Khatchaturian violin concerto, or the double amputee to run a 100 yards dash in record time. Each situation will have in addition to these general limitations a number peculiar to the individual case which can be additionally restrictive. Thus if 'I' am gagged 'I' cannot shout a warning to my friend about to enter a trap, nor can 'I' warn him telepathically. However, possibly 'I' can at least alert him by kicking on the floor. If 'I' am thoroughly bound as well as gagged 'I' cannot kick the floor, but possibly 'I' can attract his attention by some other means. If all of these fail 'I' do not feel responsible.

The sum total of all these restrictions, both general and specific, limits the number of different actions 'I' can in fact perform, and in consequence my effective freedom of choice. We have thus an opposition between immediate external compulsion and my self-origination of behaviour, my freedom, in any situation.

*   *   *

For Schlick and a number of philosophers following him this is the end
of the story as far as 'freedom' is concerned. For them a free act is a non-
compelled act. This permits them a simultaneous belief in determinism and
freedom. They believe that the total past space-time environment determines uniquely the choice the individual will make in any situation, but
that so long as the sum total of all immediate compulsions acting upon
him leave a variety of paths open to him, he is free. Now certainly freedom
from absolute external constraint is a necessary condition for feeling
'free', as the word is understood by common-sense man, but it is not nearly
a sufficient condition. Past environmental compulsions acting upon the
individual have modified his psychological constitution and are extended
in fact into the present through this modification. This is an exact analogy
to modifications in his physical constitution. We admit that a past physical accident resulting, say, in an amputation inhibits a man's present
ability to run a 100 yards dash. This accident although years in the past
acts as a contemporary compulsion. Similarly there is little effective
difference between a dog's refusing to go into a car because someone
inside is threatening him with a whip (present compulsion), and his refusing because every time he had tried to take a ride in the past he had
been whipped (past compulsion).

*   *   *

Psychology has enormously extended our awareness of the effect of
apparently totally forgotten earlier events and wishes. ' "A dozen times
Hamlet could have killed Claudius easily; but every time Hamlet decided
not to." A free choice moralist would say . . . (since no immediate compulsion or general limitations prevented the killing) . . . but no, listen to the
super-ego: "What you feel such hatred towards your uncle for, what you
are plotting to kill him for, is precisely the crime which you yourself
desired to commit: to kill your father and replace him in the affections
of your mother". Consciously all he knows is that he is unable to act;
this conscious inability he rationalizes giving a different excuse each time.'
(Hosper, *Free Will and Psychoanalysis.*)

   Whether or not we are willing to accept such a psychoanalytic dredging
into the past for causes, we are still forced to admit past compulsions to an
equal footing with contemporary restrictions in limiting our freedom
of choice in a given situation. When 'I' have an introspective feeling that
'I' can exercise my own free-will, that not only the decision but also the
choice 'I' am making is in some sense my own, 'I' am asserting my belief
that the sum total of all compulsions, present and past, has not been suf-

ficient to reduce the number of real alternate choices 'I' may make to one, and that no external observer, no matter how 'omniscient,' can consistently make accurate advance predictions of my actual choices.

* * *

Now although there is no doubt that an introspective belief in their personal free-will is held by a majority of people, at least at the common-sense level, there is equally no doubt that most of us have from time to time the nagging fear that this apparent free-will may be an illusion; that if we had a more complete view of the totality of all compulsions acting upon us, we would see that in actuality there is only one course of action open in each situation, and our apparent freedom is only a result of our necessarily incomplete knowledge of the real state of affairs. Whether this is so or not can never be discovered by direct personal introspection, and, in fact, all our previous analysis has led to the conclusion that the 'real' state of affairs is fundamentally unknowable. However this latter is characteristic of all parts of 'human knowledge', and it has not hindered us elsewhere from building up the best possible world picture compatible with the manifold aspects of experience. In any event there are additional sources of evidence which may at least bolster up or deflate our internally based belief in free-will. We turn to consider much more generally the way in which the environment acts upon the individual. Instead of making use of introspective evidence we must investigate the structure of physical and biological theory in its description of the behaviour of the human animal in interaction with his environment. This requires a shift in viewpoint from the individual introspectively aware of the considerations involved in working through to a particular decision to an external observer studying the individual and his actions from the outside.

Now the earlier chapters of this book have been devoted to a study of the sort of prediction such an external observer is able to make. Let us remind ourselves of some of the results obtained there.

(1) When we talk about 'reality' we are in fact discussing a certain conceptual scheme held by some individual and used by him to organize his experiences into a consistent picture. The 'reality' we are working with in this book includes the theoretical structure of science as it exists today.

(2) When we talk about determinism or indeterminism we are not discussing some aspect of experience itself. Rather we are examining the postulational structure of our 'reality'. To say that science is deterministic or indeterministic is to say that its semantic and syntactic structure

is so constructed that its predictions for the future values of observables are respectively a single value or a set of possible values. The question is not whether in every case enough information can in practice be gathered to make a detailed prediction, but rather whether it is possible in principle. Of course a good theory is one whose predictions can be checked and have been repeatedly verified by past observations.

(3) A theory is always tested as a whole and not in part. This means one cannot test for determinism or indeterminism directly. The test would be between two total theories, one of them deterministic and the other indeterministic.

(4) Physical theory as it exists today is indeterministic at the microscopic level but deterministic at the inanimate macroscopic level. In its entirety then it must be considered to be indeterministic.

(5) Man, although in size a phenomenon belonging to the macroscopic level, is affected by certain divergent chain reactions emanating from microscopic-sized events. This means that the bulk of his behaviour is predictable and deterministic but there is an irreducible residue of unpredictability. Though this is in general very small, over a long period of time these small indeterminacies can cumulate to make very large-scale divergencies from a determinate pattern.

*　*　*

Before going on to applying these findings to the question of free-will it is necessary to clear up a misunderstanding of quantum indeterminacy which has been responsible for much of the confusion in many contemporary discussions of the indeterminism—free-will problem, namely the equating of indeterminism with chance. The reason for this mistake is obvious enough. Probabilistic reasoning with its resultant multiple-valued statistical predictions had its historical origin in the analysis of games of chance—cards, roulette, racing, and so on—and it is certainly true that we can assert the logical proposition 8.1. Now if indeterminism and chance are simply different words for the same thing it would be necessary for proposition 8.2 also to be true. First we must note that 8.2 cannot be logically derived from 8.1. The proposition actually derivable from 8.1 is its logical contrapositive 8.1c, some-

$$\text{Chance} \longrightarrow \text{Indeterminism} \ldots 8.1$$

This does *not* mean that:

$$\text{Indeterminism} \longrightarrow \text{Chance}. \ldots 8.2$$

8.1 is equivalent to:

$$\text{Determinism} \longrightarrow \text{No Chance} . 8.1c$$

('$\longrightarrow$' stands for 'implies')

thing not at all resembling 8.2. Second we note that there are a number of phenomenological instances in which an indeterministic theory does not imply chance. One example has already been discussed in earlier chapters: the classical theory of Brownian Motion. In the theoretical description of this no attempt is made at a detailed tracing out of the path of the Brownian particle. Only a statistical prediction is made. and the typical one is the square of the distance travelled by the average particle in a given time. Although the final prediction is statistical, and we have to recognize that the exact position of the Brownian particle is indetermined inside the theory, this does not imply that the mechanism responsible for the motion is one of chance. The classical assumption is that the particle's motion is really determined by the interaction between the particle and the molecules making up the gas, and it is only the mechanical unfeasibility of carrying out the complex analysis required that makes exact deterministic type predictions impossible. (Actually a similar argument can be applied to games of 'chance' but the justification of it is much more open to dispute.) When we move on to the problem of deriving the gas laws on the basis of Kinetic Theory the large-scale theory becomes once more deterministic.

Though we will not take the time to show it, we note that either of these two results—Brownian motion or the gas laws—can also be derived using quantum statistical mechanics, which, in contrast to the classical theory, assumes that the fundamental entities are indetermined in their motions. Thus a super theory may be deterministic or indeterministic, and in either case be based upon a more fundamental theory which may be equally well either deterministic or indeterministic.

To sum up, the fact that modern physical theory in the division of quantum mechanics is indeterministic does not in any way imply that the phenomena being investigated—and this applies to our subject under particular investigation, man—is 'ruled only by chance'. At the more fundamental level it may be or it may not be, but there is no way of knowing which is the case from a study of the nature of the super theory.

* * *

We will have to be most careful about how we apply these results to the question of free-will. To help us in seeing how this must be done let us examine what we would have said if the scientific results had been different; that is, if we had decided that our present-day scientific conceptual system was deterministic. This would mean that an external observer, knowing the totality of the environment's action upon the individual from the day of his birth to the moment of decision, and knowing the instantaneous state of the environment, could predict exactly (in theory, though only approximately in present-day practice) what action the individual would make. What is more, he could in principle make this entire prediction 37 years earlier at the time of the individual's birth.

> 'Yea, the first morn of creation wrote
> What the last eve of reckoning shall read.'

If this were the case it would seem to be nonsense to speak of any free-will. However a strong group of philosophers have attempted to maintain the possibility of human free-will while simultaneously accepting rigidly deterministic laws.

As a contemporary example of this we have Moritz Schlick. He begins with the argument that we must distinguish between descriptive and prescriptive laws. Though the laws of science that describe the world of phenomena may be deterministic in the sense considered earlier, he points out that they are not prescriptive laws. They do not actually compel an individual to act in a certain way, they only describe the particular succession of acts in which he will be involved. Since, for Schlick, 'being free' is equivalent to having freedom from immediate external compulsion, the individual can be free (notice he doesn't thereby automatically prove him free) regardless of whether the laws are deterministic or not.

Now on the first part of this we agree. One of the tasks of all our analysis has been to show that scientific laws are not 'laws' in any judicial sense. They are simply formulae (ideally) isomorphic with our perceptual experience and, if our semiotic is a good one, well-proved by many checks and predictions, we expect experience to follow the same pattern as the laws. If the laws are deterministic then we expect certain types of experience to follow others unvaryingly, but in no sense do the 'laws' compel the particular succession observed. 'Prescription' is a carry over of 'moral' cause from the child or the savage. Confusion would be avoided if the 'laws' were called by one of the less emotionally loaded alternate names: 'hypotheses', 'postulates', 'axioms', 'premises', etc.

Now while we agree with Schlick about the descriptive nature of 'law' we begin to part company with him when he goes on to discuss 'freedom' and its equation with 'being free'. Implicit in his analysis is the belief that 'being free' is a percept coming directly from our experiences, and, in consequence, being something quite different in its nature from 'law'. If this were true then his argument would have more force, but in fact the two—'being free,' and 'law'—are the same sort of semiotic elements: relational postulates belonging inside the pragmatic part of a theory and without any direct phenomenal denotata in themselves. Thus it is clear that the idea of 'prescription' is as inapplicable to the concept of 'being free' as it is to 'law'. Both of the latter are descriptive. Since it is logically essential that the various postulates inside a pragmatic be consistent with one another it is entirely possible for 'determinism' to prohibit 'being free', and much of the argument of this chapter is devoted to showing that this is the case.

The general argument demonstrating it is clear. 'Determinism' means that a sufficiently complete knowledge of the state of things at one instant permits a precise prediction to be made for the state at some other time; while our discussion of the introspective meaning of 'free-will' has shown that an individual believing in it believes that there exist not only a set of alternate actions physically possible for him in a given situation within the restrictions of his immediate environment, but also the possibility of his psychologically being able to choose any one of them, and the impossibility of any outside observer, no matter how knowledgeable, unvaryingly predicting his particular subsequent course of action in advance. The question arises of course most commonly in connection with the relationship between man and his actions, and an omniscient God. Common-sense man ordinarily finds it difficult to understand how he can be held accountable, labelled a sinner, and punished for behaviour which God knew far in advance that he would execute:

> 'Oh Thou who didst with pitfall and with gin,
> Beset the road I was to wander in;
> How now with predestination round enmesh me,
> And then impute my fall to sin.'

The two seem clearly to be incompatible.

However it is valuable to consider a particular problem and at the same time study an earlier expression of the compatibility argument. We turn to Leibnitz who adopts a solution parallel to that of Schlick. We quote Leibnitz: 'I am at liberty either to make or not make a journey, for though it is involved in my concept that I will make it, it is also involved that I will make it freely'. This can be translated into Schlick's terms to read: God knows that the journey will be made (descriptive law), but

does not actually force me to make it (which would amount to the application of compulsion—prescription. This is one of our earlier listed classes
of cause: Moral). Let us now analyse this proposition. We begin by simultaneously premising God's universal knowledge (equivalent to asserting
the accuracy of the descriptive laws), and also the principle of free choice
for the individual. We assume that God in his omniscience knows that I
will make the journey. We also assume that I, exercising my 'freedom' of
choice, choose not to make it. There are two possibilities: The first, I do
not make the journey. If this is the case then God was wrong and we have
violated the premise of God's omniscience. The second, I do make the
journey, despite my choice not to. In this case my choice had no resultant
expression in action, the postulate of free alternate choices led to an
incorrect prediction, and my belief in being free was wrong. In either case
we violate one of our fundamental premises. Thus a simultaneous belief
in 'determinism' and 'free-will', in the sense in which a common-sense
man would use the latter, results in an inconsistent pragmatic, and the
two beliefs cannot form part of the same world picture.

★   ★   ★

It is worth while considering another version of the argument for the
compatibility of Determinism and Free-Will. This has been given by
D. M. MacKay. He begins with the twin assumptions: that an individual's
observable mental and physical processes are determinate, and that
a fully informed observer can, in consequence, know the outcome
of the individual's considerations before they are made. He then goes
on to deal with the difficulty that appears if an attempt is made to communicate the prediction to the observee. He shows that in certain cases its
communication can interact so strongly with the individual's brain processes as to invalidate the prediction.

Let us consider a simple example of how this might happen. We assume
that events are physically determinate, that an optimally fully informed
observer is carrying out the calculation, and take for our subject an
individual whose behaviour is dominated by contrasuggestibility. Now a
little reflection should convince the reader that it is impossible for the
observer to work out a prediction for a future action (take some simple
question like 'Will he eat pork chops or pork sausages for supper'), tell
it to the observee and have the prediction confirmed. Of course there is no
difficulty, assuming determinism, in making a correct prediction and

having it confirmed, providing the observer keeps the prediction strictly to himself. He could even theoretically take into account the chain of brain processes the contrasuggestible subject will follow while thinking about what the observer is thinking. Nor is there any difficulty in ensuring that the subject would carry out a specific action. All that is necessary for this is to make the (lying) statement to him that: 'The prediction is that he will carry out action A', and the observer can be certain that he will carry out the opposite.

Note that it is not always true that a valid prediction cannot be communicated. The simplest example of this would occur with the extremely suggestible subject. Even though his thought processes are interfered with as strongly as in the first case there is no problem in telling him a valid prediction. In fact you cannot, within already mentioned limits, tell him an invalid one.

Thus we can see that under certain circumstances it is impossible for an observer however 'omniscient' to tell an individual, whose behaviour is deterministic, what his future actions will be and be certain that the predictions will come true. Now, this is really not at all surprising. We are involved here with an instance of observer-observee interaction in some ways analogous to the situation in microscopic physics. In the latter case, the nature of our world picture made it impossible to reduce the effect of this interaction to zero, and we were forced to give up the hope of finding a deterministic description of the events concerned. The situation is different in MacKay's example in that we are voluntarily introducing an interaction. The result, however, will be the same. The two, observer and observee, can no longer be considered separately; only the joint state exists. Thus one of the initial premises is violated, namely, that the observee is a deterministic system, in himself, and MacKay's argument breaks down.

Notice that there is no difficulty in restoring determinism if we consider the first pair as constituting a super-system, and we introduce a new non-interacting external observer. In this case we recognize that the first 'prediction' was in reality only a communication passing between the initial observer and observee and, in consequence, simply constitutes part of the phenomena for the super-observer. The apparent paradox has been fully resolved.

However, there is more to learn from MacKay's argument. Accepting the necessity of preventing the individual from coming to know what the prediction is until after the event, MacKay goes on: 'Since in general

H

the individual has nothing to learn from the onlooker that is predictively valid for him, any purported prediction of his choices as 'certain' is logically indeterminate until he actually makes it'.

Now there is no doubt that MacKay has made an important point which resembles in a way some of our earlier arguments. The observer and the observee, though they are concerned with the same situation and meet on the common ground of talk and action, work with entirely different sets of facts and evidence when they are discussing the observee's own mental processes, and there is certain 'evidence' which is distinctive to each and cannot be held in common. However they do meet on the plane of physical action, and the purpose of each of their considerations is to establish a relation between certain initial physical circumstances and a future physical event. Once this is realized we can see that we are up against a variation of the Leibnitz-Schlick argument. The external observer's calculations (held private so they do not bring about an uncontrollable interaction with the individual's mental processes) correspond to the descriptive laws we were discussing there, and the fully informed observer to God. Our previous argument, that if the individual is really free it must be possible for him to make a choice contrary to that predicted, applies. Since such a contrary choice would violate the initial determinist assumption that the observer can make an accurate private prediction, we see that the individual in fact can only make the one choice. A freedom in which only one choice is possible is no freedom at all.

*　*　*

Thus we have decided that if our conceptual world picture included the postulate that the environment totally determined the individual and his actions, we would certainly deny that there is any real sense in which the individual can be said to 'possess' free-will. Let us express the above proposition in logical terms. It would be written: 'Determinism', 'D', implies 'No Free-will', '$\bar{F}$'. (The bar through the F will stand for the negation of the quantity; and similarly '$\bar{D}$' will stand for the opposite of determinism: indeterminism.) Equation 8.3 shows the proposition in symbolic form. However, the analysis carried out in the earlier chapters has shown that our contemporary scientific world picture requires that man's behaviour be considered to be (to a small extent) indeterministic. To decide what is the implication of this it is necessary to use the established proposition 8.3 to derive a proposition that contains

'Indeterminism' as one of its elements.

Now the problem would be solved quite simply if it were logically permissible to take the negative of both terms in 8.3 and obtain equation 8.4. This reads that 'Indeterminism' implies 'Free-will'. Unfortunately the procedure is logically invalid. The way in which one obtains the desired proposition containing 'D̄' from 8.3 is to take what is called its logical contrapositive. This amounts to negating both terms and inverting the order. The result is equation 8.3c. The reader can verify that 8.3 and 8.3c are logically equivalent by constructing a truth table for both propositions and showing that they have the same set of ultimate truth values. This is shown in the table on the right hand side of the page.

In words, the proposition 8.3c that we have been looking for reads: 'Free-will', 'F', implies 'Indeterminism', 'D̄'. We have now to interpret this result.

Our truth table will help in this.

$$D \longrightarrow \bar{F} \quad \dots \dots \dots \dots \dots 8.3$$

From 8.3 one can *not* derive:

$$\bar{D} \longrightarrow F \quad \dots \dots \dots \dots \dots 8.4$$

$$F \longrightarrow \bar{D} \quad \dots \quad 8.3c$$

	D	F	$D \rightarrow \bar{F}$	$F \rightarrow \bar{D}$
	t	t	f	f
	t	f	t	t
*	f	t	t	t
†	f	f	t	t

t stands for 'true'

f stands for 'false'

It shows that wherever free-will exists indeterminism will also be present (note the line marked with an asterisk in the truth table, but the converse is not true—indeterminism may hold without free-will being also present (note the line marked with a † in the truth table). In other words, our argument has demonstrated that indeterminism is a necessary but not sufficient condition for free-will. Spelled out in more detail: for the maximally (in terms of the theoretical possibilities) omniscient and omnipotent external oberver a necessary criterion that an entity under investigation by him be describable as exercising free-will is that regard-

less of the amount of theoretical and technical equipment he may bring
to bear upon it there is an irreducible indeterminism, and consequently
unpredictability and uncontrollability, in its behaviour. Remember, as
we have explained earlier in this chapter, this does not imply that in any
absolute way the entity's behaviour is 'governed by chance'. It means
that the contemporary world picture for the external observer limits him
in his description of an observee's behaviour to calculating a set of
alternative possible behaviours and giving the probability for each of
these. There is no reference at all to the chance or non-chance characteristics of any fundamental mechanism. In particular, the introspective
considerations of the subject are entirely outside the scope of his analysis.

We have established that indeterminism is a necessary condition for
free-will. To see that it is not a sufficient condition we can take some
simple examples: the space-time motion of an electron through a set of
slits is undetermined, the path of an atlas rocket leaving Cape Cana-
veral on its peaceful intercontinental ballistic missile path is determined,
according to our present-day physical theories. However, in the first case
we would not speak of the electron's free-will, nor in the second would
anyone be concerned about the rocket's lack of free-will. The reasons are
quite simply that one just doesn't use such a category of description with
reference to such entities.

A second necessary condition for free-will then is that the entity under
investigation be one about which free-will might or might not be legitimately attributed according to our prevailing world picture. In this,
electrons and rockets would be excluded. As better and more 'introspective' mechanical 'brains' are developed it may become difficult to decide
exactly where to draw the line, but for the moment we can certainly
restrict our free-will consideration to living entities. In most semiotics it is
further limited to animals, and often to human beings alone. There is no
point in entering into any discussion as to the range of applicability of the
concept 'free-will'. It is sufficient to agree that it is applicable to man.

★   ★   ★

We will not attempt to derive other necessary conditions for free-will.
The two, indeterminism and applicability, are the principal ones. These
are both satisfied for the world picture we have been developing in
this book, and in consequence our external observer is justified in con-
ceding free-will to man.

Now notice that this does not in any absolute way assert that man has free-will. It merely admits the possibility. This may seem to be a very small conclusion after so much work. And yet this result is of considerable importance. Let us see why: The ordinary common-sense man has always had a belief in his personal free-will and, as soon as he acquired some knowledge of philosophy and theology with its concept of a superhuman God, has also usually become concerned with the validity of his belief. Up to the seventeenth century this validity was not really denied. Though Christian theology might talk about an omniscient and omnipotent supreme being, it was a highly abstract theory. At the practical level the churches acted as if man did possess free-will and hence was responsible for his sins. The situation changed with the development during the seventeenth, eighteenth, and nineteenth centuries of physical science. Here for the first time in the history of man's thought appeared a rigorously deterministic theory, extending its range of application in all directions without encountering any apparently insurmountable obstacle; and by the middle of the nineteenth century there was every good reason to believe it would be eventually extended to a detailed description of man himself. What to do with man's belief in free-will when considered against the background of a universal deterministic physics? The continuing success of physics resulted in the abandonment of any direct attacks upon its determinism. Instead, efforts were made in the direction either of arguing that man was more than a purely physical being, and that consequently his behaviour would not be entirely explicable in physical terms, or of showing that physical determinism was compatible wth human free-will. Part of our efforts throughout this book have been devoted to eliminating these possibilities. The fact is that man's belief in his free-will seemed to have become untenable.

This then is the significance of our discussion in this book. In contrast to nineteenth-century physics and the world picture based upon it which denied the possibility of free-will for man, the new physics reopens the question. When common-sense man, with his introspective belief in free-will, now turns to science for an opinion he receives an entirely new answer. Modern physics, while being unable to prove that he has free-will, at least now concedes the possibility. In general then, a contemporary world picture including both our immediate introspective understanding of what goes on in our mind when we are involved in making decisions, and modern science, is justified in including the concept of 'free-will'.

*   *   *

The argument has now been completed but a few comments on it still need to be made.

For the first, we must note that 'free-will' has not been defined in anything like so satisfactory a way as was possible for 'determinism' and 'indeterminism'. Like these latter, 'free-will' is a relational concept, and can only be defined by showing how it is used to combine simpler concepts to produce meaningful statements. This made definition difficult enough for 'determinism', where we had the advantage of the explicitly organized semiotic of Physical Science. With 'free-will', we are dealing with a concept existing entirely within the semiotic formed around our introspective common-sense-language world picture. In this realm of discourse nothing like the same precision is possible. Much more could undoubtedly be done than we have attempted. For the argument of this book it is sufficient to establish that an essential part of a maintenance of 'free-will' is a belief in the essential unpredictability of one's actions.

Next, since we agree with Karl Popper that an essential characteristic of any useful theory is its refutability, let us state the grounds on which our argument might be rejected. Since we have not been developing a theory about Nature, our theory cannot be tested at the perceptual observational level. Rather, we have been analysing theories; in particular, the structure of Physics, the structure of our common-sense world picture, and the relationship that does or should hold between the two. Thus, rejection requires quarrelling with our analysis, our definitions, or our logic. This can most certainly be done.

Finally, it may very rightly be asked what is the pragmatic usefulness of it all? There are two aspects to this. Firstly, we have shown that the schizophrenia existing in a simultaneous belief in 'free-will' and the universal applicability of Physical Science, which was inherent in the status of nineteenth-century science, has vanished with the development of the science of this century. Secondly, without attempting to document the evidence, the author feels that there is a difference in the behaviour of people which is functional upon their belief in 'free-will' or upon its opposite (which might be taken to be 'fatalism' or something similar). The 'free-willer' tends to be aggressive in his relation to the world, treats it as something to be comprehended, manipulated, and dominated. His opposite number tends rather to accept the world and events as they come. The contrast is most obvious in the up-to-now Oriental attitude and that of the west, particularly as the latter has developed since the Renaissance.

We will not dare any evaluation of the relative merits of the two approaches. Western Science has produced encyclopedias of factual and organised knowledge, and has amply demonstrated its ability to produce a standard of living for the poorest man unequalled throughout the world's history. It has also demonstrated its capacity to wipe man and the larger part of the rest of living creatures off the Earth.

Bibliography

INTRODUCTION

No attempt will be made in this bibliography to include an exhaustive list of all the material consulted in the course of this study. The literature dealing with this subject is so extensive that a complete bibliography would run on for many pages, and most of it would be repetitious and far too specialized for most readers, who would simply end up discouraged from doing any further reading. It is necessary to include any material to which reference is specifically made in the body of the book. Other than this, only books that can be profitably read by the general reader are listed. The specialist will have no difficulty in using these to prepare a more detailed bibliography dealing with any particular phase of the problem.

GENERAL

Cassirer, E., 'Determinism and Indeterminism in Modern Physics', New Haven, Yale Press, 1956.
'Determinism and Freedom, A Philosophical Symposium', New York, New York University Press, 1958.
Heisenberg, W., 'Physics and Philosophy', New York, Harper and Brothers, 1958.
Margenau, H., 'The Nature of Physical Reality', New York, McGraw-Hill, 1950.
'Observation and Interpretation, A Symposium of Philosophy and Physics', London, Butterworth, 1957.
Taube, M., 'Causality and Chance Determinism', London, Allen, 1936.

CHAPTER 1

La Barre, J., 'The Human Animal', Chicago, University of Chicago Press, 1954.
Piaget, J., 'The Child's Concept of Causation', London, Routledge and Kegan Paul, 1930.
Piaget, J., 'The Child's Concept of the World', London, Routledge and Kegan Paul, 1929.

Malinowski, B., 'Freedom and Civilization', London, Allen and Unwin, 1947.

CHAPTER 2

Hebb, D., 'The Organization of Behaviour', New York, Wiley, 1949.
'International Encyclopedia of Unified Science', Chicago, Chicago University Press, 1946.
Northrop, A., 'The Meeting of East and West', New York, Macmillan, 1946.

CHAPTER 3

Brigman, A., 'The Nature of Our Physical Concepts', New York, New York Philosophical Library, 1952.
Lenzen, V., 'The Nature of Physical Theory', New York, Wiley, 1931.

CHAPTER 4

Robertson, J. K., 'Atomic Artillery and the Atomic Bomb', New York, Van Nostrand, 1945.
Richtmyer and Kennard, 'Introduction to Modern Physics', New York, McGraw-Hill, 1947.

CHAPTER 5

Neumann, J., 'Mathematical Foundations of the Quantum Mechanics'.
Reichenbach, H., 'Philosophical Foundations of Quantum Mechanics', Los Angeles, University of California, 1944.
Rojansky, V., 'Introductory Quantum Mechanics', New York, Prentice-Hall, 1938.

CHAPTER 6

Bohm, D., 'Causality and Chance in Modern Physics', London, Routledge and Kegan Paul, 1957.
Cooper, J., 'The Paradox of Separated Systems in Quantum Mechanics', Proc. of the Camb. Phil. Soc. 46, pp. 620-, 1950.
de Broglie, L., 'La Physique Quantique, Restera-t-elle Indeterministe?', Paris, Gautier-Villers, 1953.

des Touches, J., 'Principes Fondamenteaux de la Physique Theorique', Paris, Herman et Cie., 1942.

'Albert Einstein, Philosopher-Scientist', Evanston, Ill., Library of Living Philosophers, 1949. (Particularly the article by N. Bohr.)

Schroedinger, E., 'Are there Quantum Jumps?', British Journal for the Philosophy of Science, May and Nov., 1952.

Einstein, Podalsky, and Rosen, 'Can the Quantum Mechanical Description of Physical Reality be Considered Complete?', Phys. Rev. 47, 1935.

CHAPTER 7

Schroedinger, E., 'What is Life?', Cambridge, Cambridge University Press, 1946.

Milne and Margery, 'On the Sensitivity of the Eye', Scientific American, December, 1956.

Barlow, H., 'Increment Thresholds at Low Intensities . . .', Journal of Physiology, 1957, Volume 136, pp. 469-488.

Rashevsky, N., 'Mathematical Biophysics', Chicago, Chicago University Press, 1948.

Ryle, G., 'The Concept of Mind', London, Hutchinson's University Library, 1949.

Eccles, J., 'The Neurological Basis of Mind', Oxford, Clarendon Press, 1953.

Scholl, D., 'The Organization of the Cerebral Cortex', London, Methuen, 1956.

Burns, B., 'The Mammalian Cerebral Cortex', London, Edward Arnold, 1958.

CHAPTER 8

Campbell, N., 'Is Free Will a Pseudo Problem?', Mind, Vol. LX, pp. 441*, October, 1951.

Schlick, M., 'A Philosophy of Nature', New York, Philosophical Library, 1949.

Hospers, J. 'An Introduction to Philosophical Analysis', New York, Prentice-Hall, 1953.

Mackay, D. M., 'On the Logical Indeterminacy of a Free Choice,' Mind, Vol. LXIX, No. 273, January, 1960.